The 1956 Hungarian Revolution:
Hungarian and Canadian Perspectives

The University of Ottawa Press acknowledges with gratitude the support
extended to its publishing list by the Department of Canadian Heritage through
its Book Publishing Industry Development Program, by the Canada Council for
the Arts, by the Canadian Federation for the Humanities and Social Sciences
through its Aid to Scholarly Publications Program, by the Social Sciences and
Humanities Research Council, and by the University of Ottawa.

u Ottawa

We also gratefully acknowledge the Institute of Canadian Studies at the
University of Ottawa and the Embassy of the Republic of Hungary in Canada
whose financial support has contributed to the publication of this book.
www.press.uottawa.ca

LIBRARY AND ARCHIVES CANADA CATALOGUING IN PUBLICATION

The 1956 Hungarian Revolution : Hungarian and Canadian perspectives /
edited by Christopher Adam ... [et al.].

Based on papers presented at the conference: The 1956 Hungarian Revolution 50
    Years Later -- Canadian and International Perspectives, held at the University
    of Ottawa, Oct. 12-14, 2006.
Includes bibliographical references.
ISBN 978-0-7766-0705-4

1. Hungary--History--Revolution, 1956. 2. Canada--Foreign relations--
Hungary. 3. Hungary--Foreign relations--Canada. I. Adam, Christopher

DB957.N55 2010   943.905'2   C2010-902041-3

The 1956 Hungarian Revolution: Hungarian and Canadian Perspectives

Edited by Christopher Adam, Tibor Egervari,
Leslie Laczko, Judy Young

Contents

Preface

From October 12th to the 14th, 2006, an international scientific colloquium was held at the University of Ottawa to highlight the fiftieth anniversary of the Hungarian Revolution. Entitled *1956 – The Hungarian Revolution 50 Years Later, Canadian and International Perspectives*, the colloquium was organized by the Faculty of Arts' Institute of Canadian Studies and the Faculty of Social Sciences in collaboration with the Hungarian Studies Association of Canada. The objective of the colloquium was to establish the state of recent research on the event itself, as well its impact in Canada and around the world.

This scientific gathering took place within a series of commemorative reflections undertaken in Ottawa and across Canada throughout 2006. With the encouragements of His Excellency Dénes Tomaj, then ambassador of the Republic of Hungary, Mr. Peter Herrndorf, president and chief executive officer of the National Arts Centre, and Dr. Gilles Patry, then president of the University of Ottawa, the National Capital remembered the revolution, the exceptional welcome that Canada reserved for Hungarian refugees, and the national and international events triggered by this first post-war European uprising.

To this list of supporters we must add Library and Archives Canada (including the Portrait Gallery of Canada), the Canada-Hungary Educational Foundation, the Canadian Film Institute, and the Canadian Museum of Civilization, which all organized activities that combined commemoration of the past with celebration of the present.

The Orion Quartet and the National Arts Centre Orchestra presented programs prepared from the works of Béla Bartók, Zoltán Kodály, and Johannes

Brahms. The public was invited to view an important selection of films on the Hungarian Revolution and its consequences, among which could be found *Freedom's Fury* by Canadians Colin K. Gray and Megan Raney. Finally, the National Arts Centre organized a portrait exhibition of fifty Canadians of Hungarian origin produced by the photographer Tony Hauser. These events brilliantly highlighted the academic, artistic, and social ties that link Canada and Hungary, now a member of the European Union.

The colloquium's organizing committee wishes to express its gratitude to all those who, from near or far, contributed to the success of the three days of intense exchanges. We leave it to the reader to establish the merit of our reflections, though we are convinced that the participants, coming from the four corners of the world, took part in an exceptional moment of exchange and mutual understanding.

Introduction

In October 1956, a spontaneous uprising took Hungarian Communist authorities by surprise. In a matter of days, a new regime, led by reformist Communist leader Imre Nagy, was put in place. The government immediately manifested its intention to install a democratic, multi-party republic, to withdraw Hungary from the Warsaw Pact, and to liberalize the economic system of the country, all the while maintaining its socialist orientation. This prompted Soviet authorities to invade the country. After a few days of violent fighting, the revolt was crushed. In the wake of the event some 200,000 refugees left Hungary and over 38,000 of those made their way to Canada. This would be the first time Canada would accept so many refugees of a single origin, setting a precedent for later refugee initiatives.

A major political event of the Cold War period, the 1956 Hungarian Revolution continues to be of interest to scholars, as evidenced by a number of recent works (cf. Lessing 2006; Sebestyen 2007; Eörsi 2006; Gati 2006; Gough 2006; and the review of these works by Deák in 2007). This publication offers a selection of the papers presented at the conference "The 1956 Hungarian Revolution 50 Years Later – Canadian and International Perspectives" held at the University of Ottawa, October 12–14, 2006. The nearly two dozen academic presentations and the active participation of scholars and specialists from around the world helped give this conference a significant international and multidisciplinary aspect. Many of the contributions to this book draw upon new archival data from Hungary, the USSR, Canada, and the United States, as well other documents not available until relatively recently, and they attempt to cast new light on a number of issues. The chapters reflect a range of perspectives from the disciplines of history and the social sciences. The book is divided into two main sections: the first one reviews the 1956 Revolution from the Hungarian and international perspective, while essays in the second section focus on Canadian perspectives.

Part I: The Revolution, Hungary, and the World

In the opening chapters, conference keynote speakers János Rainer and Csaba Békés, two leading Hungarian researchers of the period (cf. Békés, Byrne and Rainer 2002) contextualize the uprising, albeit from different angles. Rainer situates the events of October–November 1956 within the context of Hungarian domestic politics. Rainer argues that most revolutionaries of all stripes and backgrounds seemed to agree when it came to the political elements of a post-revolutionary Hungary. The revolutionaries essentially wanted to maintain a welfare state—with limited privatization—alongside a multiparty democratic system. Csaba Békés, by contrast, approaches the revolution from both the perspectives of historiography and international politics. One of the key controversies surrounding the revolution was the lack of intervention on the part of the West, specifically the United States, which had implied that military aid might be forthcoming through its anti-Communist rhetoric. Yet Békés argues that there was no chance that any type of military intervention would materialize, as the goal of American foreign policy was to maintain, rather than destabilize, the postwar political and diplomatic situation in Europe.

Susan Glanz turns the discussion to economic history and provides a survey of the fiscal policies and platforms of the resurrected political parties that played a role in the revolution and the formation of a new multi-party government. Glanz concludes that all major parties agreed that the redistribution of land through the division of large estates in 1945 was a positive development for Hungary and that they also arrived at a consensus on the public ownership of mass industry, with reintroduction of limited private ownership.

Mária Palasik's contribution focuses on social history, looking at gender issues and specifically the role that women played in the revolt. By analyzing a series of archival photographs, Palasik finds that while in half of these photos women appear to be leaving scenes of potential conflict and violence during the days of the revolution, many were openly critical of the Communist regime in a vocal way, which in a number of cases led to persecution after the supression of the revolt. Some women did participate actively in armed clashes, but Palasik finds that the majority of these were either teenagers or women in their early to mid-twenties. She shows that many women occupied the traditional roles of nurses and care-givers, assisting the action in the background.

Sociologist Júlia Vajda, who was unable to attend the conference in person but had her paper presented, examines how some Holocaust survivors viewed the 1956 revolution. Basing her arguments on oral testimonies, Vajda concludes that it is not helpful to categorize Holocaust survivors as anti-Communist middle-class Jews who soon emigrated, or active Communists in positions of power, or those sympathetic to the Communist cause but without a place in the party. Instead she tries to evaluate the psychological reactions to the revolution of individial Shoah survivors. Vajda finds that when two hundred Shoah survivors were asked to tell their life story during lengthy interviews, the majority barely talked about 1956 as a significant event in their personal lives. When 1956 is mentioned, it is usually tied into the broader context of the Holocaust, which remains the defining event in the lives of most interviewees.

Judith Kesserű Némethy examines the impact of the 1956 revolution on Argentina and on that country's Hungarian immigrant communities. According to Némethy, the uprising created a sense of solidarity in an otherwise politically and ideologically fractured émigré community.

Finally, Heino Nyyssönen examines 1956 from the perspective of public memory. How do societies choose to publicly remember important historical events? This question is especially interesting and important in contexts where the macro historical context and the political regime have recently changed. Nyyssönen looks at how memory of the revolution lived on in Hungary following the collapse of the single-party regime in 1989. This presentation was especially timely, as the conference took place within the context of riots and violent demonstrations in Budapest, in which the anti-government rioters overtly referred to the heritage of the revolution and claimed ownership of it.

Nyysönnen examines the politicisation of the revolution, starting in 1989, and looks at how this left its mark on public commemorations and celebrations.

Part II: The Canadian Context

Harold Troper's chapter locates the arrival of the 1956 refugees in the context of Canadian immigration history. As Troper notes, few would have predicted at the end of World War II that ten years later Canada would be one of the world's main immigrant-receiving societies and a leader in the intake of Hungarian refugees. In the 1950s Canada had only recently re-opened its doors to massive immigration. Canada was undergoing a period of economic expansion and the outlook was positive on many fronts. Pressure from employers in need of workers prodded the Canadian government to cautiously open its doors to immigration. A relative shortage of candidates from the historically preferred source countries of Britain and Northern Europe led to a cautious willingness to admit more Eastern and Southern Europeans and a gradual relaxation of the ethnic preference hierarchy that had long explicitly guided Canadian policy. Troper argues that the Cold War context shaped the way Canada and Canadians reacted to the 1956 Revolution, with televised news reports of the struggle of the Hungarian Freedom Fighters leading to widespread sympathy for Hungarian refugees, pushing the government to move more quickly to take in refugees than it might have done otherwise. The Hungarian refugee intake of 1956–1957 became a precedent and a model for later Canadian initiatives involving Czech, Ugandan, and Southeast Asian refugees.

Nándor Dreisziger's contribution looks at the 1956–1957 refugee wave in the context of a century and a half of Hungarian immigration to Canada. The main earlier waves included those arriving before 1914, those arriving between 1924 and the early 1930s, and the post–World War II "displaced persons." Each of these four waves included immigrants whose main motivations were economic and those whose main motivations were political, with a higher proportion of economic immigrants in the first two waves and a higher proportion of political immigrants among the post–World War II DPs (displaced persons). Within the 1956–1957 cohort, the very first arrivals included many political refugees, with many of the later arrivals being motivated by economic as well as other factors. Compared to the three earlier waves, the 1956–1957 stream had a similar age composition with slightly more women than in the earlier streams. The 1956–1957 stream was also more educated than the earlier groups, with many of its members being professionals and students. The 1956–1957 refugee group, as with the post–World War II DP group, had higher proportions of Protestants and Jews than the two earlier waves, reflecting the more privileged class background and higher educational qualifications of the later arrivals. A distinctive feature of the 1956–1957 group is the very short time period its members had to decide to leave Hungary and settle in Canada.

In Peter Hidas's chapter, we find a detailed description, based on historical documents, of the almost daily arrivals of Hungarian refugees in Canada in the fall of 1956 and the first half of 1957. Some arrived by ship and others by plane in the largest airlift in Canadian aviation history. The government's plan included an attempt to disperse new arrivals across the country, with each province being assigned a target number of newcomers in approximate proportion to each province's share of the Canadian population. The refugees' own preferences as to where to settle did not always coincide with the government's plan. Hidas's essay also details the collaboration between government and a number of private agencies that were key actors in the settlement process, as well as the ongoing bargaining between the federal government and various provincial governments over settlement targets and funding. On the whole, within a few months a vast majority of the 1956–1957 refugees had found jobs and were beginning their integration into the larger Canadian fabric.

Turning to Greg Donaghy's contribution, we find an examination of Canada's response to the Hungarian Revolution from the perspective of Canada's diplomatic policy and international relations. Drawing on government documents from the period, Donaghy paints a picture of a hesitant and uncertain Canadian government trying to come to terms with the 1956 Hungarian crisis. An evolving Canadian policy of constructive engagement in dealing with the Soviet Union involved setting aside the goal of liberating the satellite countries of Eastern and Central Europe. This policy led to a complex Canadian response to the Soviet Union's sending troops into Budapest, with public opposition to Soviet actions being moderated by a range of other considerations. On the whole, the Hungarian crisis reinforced the shift in Canada's foreign policy in the direction of constructive engagement with the Soviet Union.

Christopher Adam provides an analysis of how the 1956 Hungarian Revolution was covered by the Hungarian Canadian press, and specifically by one newspaper, the *Kanadai Magyar Munkás* (Canadian-Hungarian Worker). The *Munkás* was the second largest Hungarian weekly printed in Canada and was openly affiliated with Canada's communist party and supportive of Hungary's post-war Communist regime. Adam explains the delicate position the paper found itself in after the 1956 events. The *Munkás* told its readers that the 1956 refugees were being brought in as cheap labour and competition to Canadian workers and union members, and that their arrival was not welcomed by Canadian workers. The paper attempted to persuade the refugees to return home to Hungary. Until its eventual demise, the *Munkás* never relinquished its goal of persuading readers that Canada's Hungarian refugee movement was part of a government plot to weaken the Canadian labour movement and at the same time strike a blow against the Soviet Union.

*

In its focus on the Canadian connection, this book builds upon and updates the picture sketched by Keyserlingk's *Breaking Ground* (1993) and Donaghy and Stevenson's *Canadian Diplomacy and the Hungarian Revolution 1956-1957* (2006). As we look back over the past half-century, the dynamic character of Canada's evolution and the speed with which Canadian society has changed stand out. Canada was among the leaders in its intake of Hungarian refugees in 1956–1957. Yet, as Troper's contribution makes clear, this could not have been predicted, given the country's very restrictive policies and closed doors until after World War II. Canada's mobilization to welcome the 1956–1957 Hungarian arrivals, occurring as it did a full decade before the many changes of the 1960s, including the adoption of a less restrictive "points system" for immigrant admissions and the adoption of a policy of multiculturalism, set the stage for making refugee admissions a more permanent component of Canada's immigration system.

Was the Canadian government's rapid mobilization to so quickly accept the 1956 refugees a result of initiatives originating within the government, or was it a response to public opinion and community proposals—a question visited by earlier analyses (cf. Keyserlingk 1993, Dirks 1993, and Donaghy and Stevenson 2006)? The papers of Hidas and Troper suggest that it was both—and these two contributions spell out some of the complex ways that these and other factors combined to shape the outcome.

What was the role of foreign policy considerations in shaping Canada's response? Was rapid action at home a way of deflecting attention from embarrassing events occurring elsewhere, as Adelman (1993) has suggested? Or rather, that a crisis elsewhere occurring at the same time facilitated or presented an opportunity for rapid action on the home front? The chapters by Donaghy and Troper highlight the way external events and foreign policy considerations combined with domestic developments in their influence on government actors.

We hope this work will be useful to those interested in locating the experience of the 1956 Hungarian arrivals according to a comparative perspective. This cohort's relatively rapid and successful integration into the larger Canadian fabric suggests possibilities for comparative analysis of earlier cohorts of arrivals to Canada, Hungarian emigrants to other countries, and other Cold War refugees, such as Cuban-Americans and Vietnamese-Americans.

In this connection, the 1956 Hungarian refugee movement to Canada is relevant to research on the trajectories of various Canadian categories of refugees and immigrants. As several authors in this volume argue, the 1956 Hungarian experience set the ground for the intake of later waves of refugee claimants. It also set the stage for large numbers of refugees being admitted alongside the increasingly larger numbers of immigrants. In terms of logistics, it is interesting that the Air Bridge to Canada, or ABC scheme, that was used to bring a large number of the Hungarian arrivals to Canada, discussed in Hidas's contribution, was in fact set up to transport the much larger group of British immigrants to Canada, and that the Hungarian refugees were piggy-backed and integrated into this series of flights (cf. Dreisziger 1993). Also striking in hindsight is that the category of British immigrants was still by far the single largest group of admitted newcomers to Canada in 1956–1957, numbering over one hundred thousand.

As Hawkins (1993) has noted, Canada's rules regarding refugees have evolved in such a way that admitted refugees have been expected to become landed immigrants as soon as possible, and most over the years have done so. Given this context, do refugees and other categories of immigrants display similar or different outcomes over time in terms of their ease of integration? The 1956 Hungarian refugees have been relatively successful in their integration into the larger Canadian fabric. Yet, over the past two decades, much evidence suggests that many recent refugees are having a much more difficult time in the Canadian labour market.

Acknowledgements

The editors would like to acknowledge the collaboration and support of our colleague Pierre Anctil of the University of Ottawa's Institute of Canadian Studies as a fellow member of the conference organizing committee, as well as the assistance of Houria Messadh of the institute's staff. Also we are grateful for the generous contributions of the University of Ottawa's Faculty of Social Sciences, Faculty of Arts, and Office of the President. Further funding was provided by Social Sciences and Humanities Research Council of Canada, the Hungarian Studies Association of Canada, and the Canada Hungary Educational Foundation. We would also like to thank the Embassy of the Republic of Hungary for their grant that contributed to the cost of publishing this book.

References

Adelman, Howard. "An Immigration Dream: Hungarian Refugees Come to Canada—An Analysis." 25–44. In Robert H. Keyserlingk, ed. *Breaking Ground: The 1956 Hungarian Refugee Movement to Canada*. Toronto: York Lanes Press, 1993.

Békés, Csaba, Malcolm Byrne, and János Rainer, eds. *The 1956 Hungarian Revolution: A History in Documents*. Budapest: Central European University Press, 2002.

Deák, István. "Did the Revolution Have to Fail?" *The New York Review of Books*. Volume LIV, Number 3 (March 1, 2007).

Dirks, Gerald E. "Canada and Immigration: International and Domestic Considerations in the decade Preceding the 1956 Hungarian Exodus." 3–12. In Robert H. Keyserlingk, ed. *Breaking Ground: The 1956 Hungarian Refugee Movement to Canada*. Toronto: York Lanes Press, 1993.

Donaghy, Greg, and Michael Stevenson. *Canadian Diplomacy and the Hungarian Revolution 1956-1957*. Ottawa: Historical Section, Foreign Affairs Canada, 2006.

Dreisziger, Nándor. "The Refugee Experience in Canada and the Evolution of the Hungarian-Canadian Community." 65–85. In Robert H. Keyserlingk, ed. *Breaking Ground: The 1956 Hungarian Refugee Movement to Canada*. Toronto: York Lanes Press, 1993.

Eörsi, László. *The Hungarian Revolution of 1956: Myths and Realities*. Mario D. Fenyő, trans. New York: East European Monographs, Columbia University Press, 2006.

Gati, Charles. *Failed Illusions: Moscow, Washington, Budapest, and the 1956 Hungarian Revolution*. Stanford: Stanford University Press, 2006.

Gough, Roger. *A Good Comrade: Janos Kadar, Communism and Hungary*. London: I. B. Tauris, 2006.

Hawkins, Freda. "Canada's Hungarian Movement: A Personal Recollection." 109–113. In Robert H. Keyserlingk, ed. *Breaking Ground: The 1956 Hungarian Refugee Movement to Canada*. Toronto: York Lanes Press, 1993.

Lessing, Erich. *Revolution in Hungary: The 1956 Budapest Uprising*. London: Thames and Hudson, 2006.

Keyserlingk, Robert H., ed. *Breaking Ground: The 1956 Hungarian Refugee Movement to Canada*. Toronto: York Lanes Press, 1993.

Sebestyen, Victor. *Twelve Days: The Story of the 1956 Hungarian Revolution*. New York: Random House, 2006.

Part I

The Revolution, Hungary, and the World

1.

The Hungarian Revolution of 1956: Causes, Aims, and Course of Events

János M. Rainer

On October 23, 1956, a revolution broke out in Budapest and spread all over the country in just a few days. The demonstrators, strikers, armed insurgents, leaders of the organizations of the revolution, and their sympathizers, demanded democratic freedoms and national independence. The first modern anti-totalitarian revolution in Europe lasted for practically two weeks, with another four weeks of rear-guard actions. Its impact could, however, be felt directly or indirectly for decades to come, right up to the change of regimes in 1989–1990.

I offer here a survey of the antecedents of 1956 from the point of view of political and social history, as well as the history of ideas. This is followed by a brief history of the revolution and an outline of the strata of active participants. Finally, I attempt to characterize the revolutionaries' aims.

Antecedents

The need for political, economic, social, and mental change became a constant concern of Hungarian public life from the early 1930s, when the Great Depression began to make an impact in Hungary. The solution to the agrarian question, in the form of land reform, was a perennial topic from the end of World War I onward. The great economic crisis and the outbreak of World War II gave an impetus to reformist thinking, as it became obvious that Hungary would necessarily emerge from the war a different country. The dimensions of the war made it clear that Hungary's subsequent fate would be greatly determined by the superpower in control of the East-central European region.

In 1944 Hungary became part of the Soviet sphere of influence. This fundamentally determined Hungary's domestic and foreign policy, as well as its social and economic development between 1944 and the late 1980s. All issues that were believed to interfere with Soviet military and political interests and security were decided by the Soviets. Hungarian political life was independent as long as it did not go beyond the limits of this system and remained in harmony with Soviet demands. Whenever a conflict arose, Soviet interests enjoyed absolute priority.[1]

The "people's democracy" established in 1944–1945 was a political system that corresponded to both the interests of Soviet security and the requirements of the proclamation formulated at Yalta in February 1945. The former were ensured by the dominance of the Communists in parliament, in the government, and in certain key positions (primarily in the form of the Interior Ministry and political police). The latter were, in turn, satisfied by temporary coalitions with the participation of all democratic political parties. The 1945 parliamentary elections revealed that the Hungarian people wanted democracy and a welfare economy, as well as a mixture of both Hungarian and Western traditions. However, the radical left managed to obtain considerable support in a very short time. Many people, especially the young, felt that the catastrophic four years they had experienced of World War II demanded a radical break with the former regime.

The Communist Party of Hungary drew the conclusion from the 1945 elections that its task was to "set the election results right" by means of extra-parliamentary measures or even by force. This intention of the Communists met with the understanding of Moscow. Total social and political control came only when, in 1947, the Small-holders' Party was destroyed,[2] Communist victory at the elections was obtained by fraud, and the show trials began. This trend turned into a conscious political course after the formation of the *Cominform*.[3] Then came the merger of the Social Democratic Party with the Communists in June

1948, the arrest of Cardinal Mindszenty at Christmas 1948, his show trial in February 1949, and finally, the first single-party elections in May 1949.[4]

During the period of the Cold War, Hungary, a state bordering both the Soviet Union and the Western world, became an important element of the Soviet *cordon sanitaire*. Neither Western orientation nor non-alignment was acceptable to the Soviets. The Soviets became less and less tolerant and considered even a differing social order in neighbouring states a menace.[5] All East-Central European Communist Party leaders of the period considered Soviet policy of the 1920s and 1930s to be their model. It included forced industrialization, an emphasis on heavy industry, an exaggerated development of the defence industry, the forced collectivization of agriculture, the misuse of education and culture for the purposes of everyday politics, an irrational cult of the country's leader, and a ritual, degrading, and emphatic assertion of the Soviet model. War psychosis was coupled with constant hostility and campaigns of reckoning.

The pursuit of irrational economic plans resulted in a rapid decrease in the standard of living. These factors taken together led to increasing tension and later to mass discontent. Rákosi's leadership entered into an actual state of war against society. It identified its "enemies" based on certain social and political criteria. (Members of the former elite, wealthy peasant farmers—"kulaks"—non-party intellectuals, religious people, etc.) In the early 1950s, the state security police (*ÁVH*) kept on record nearly 1.3 million people. The state condemned 387,000 persons for various "offences" (30,000 for alleged anti-state activities and 120,000 for endangering public supply); 22,000 were relocated/assigned to forced residence outside their domicile; and 6,000 were interned without having been sentenced in court. By 1953 nearly 500 persons had been executed for political reasons. Even the Communist political elite was decimated by purges, including show trials (such as the Rajk case – more on this at the beginning of the next section).[6]

When Stalin died on March 5, 1953, Soviet leaders realized that the regime was threatened by a serious internal crisis and could not be maintained unless changes in policy were introduced. In order to be able to settle the question of succession and normalize conditions within their empire, the Soviets had to resolve the crisis that was arising in the peripheries. In the middle of June

1953, Soviet party leaders ordered a delegation of the Hungarian Party to go to Moscow to receive new political directives. General Secretary Mátyás Rákosi had to resign his post as prime minister in favour of Imre Nagy.[7] Nagy pursued three main objectives between 1953 and 1955. First, he attempted to rectify the excesses committed between 1948 and 1953 in economic and social policy. He prepared a new economic policy strategy, which gave priority to light industry, agriculture, and consumption. An amnesty was announced, releasing the interned and restoring the freedom of deportees. He terminated forced collectivization and cleared the way for voluntary withdrawal from collective agriculture. Second, he planned to introduce a more democratic political process. He cautiously suggested the revival of limited activity for parties that had been suppressed earlier by including them in the People's Front movement. Third, he supported the preparation of professional studies on future economic policy. These studies resulted in the coining of the famous key phrase of the economic reforms of the 1960s: "economic mechanism" ("gazdasági mechanizmus").

All of this went far beyond what could be tolerated by the Soviets. With their support, and relying on the old apparatus, Rákosi managed to overthrow Nagy in March 1955. Total "re-Stalinization" and retaliation against the "deviationists" were eventually prevented, however, by further struggles for power in the Soviet Union and by the continuation of *detente*, especially after reconciliation with Yugoslavia in May 1955. The party opposition gathering around Nagy gradually gained ground in the press in 1955–1956, and Rákosi's leadership slowly disintegrated.[8]

In February 1956, Khrushchev's "secret" anti-Stalin speech at the 20th Party Congress, aroused hopes all over the world for a peaceful democratization of the Communist regimes. After the workers' revolt in Poznan, Poland, the Soviets dismissed Rákosi but replaced him as head of the Party with Ernő Gerő, formerly second in rank among the leading group of "Muscovites" who came to an understanding with the moderate Stalinists led by János Kádár. Old and new at the same time, the leadership set up in this way followed the same course as its predecessor. In the meantime, a democratic mass movement arose, going far beyond the goals of the opposition within the Party.

What was Hungarian society like in 1956? First of all, it was a frustrated society. In 1945 the population was happy that the war was over, although, for most, the end of the war provided a deliverance from horror and mortal fear rather than liberation. Outside coercion was certainly the decisive factor in the transformation of Hungary after 1945. But László Péter had warned more than twenty years ago that "the people's democracies did not fall out of the sky onto the countryside beyond the Elbe; it was not alien bayonets that forced this upon a resisting population, for everywhere without exception, they came into being through the active (and how active) cooperation of tens and even hundreds of thousands of the local population."[9] Such cooperation obviously presupposes that the Soviet-type system possessed a measure of legitimacy for many groups, at least at some point in history. Behind this, and in the longer term, Péter saw the specific features of social development in Eastern Europe and, as a direct antecedent, the institutions and political traditions that had developed in the nineteenth century. These included, for instance, the system of large landed estates, the one-sided industrial system, the tradition of étatism, the weak constitutional forms, the discretionary form of government, and the narrow and ever narrowing scope for autonomous social action. But the majority of Hungary's population found the years of classical Stalinism to be unbearable. Resistance did not assume the form of sabotage, "White" partisan actions, or secret plots. There were, however, important phenomena that involved large masses. The continuing practice of religion, the resistance against the organization of collective farms, and the migration of the labour force indicated the healthy attitude of society, its ability to survive and even to make things difficult for the regime. Terror could not undermine solidarity totally; it even created and strengthened it.[10]

Nagy's platform of 1953 was received with joy, relief, and high hopes. This hope lasted, however, for less than a year and a half. While the New Course had mobilized public opinion, the self-confidence of the Stalinist leaders of Hungary had subsided. Party functionaries and the Party intelligentsia began to feel uncertain and realized the need to examine their conscience and reconsider their attitudes. In those days, Nagy attracted Communist reformers, as well as others. His personality and the New Course became a focal point for all those who could accept nothing but a change of regimes. Nagy and his "Communism with a human face" seemed for them the first step toward their final aim: democracy.

By 1956 Hungarian society had been through a sweeping social change and was still in the midst of one. The pre-war elite (the aristocracy, the capitalists, the civil servants, and the army officers, among others) lost its former social status and was fully excluded from political life. It was replaced first by a plebeian stratum of democrats, which, in turn, was ousted by a new elite of Communist functionaries. Forced industrialization in the early 1950s launched the process of cultural disintegration in rural society, as well. In contrast, the industrial workers had greatly grown in strength, the number of civil servants had increased, and a mass migration to the towns had begun. This process of urbanization terminated as late as the middle of the 1960s. By 1956 Hungarians had become accustomed to a decade and a half of rapid and often unforeseeable changes, the uncertainty of the conditions of individual life, and the need for immediate and energetic responses to whatever situation confronted them. Social conditions in 1956 were far from being consolidated. Hungarian society was loose and pliable, multi-layered, and, above all, uncertain both on the material and the mental level.[11]

The Revolution[12]

On October 6, 1956, László Rajk, the most famous Communist victim of the Rákosi regime, was solemnly reburied. The attending crowd of a hundred thousand saw in the funeral a prelude to the end of Stalinism, as well. On October 16, a meeting of students in Szeged decided to found the MEFESZ (Hungarian abbreviation for the Unified Organization of Hungarian University and College Students), an organization independent of DISZ (*Dolgozó Ifjúság Szövetsége,* Association of Working Youth).[13] At this point, the monolithic system of political institutions started to break up, and this process proved unstoppable in the following days. On October 22, rumours circulated about replacements at the head of the Polish Party and the victory of Wladyslaw Gomulka, who represented a trend similar to that of Imre Nagy in the struggle for power against Stalinist leadership. Khrushchev flew to Warsaw; Soviet troops were mobilized; but the threat of an intervention was weakened by the unified attitude of the Polish leaders and Gomulka's profession of allegiance to the Warsaw Pact. Upon learning of developments in Poland, students at the Technical University in Budapest drafted a list of demands, such as the withdrawal of Soviet troops stationed in Hungary, free general elections with the participation of several parties, and the prime ministry of Imre Nagy. They also called for a demonstration, both as an expression of solidarity with the Polish people and to make their demands even more emphatic.

On October 23, Party leaders forbade the demonstration but later changed their minds. The demonstration of students started anyway and soon turned into a mass demonstration, joined by workers. Gradually the whole population of the capital became involved. The slogans of the Party opposition were soon replaced by ones demanding national independence and democracy—without the adjective "Socialist." The procession, coming from various parts of the city and heading toward the statue of General Bem, snowballed into a crowd of about two hundred thousand, waiting for the appearance of Nagy at the Parliament. Others pulled down the statue of Stalin, and still others marched in front of the Radio Building, clamouring for a broadcast of their demands.

Early in the evening, Gerő turned to the Soviet Embassy for military aid. The Soviets were only too willing to help, their troops having already been mobilized. ÁVH men opened fire on the crowd preparing to occupy the Radio Building, thereby triggering an armed revolt.

Late in the evening, Party leaders decided to suppress the "counter-revolutionary rebellion" by force. At the same time, they took Nagy back into their ranks. Seeing the turbulence of the crowd, the leading figure of the opposition was embarrassed but accepted the call of his opponents to resume the office of prime minister on October 24. At first, Moscow refrained from a military intervention, and later, when the intervention did take place, Moscow tried to put a check on it. The Budapest youth, the freedom fighters, did not withdraw on October 24 when they saw the Soviet tanks approach.

With the exception of certain units of the security police, the Stalinist state collapsed within a few days. An autonomous system of revolutionary institutions was spontaneously set up in the following few days. Revolutionary commissions were formed all over the country in the wake of demonstrations in the country towns, and workers' committees were elected in the factories. A general political strike began. The revolutionary organizations and the insurgents of the capital insisted upon the demands of October 23. At the same time, Party headquarters became the scene of a fierce political struggle between the orthodox line and the adherents of Nagy, who urged a peaceful solution by negotiations. Moscow sent a delegation to Budapest that included Mikoyan, Suslov, and KGB Chief Serov.

On October 25 and 26, the orthodox group seemed to be able to curb the escalation of events with the help of armed units under its control. On October 25, a massacre took place in Kossuth Square in Budapest when a crowd of unarmed demonstrators was shot at. Several country towns witnessed similar bloody events. However, on the night of October 27–28, Nagy and the supporters of a peaceful solution managed to proclaim a cease-fire. In the following few days, Party leaders and the new government met some of the demonstrators' demands. Soviet troops withdrew from Budapest, and on October 30 Nagy declared a return to a multi-party system.

In this critical period, Hungary's situation was a prominent issue worldwide. Many people in Hungary believed that support would come from the West. However, the Suez Crisis breaking out on October 29 divided the attention of the world and exposed the fate of the Hungarian Revolution to the bargaining of the Great Powers. The leaders of the United States believed that no Western-led intervention was possible that would not involve the risk of another world war, a nuclear one this time. The Suez war was their chief strategic interest. The only thing they could do was assure Moscow that they did not intend to integrate Hungary into the Western bloc. On the other hand, Moscow realized that the political solution was leading to Hungary's drawing away from its own standards, in terms of both domestic and foreign policy, and that the institutions of vital importance from the Soviet point of view (the Party leadership and apparatus, the organs of state security, and the army) were on the brink of collapse or had already become unreliable. As a result, the Soviets eventually decided on military intervention. Moscow interpreted the American message as a promise by the West to refrain from any military step. At the first sign of a second Soviet intervention, Nagy declared Hungarian neutrality and withdrawal from the Warsaw Pact. This step did not meet with any response in the West. Although there were signs of consolidation in Budapest after this proclamation, the Soviets did not change their minds about stepping in.[14] At dawn on November 4, the Soviet army attacked the city and suppressed the resistance of the heroically fighting insurgents in a few days.

Participants

In 1959–1960, the organs of state security prepared large-scale surveys of the events and their participants, on the basis of the documents of retaliation after the revolution. They found that the students' demonstration of October 23, beginning with 10,000–20,000 participants, had grown into a mass demonstration of about 250,000 people. In the following days, there were over a hundred demonstrations all over the country, including between 100,000 and 200,000 participants. The number of the armed groups of freedom fighters (National Guard units) was 160, 14,178 members of whom became known by name. There were 2,100 workers' councils, with 28,000 members, all known by name. Almost every settlement had its own local revolutionary council with at least 20,000–30,000 members. (At that time there were nearly 4,000 independent localities of different kinds in Hungary.) The direct democratic local elections, resembling a national assembly, were attended by 10–15 per cent of the population.[15] The number of active participants in the revolution can, therefore, be estimated to have been about one million even by a moderate estimate. The re-election of the workers' councils probably involved even more people. The great dimensions of popular activity are demonstrated also by the large number of emigrants after the revolution (200,000 persons).[16]

Imre Nagy faced the revolution of October 23, 1956, as a reformist Communist politician. For him, the revolution was something that he had long feared, the outbreak of which he had tried to avoid by all means. But he gradually recognized that he was unable to set the country on the track he preferred. When all his efforts to do so failed, he understood that he could save the country, the people, and the cause of Socialism, everything he felt important to save, only if he joined the revolution and tried to keep it under control. He still wanted to consolidate the country, but could not find any other way out than adopting the demands of the people. His declaration of the country's neutrality and its withdrawal from the Warsaw Pact were responses to the challenge of Soviet intervention and at the same time expressed a historic resolution: Nagy identified himself with the demands of the nation as opposed to the interest and dogmas of the Party and the international Communist movement. As the most well-known politician of the revolution, he became one with it. His trial and execution in 1958 forever fixed this image of Nagy. The actual protagonist in the revolution was, however, not a single person but Hungarian society itself. Other important roles in the play were played by the students, the armed freedom fighters, and the members and activists of the revolutionary organs.

The Students

Hungarian universities were radically transformed by Communist power in the late 1940s, when teaching staff and the students were purged of "bourgeois elements." Teaching became deeply saturated with politics, and the number of students increased. The student population was controlled by entrance examinations in order to ensure that students of working-class and poor peasant origin would dominate in the institutions of higher education. Given this family background, the students were directly aware of all the uncertainties of the social transformation and the distress caused by the introduction of a Soviet regime. Their social and political training had begun before the war and was determined by middle-of-the-road populist literary and political ideas. Their young professors, several of whom had formerly belonged to and studied at the so-called "people's colleges" of the late 1940s, where Hungarian populism and Communist messianism dominated, represented the same trends. Most of them felt they were rising socially; consequently, they felt that they belonged to the *avant-garde* or elite. They understood the criticism of the opposition within the Party and were able to formulate the promises of Communist ideology and explain the discrepancies between the social demands emerging at the end of the war and the actual developments of the day. The students broke the monolithic political structure and called for a demonstration for the first time. Although the students' activities did not subside after October 23, they ceased to be the *avant-garde*. This was reflected, for example, in the fact that they were unable to set up a central organ for themselves. However, their moral prestige allowed their political attitudes to carry weight in the future.[17]

The Armed Freedom Fighters

There is no other armed revolt in the history of the Soviet regime in East-central Europe that reached the dimensions of the Hungarian one. The armed uprising made the incapacity for action of the old regime manifest and cleared the way for revolutionary self-organization. It made the political changes taking place in the wake of the revolution more radical. Our knowledge of the armed insurgents is highly ambiguous. Their political role was of crucial importance, but they represented the least politically motivated group of participants. In general, they came from the peripheries of Budapest society, were hardly touched by social change, and were disadvantaged in many ways. They lived under unfavourable financial, cultural, and mental conditions.[18] The freedom fighters had nothing to lose. Their behaviour in battle was motivated both by despair and their habitual reactions to dangerous situations in the street. This latter mentality accounts for their sometimes reckless heroism when facing superior numbers and also for their extreme viciousness when they took the law into their own hands. They fought in perfect unison, but at times of cease-fires they immediately started to argue and quarrel with one another. During the fights, their leaders were selected according to age, inventiveness in battle, and natural authority, but afterward they could be easily manipulated politically. Noisy and overbearing behaviour became the criterion of leadership.

The composition of freedom fighters is known mostly from the documents of post-revolutionary retaliation and from memoirs written much later, which are consequently not quite trustworthy.[19] It can be taken for granted that the armed freedom fighters were those who emigrated in the largest numbers, whereas the less conscious or deliberate elements, the most downcast and disadvantaged of this group, remained. It was this group that yielded most of those sentenced to death, to life imprisonment, or imprisonment for longer than a decade.

The Revolutionary Organs

The revolution in the capital and in smaller settlements in the country proceeded in different ways. The most important element of the revolution in the country was not armed resistance but a manifold organizing activity. Its outstanding figures were not demonstrators and freedom fighters but revolutionaries struggling to set things right and restore public order.[20] Local society still maintained its internal cohesion; consequently, everyone knew whom to elect as leaders, dismiss, or take into custody. In the newly organized local organs there were many workers and young people in their twenties and thirties. The revolutionary committees included an extraordinarily high number of army officers. However, the fact that few former Party members were part of the committees indicates that the transformation of local society had not come to a halt with the end of the coalition era. At the same time, the still-respected former leaders of the parties of the post-1945 coalition were included in the committees in large numbers. The workers' councils reacted to the extraordinary challenge in the same manner as the local revolutionary committees and were organized on a similarly democratic basis. They played an actual political role after November 4, 1956, when the revolution lost its armed forces in a few days' time.[21] The political centre of gravity, the Nagy government, was similarly lost. But November 4 did not abolish all of the self-organized bodies of the revolution. Although a National Workers' Council could not be established on November 21, because of the political police and Soviet army units, the Budapest Central Workers' Council worked *de facto* as a national body.

The Vision of 1956

The aims and ideas of 1956 were a long time forming. Some were responses to challenges of the moment, but some—democratic transformation of the country and restoration of the independent nation-state—had been occupying politically minded Hungarians for decades.

The demands drawn up around October 23 show a rare degree of unanimity regarding the common ground in Hungarian society. They covered the negative program of dismantling the communist political system. The demands also covered independence, re-expression and fostering national traditions, respect for basic democratic rights and freedoms, restoration of a multi-party system, and the holding of free elections. Most of the political programs stated plainly the new property relations that had developed since 1949 (land reform and the situation with nationalization of manufacturing, wholesale trading and the banking system) were not to be reversed: reprivatisation was firmly rejected. In other words, the revolutionary program envisaged retaining state ownership and the state's role in directing the economy, or, as another, quite unclear solution, subjecting both to real socialization (based on collective ownership rights for the workers, exercised through the workers' councils.) The system of workers' councils itself developed all over the country with astonishing speed, so that it was able to turn into an alternative base of power after November 4.

The revolutionaries saw before them a kind of third-way "vision": a political system based on representative democracy (with some direct, "self-managing" forms, as well) and a state-run welfare economy based on broad public ownership. Although Soviet socialism had very few advocates in 1956, socialism, especially Hungarian socialism, seems to have had quite a few supporters for reasons that need to be sought mainly in the antecedents to the revolution. The political experience of the participants had been obtained under the pre-war and wartime system and in the coalition period of 1945–1946. The Horthy regime had been quite discredited by its ignominious end and the painful memories it left behind. All were anxious to dissociate themselves from any "restoration," while the coalition period could serve only as a starting point. No one wanted to return, as such, to conditions that had prepared the way for the Communist takeover.

The revolution's political program embraced the Western pattern of democracy, complete with its institutional and legal framework. But this Western democracy would have been peopled by Hungarians who seemed reluctant to make fundamental changes in the pattern of socio-economic arrangements typical of Stalinist socialism. Capitalism and the market economy were classed as a legacy of the past doomed to oblivion. Illusions about a state-run economy were also widespread in the West before the war and for decades afterward. There were still, in 1956, very lively expectations of "socialism" as a system that would approximate better than any other to the ideal of justice. It was as if people were thinking they could create their own Hungarian socialism once the country was independent again and not obliged to adopt Soviet patterns. The political and social program of 1956 certainly seemed to have a third-way, democratic, and left-wing character.

However, it is worth considering some special factors that can modify this picture. Political discourse and mass communications in the few short days when full freedom of speech applied were largely exercised by the Communist Party opposition or its former members. The party opposition also had the best-known politician: Imre Nagy. The demands that gained publicity were so uniform because the new language of public discourse had been developed by the party intelligentsia, and they, of course, were best at speaking it. The non-Communist participants in political life had just emerged from long years of oppression or, in many cases, long prison sentences. They, understandably, spoke in a cautious or restrained tone if they said anything at all. The middle class of the interwar period had proved unable to rally after 1945. There was still an element of self-restraint and self-censorship in the revolution, on the grounds that an independent Hungary might be more acceptable to the Soviet Union, if it was socialist at least, an idea probably influenced by the example of Tito's Yugoslavia. The speed of events and short duration of the revolution left no time to work out demands in full, let alone thrash out opposing views. Everything that called for a longer period of elaboration was lacking. For instance, no detailed economic or economic-policy ideas were devised. Nor was there a foreign-policy program for 1956—withdrawal from the Warsaw Pact and the call for neutrality were just responses to preparations for a second Soviet invasion.

As for the ideology of the populist writers—the last, great, specifically Hungarian current of political ideas—it had never shaped up into a coherent political program. István Bibó, its most conscious representative, had tried to do so in 1945–1948, but the developing conditions of Stalinism had prevented him from finishing his attempt. But Bibó's political vision at the end of the 1940s was an anticipation of 1956. A democrat with socialist features, closed to the right but open to the left, and with ideas taken from people with a more moderate, middle-of-the-road view, Bibó probably exerted the decisive influence on the most active, politically conscious actors and observers of 1956. There is probably truth in what one pair of Hungarian authors, a historian and a political scientist, said in 1989: the closest that the utopia of the "people's" movement came to Earth in the twentieth century was in 1956.[22]

By the mid-twentieth century it had become apparent that the totalitarian responses to the crisis of the previous century were unacceptable in their entirety, but, in 1956, certain elements of them still seemed as if they might be adapted to a system that was essentially anti-authoritarian. Such elements were direct democracy, collective ownership or a planning, paternalistic state, all of which might also be viewed as necessary correctives to crisis-ridden market coordination and liberal democracy.

There is no knowing how much resemblance the political formula of 1956, if it had been applied, would have borne to that of 1945 or of 1947, or even to the political map of Hungary after 1989. It was a failed revolution, not a victorious one, that defined the political debates that the revolution's participants held in exile and that were held after the change of system in 1989. These debates did not derive from the political debates of 1956, because no such debates were then held. Nor did any political thinking, party, or school of thought survive that was specific to 1956. Yet 1956 did leave a positive political tradition that survives to this day. The democratic transformation of 1989–1990 drew not only political aims and ideas but also moral strength from the memory of 1956. This spiritual relationship between the earlier and later changers of the system was especially strong in the first stage of the system-changing process, when the Kádár regime was being dismantled. To that extent, the new Hungarian democracy is a direct heir to the 1956 revolution, a fact that later disputes cannot alter.

Notes

1. On the postwar years in Eastern Europe, see: Tony Judt, *Postwar: A History of Europe Since 1945* (Toronto: Penguin, 2005); and John Lewis Gaddis, *We Now Know: Rethinking the Cold War* (New York: Oxford University Press,

1997). On Hungary, see: Romsics Ignác, *Hungary in the Twentieth Century* (Budapest: Corvina, 1999); and Peter Kenez, *Hungary from the Nazis to the Soviets: The Establishment of the Communist Regime in Hungary 1944-1948* (New York: Cambridge University Press, 2006).

2. István Csicsery-Rónay–Géza Cserenyey,*Koncepciós per a Független Kisgazdapárt szétzúzására 1947* (Show Trial to Smash the Independent Small-holders' Party, 1947) (Budapest, 1956 Institute, 1998).

3. Grant M. Adibekov, *Kominform i poslevoennaya Evropa* (Cominform and Post-War Europe) (Moscow, 1994), 23; Leonid Gibyansky, "Kak voznik Kominform. Po novym arkhivnym materialam" (How the Cominform Was Formed. On New Archive Material) *Novaya i noveyshaya istoriya* 4 (1993); Grant Adibekov, "How the First Conference of the Cominform Came About," in *The Cominform: Minutes of the Three Conferences 1947/1948/1949* (Milan, 1994), 3–9; Anna Di Biagio, "The Establishment of the Cominform," in *The Cominform: The Minutes of the Three Conferences 1947/1948/1949* (Milan, 1994), 11–34.

4. Mária Palasik,*A jogállamiság megteremtésének kísérlete és kudarca Magyarországon 1944–1949* (Attempt at Creating the Rule of Law and its Failure in Hungary, 1944–1949) (Budapest, 2000).

5. John Lewis Gaddis, *We Now Know: Rethinking Cold War History*; Vojtech Mastny, *The Cold War and Soviet Insecurity: The Stalin Years* (New York, 1996); Vladislav Zubok and Constantine Pleshakov, *Inside the Kremlin's Cold War: From Stalin to Khrushchev* (Cambridge, MA, 1996). The debate on the Cold War in the United States and elsewhere is dealt with in detail and based on a wide range of special literature in Melvyn P. Leffler, "The Cold War: What Do 'We Now Know'?" *American Historical Review* (April 1999): 501–524; see also Csaba Békés, "A hidegháború eredete" (The Origins of the Cold War), in *Évkönyv VII* (1999). *Magyarország a jelenkorban* (Yearbook VII, 1999. Hungary's Recent Past) (Budapest, 1956 Institute, 1999), 217–226.

6. Révai Valéria, et al, eds., *Törvénytelen szocializmus. A Tényfeltáró Bizottság jelentése* (Unlawful Socialism. Report of the Fact-Finding Commission) (Budapest, Zrínyi Kiadó - Új Magyarország, 1991).

7. János M. Rainer, *Nagy Imre. Politikai életrajz* (Imre Nagy. A Political Biography) *Vol. 1, 1896–1953* (Budapest, 1996), 509–543.

8. On this process, see János M. Rainer, *Nagy Imre. Politikai életrajz* (Imre Nagy. A Political Biography) *Vol. 2, 1953–1958* (Budapest, 1999), 9–233.

9. László Péter, "Miért éppen az Elbánál hasadt szét Európa? (A népi demokratikus rendszer társadalmi gyökerei)" (Why did Europe split right along the Elbe? [The social roots of the people's democratic system]), in Miklós Tóth and Lóránt Czigány, eds., *Önarcképünk sorsunk tükrében 1945– 1949. Sine ira et studio* (Our self-portrait in the light of our destiny...), (Amsterdam: Hollandiai Mikes Kelemen Kör, 1984), 21.

10. János M. Rainer, "Violence and Resistance in Hungary before 1956," in Péter László and Martin Rady, eds., *Resistance, Rebellion and Revolution in Hungary and Central Europe: Commemorating 1956* (London: Hungarian Cultural Centre, University College London, 2008), 191–198.

11. Gábor Gyáni, "Socio-psychological roots of discontent: paradoxes of 1956," *Hungarian Studies* 20, 2 (2006): 65–73.

12. For the literature on the revolution, see András B. Hegedüs, ed., *1956 kézikönyve* (1956: A Manual), Vol. 2 *Bibliográfia* (Bibliography) (György Litván, ed.) (Budapest, 1996), 51–69. In what follows I have relied mostly on the following: Tibor Méray, *Nagy Imre élete és halála* (Life and Death of Imre Nagy) (Paris, 1983); Miklós Molnár and László Nagy, *Reformátor vagy forradalmár volt-e Nagy Imre?* (Was Imre Nagy a Reformer or a Revolutionary?) (Paris, 1983); Peter Unwin, *Voice in the Wilderness. Imre Nagy and the Hungarian Revolution* (London, 1991); János M. Bak, Gyula Kozák, György Litván, and János M. Rainer, *Az 1956-os magyar forradalom. Reform, felkelés, szabadságharc, megtorlás* (The Hungarian Revolution of 1956. Reform, Revolt, War of Independence, Repression) (Budapest, 1991); László Varga, *Az elhagyott tömeg. Tanulmányok 1950–56-ról* (The Forsaken Crowd. Essays on the Years 1950–1956) (Budapest, 1994); György Litván, János M. Bak, and Lyman H. Legters, eds., *The Hungarian Revolution of 1956. Reform, Revolt, and Repression 1953–1963* (London–New York, 1996); László Gyurkó, *1956* (Budapest, 1996); Zoltán Ripp, "A pártvezetés végnapjai" (Last Days of the Party Leadership), in Julianna Horváth and Zoltán Ripp, eds., *Ötvenhat*

októbere és a hatalom (October 1956 and the Political Power) (Budapest, 1997).

13. Following the logic of the monolithic political structure since 1950, DISZ was the single youth organization in Hungary, under the control of the Communist Party.

14. On the international aspects, see the following: Csaba Békés, *Az 1956-os magyar forradalom a világpolitikában. Tanulmány és válogatott dokumentumok* (The Hungarian Revolution of 1956 in International Politics. Essay and Selected Documents) (Budapest, 1996); Mark Kramer, "New Evidence on Soviet Decision-Making and the 1956 Polish and Hungarian Crises," *Cold War International History Project Bulletin* 8, 9 (Winter 1996–1997): 358–384; János Bak, ed. "Az 1956-os magyar forradalom a világpolitikában. Az 1996. szeptember 26–29-i budapesti nemzetközi történészkonferencia előadásai és vitái" (The Hungarian Revolution of 1956 in World Politics. Lectures and Debates at the International Conference of Historians at Budapest, September 26–29, 1996) *Évkönyv 1996/1997* (Budapest, 1997), 9–321; János M. Rainer, "Szovjet döntéshozatal Magyarországról 1956-ban" (Soviet Decision-Making concerning Hungary in 1956), in *Évkönyv II. 1993* (Budapest, 1993), 19–38; János M. Rainer, "Döntés a Kremlben, 1956. Kísérlet a feljegyzések értelmezésére" (Decision-Making in the Kremlin, 1956. An Attempt at Interpreting Documents), in *Döntés a Kremlben* (Decision-Making in the Kremlin), 111–154; Valeri Musatov, *Predvestniki buri. Politicheskie krizisi v Vostochnoy Evrope (1956–1981)* (Harbingers of the Storm. Political Crises in Eastern Europe, 1956–1981) (Moscow, 1996), 11–113. For the fullest Soviet documents relating to the decision to intervene, see the following: Jelena Orehova, Vyacheslav Sereda, Aleksandr Stykalin, eds., *Sovetski Soyuz i vengerski krizis 1956 goda* (The Soviet Union and the Hungarian Crisis) (Moscow: Rosspen, 1998), 339–557; John P. Glennon, Edward C. Keefer, et al, eds., *Foreign Relations of the United States, 1955–1957 Eastern Europe*, Vol. 25 (Washington: US Government Printing Office, 1990).

15. File V-150.352 at *Történeti Hivatal* (Historical Bureau) on *Az 1956-os magyarországi ellenforradalom az állambiztonsági munka tükrében* (The

Hungarian Counter-Revolution of 1956 as Reflected by State Security Activities).

16. See the top secret report on defection by the Central Statistic Office in 1956, prepared in 1957 in *Regio* 4 (1991): 174–211.

17. For the students' movements, see Tibor Beck and Pál Germuska, *Forradalom a Bölcsészkaron* (Revolution at the Faculty of Arts) (Budapest, 1997).

18. Gábor Kresalek, "Mit akartak a felkelők?" (What did the Insurgents Want?) *Világosság* 10 (1991): 734–738; Gyula Kozák, "Szent csőcselék" (The Sacred Mob), *Évkönyv VI, 1999. Magyarország a jelenkorban* (Yearbook VI, 1999. Hungary's Recent Past) (Budapest, 1999), 255–281.

19. László Eörsi, *Corvinisták, 1956* (Fighters of the Corvin Block, 1956) (Budapest, 2001); László Eörsi, *Ferencváros, 1956* (The Budapest District of *Ferencváros*, 1956) (Budapest, 1996); Bindorffer Györgyi and Gyenes Pál, eds, *Pesti utca. Válogatás fegyveres felkelők visszaemlékezéseiből* (The Streets of Pest. Selected Memoirs of Armed Insurgents) (Budapest, 1956 Institute, 1996).

20. Bálint Magyar, "1956 és a magyar falu" (1956 in Rural Hungary), *Medvetánc* 2, 3 (1988): 209; János M. Rainer, "The 1956 Revolution in the Provinces," *Budapest Review of Books* Vol. 2 (Summer 1992) 2, 64-68; János M. Rainer, "Budapest és vidék 1956-ban" (Budapest and the Countryside in 1956), in Zoltán Simon, ed., *A vidék forradalma* (Revolution in the Countryside) (Debrecen, 1992), 37–48.

21. For the resistance led by the workers' councils and the Central Workers' Council, see László Varga, "Munkástanácsok 1956" (Workers' Councils in 1956), in *Az elhagyott tömeg 1950–1956* (The Forsaken Crowd, 1950–1956) (Budapest, 1994), 199–237. For the documents of the Central Workers' Council, see László Varga, "A Nagybudapesti Központi Munkástanács irataiból" (Selected Documents of the Central Workers' Council of Greater Budapest), *Társadalmi Szemle* 8–9 (1991): 142–155; and 11 (1991): 79–93. For the memoirs of some leaders of workers' councils, see Gyula Kozák and Adrienn Molnár, eds. *"Szuronyok hegyén nem lehet dolgozni!" Válogatás 1956-os munkástanácsvezetők visszaemlékezéseiből* ("It is Impossible to Work with Bayonets in Your Back." Selected Memoirs of Leaders of Workers' Councils in 1956) (Budapest, 1993). For the memoirs of Gyula Sebestyén and Ferenc

Tőke, see Gyula Kozák, ed. *Szemle. Válogatás a brüsszeli Nagy Imre Intézet folyóiratából* (*Szemle*. Selections from the periodical of the Imre Nagy Institute in Brussels) (Budapest, 1992), 50–69. See also Bill Lomax, ed., *Hungarian Workers' Councils in 1956* (New York, 1990); István Kemény and Bill Lomax, eds., *Magyar munkástanácsok 1956-ban* (Hungarian Workers' Councils in 1956) (Highland Lakes, NJ, 1990).

22. Mária Csicskó and András Körösényi, "Egy harmadikutas szocializmus – utópia földközelben. A Petőfi Párt 1956-67-ben," (A Third Way Socialism – Utopia Coming to Earth. The Petőfi Party in 1956-57) *Századvég* 1, 2 (1989): 118–183. István Bibó (1911–1979) outstanding Hungarian political philosopher, member of the revolutionary Nagy government in November 1956. He was sentenced to life imprisonment in 1958, released in 1963.

2.

Could the Hungarian Revolution Have Succeeded in 1956? Myths, Legends, and Illusions

Csaba Békés

Whether it could have been otherwise is the most frequent and poignant question for contemporaries and posterity alike when a revolution or an uprising has failed. Was defeat inevitable, or might there have been a chance of success if external and internal circumstances had been luckier? The failure of the most recent revolution in Hungary, in 1956, causes critics to pose such questions, to which Hungarian society has failed to find reassuring answers. Popular verdicts and scholarly interpretations of the viability of the revolution contain both rational elements and emotional and moral approaches; the latter have assisted at the birth of many historical myths and legends in recent decades.

The basic, still-prevalent myth about the 1956 Hungarian Revolution relates how the uprising might indeed have succeeded if events on the international policy stage had developed more favourably for Hungary.

Post-1989 historical researches, based on systematic examination of domestic and foreign archive materials made available since the collapse of Communism, give strong grounds for saying that the bipolar world system designed to stabilize the post-1945 situation left the countries of the Soviet empire with no realistic chance of ridding themselves of the Communist system. Right up to 1989, the Soviet Union viewed East-central Europe as a security zone of fundamental importance that could not be conceded. Any Western effort to detach these countries was seen as intervention, against which Soviet leadership was even prepared for direct armed conflict between the superpowers and the risk of a third world war. Yet it was quite apparent that neither the United States nor any Western country would strive or aspire to do anything of the kind, as they accepted the need to maintain the status quo in Europe. The "liberation propaganda" by the Eisenhower administration in 1953–1956 was simply rhetoric, aimed mainly at sustaining anti-communist morale behind the Iron Curtain.[1]

But this interpretation, offered by historians, clearly fails to attract those who are not content to measure what was one of the foremost events in 20th-century Hungarian history by the revolution's moral content, or by its decisively positive effect on the character of the Kádár system. Some want to believe there had been a chance of success.

Many myths, legends, and illusions about the 1956 revolution remain or recur in the public mind to this day. They are designed to explain how the failure of the revolution was not preordained and the conditions had simply been unfavourable to Hungary. Such arguments or elements of such arguments recur periodically in memoirs and reminiscences of the revolution, and above all in political journalism. It is understandable that those who took part might uphold myths about the revolution, but it is difficult to excuse such views in journalism, where even minimal perusal of specialist literature could reduce the myth-spreading and myth-making considerably. Yet the saddest thing for a historian is that the urge to mythologize does not always spare his/her own profession: myths, legends, and misconceptions sometimes crop up even in historical works with scholarly pretensions.[2]

The commonest myths and illusions about 1956 usually concern real or desired roles for the United States, the Soviet Union, and the United Nations. Many concern the Suez Crisis, which was taking place at the same time as the revolution.

The United States and the West

The main lost opportunity of the revolution, as perceived by the Hungarian public mind until very recently, was the expected help from the West that never materialized. So the focus, when subsequently weighing the chances, was almost always on what the West, above all what the United States, might or should have done in 1956 to assist the Hungarians.[3]

The main misunderstanding about the role of the West and America (still present as an illusion in many people's thinking) was that many in Hungarian society thought of the status quo and spheres of interest established in Europe in 1945 as a temporary formation, and of the Hungarian Revolution as an exceptional occasion for the Western powers to alter the country's status. Of course, it was not difficult to misunderstand the effectively targeted US propaganda broadcast by the Hungarian service of *Radio Free Europe*.[4] It might well be asked why the US administration, seen as bastion of the free world, would say what it did not mean seriously. Nobody was forcing the United States to make great promises, and if it did so, there had to be a pressing reason. Though the trend in East–West relations in 1955–1956 pointed rather to rapprochement between the two superpowers, doubters were constantly reassured by the propaganda: America had not forgotten the "enslaved nations."[5] This propaganda also fed the illusion that the West would help in the Hungarian Revolution, especially as they would not have to initiate the "liberation" but simply support an independence struggle that had arisen out of a domestic explosion. Many people may be surprised to know that according to a survey among Hungarian refugees in Austria in February 1957, 96 percent trusted in some kind of assistance from the United States and 77 percent understood this to be military assistance.[6]

It has to be added that similar illusions about the possible role of the West and the United States were current (and remain so to this day) among the Western public, who looked on the Hungarians' struggle for freedom in 1956 with general sympathy. US liberation propaganda aroused serious expectations in Western societies, as well, and it became apparent to many people after the defeat of the Hungarian Revolution that the foreign policy of the democratic countries often failed to follow the general intrinsic ideas of democracy: the decisive foreign-policy interests of *Realpolitik* were often at variance with the liberal idea of freedom.[7]

Another group of misconceptions about the role of the US administration sets out expressly (and seemingly rationally) to explain that although the United States would have liked to extend help to the Hungarian Revolution, it was unable to do so because "unfavourable conditions" prevailed at the time. The "excuses" given are usually the following:

1. Eisenhower and his administration could not give due attention to events in Hungary because of the presidential election campaign. (The election was held on November 6.)

2. The US State Department was insufficiently prepared with policy line for treating events in Hungary.

3. Secretary of State John Foster Dulles was hospitalized at the worst possible time, on November 3.

4. The US legation in Budapest was under a chargé d'affaires during the revolution. The appointed minister, Edward T. Wailes, only arrived on November 2.

5. Hungary's geographical position precluded entry by US troops without violating Austria's neutrality. (This argument even appears in Eisenhower's memoirs, although the president would have been quite aware this was not a major factor in shaping US policy,[8] especially as there is plenty of evidence that military intervention was excluded from the options at the outset. Secretary of State John Foster Dulles had distanced himself clearly in public from such a course, in connection with the events in Poland. Appearing on the popular political television program *Face the Nation* on October 21, Dulles replied to a question that the United States would not send troops to Poland even if there should be armed intervention by the Soviets.[9])

Although most of these suppositions have at least some truth in them, the problem with them remains that these circumstances did not materially affect the course of events. The behaviour of the US government was not decided by such contingencies, random in some cases, but by the mechanism of Cold War, which meant that the United States could not intervene in the imperial affairs of the rival superpower, the Soviet Union, without risking a third world war.

The Suez Crisis

The belief that the revolution could have succeeded if the concurrent Suez Crisis had not prevented the West from acting together still occupies a special place among the prevalent myths about the Hungarian Revolution.[10]

It is generally established that Israel's October 29, 1956, attack on Egypt came a few days after secret British-French-Israeli talks in Sèvres, France. According to the agreed-upon scenario, the British and French governments, as a "peacemaking force," then issued an ultimatum to the "warring parties," and when this was rejected by Egypt, the British and French air forces began on October 31 to bomb Egyptian military and strategic targets. On November 5, Anglo-French paratrooper units landed at Port Said, at the mouth of the Suez Canal.

President Eisenhower reacted angrily to his allies launching military action of such weight without the knowledge or agreement of the US leadership, indeed to them conducting it despite his prior warning. So the United States moved strongly from the outset to stop the military action. US economic and political pressure then forced the British and French governments, on November 6 and 7 respectively, to comply with an extraordinary UN General Assembly resolution calling for an immediate ceasefire.[11]

The obvious concurrence of the two crises gave grounds for speculation— not wholly unacceptable as a scholarly hypothesis—that the British, French, and Israeli politicians preparing for Suez at the secret talks at Sèvres on October 22– 24 had been swayed by news of the outbreak of the Hungarian uprising when they agreed on a date for the attack on Egypt and, that having observed with relief that Soviet attention would be tied down by events in Eastern Europe, they had advanced the planned Israeli attack on Egypt by several days.[12] It is now known that the October 29 timing of the attack had been agreed on the first day of the meeting at Sèvres, on October 22.[13] The British and French foreign ministers intervened urgently to fix a date and wanted the Israeli attack to occur as soon as possible. This was not because they thought that the Soviet Union would be preoccupied by events in Hungary, as many still think today, since the events only ensued the following day, on October 23. However, the Polish crisis had broken out a few days earlier, on October 19, and might have influenced the timing to some extent. The real, prime reason for the haste was that the British and French had already been holding expeditionary forces on alert for some time, waiting for a political decision on action against Egypt. That state of alert could not be sustained for much longer. The minutes of the secret negotiations at Sèvres were eventually signed on October 24. The October 29 date of the Israeli attack was left unchanged, so the outbreak of the Hungarian Revolution or news of it made no change in the agreed scenario. The date of the Suez action was not advanced by the uprising.

As for lack of unity in the West, the division among the Western powers caused by the Middle East conflict certainly made life easier for the Soviets. Without Suez, the world public would clearly have condemned the crushing of the Hungarian Revolution with greater unanimity, although there was no shortage of such moral support anyway. But increasing knowledge of once top-secret records of Soviet decision-making and crisis management make it possible to affirm that the Moscow leadership would have made the same decision if need be, even if there had been no Suez. And they would do so again, to salvage the Communist system in Czechoslovakia in 1968, while in 1981 only effective local crisis management (introduction of a state of emergency) forestalled a similar Soviet intervention in Poland. Similarly, passiveness in the West was caused not by the absence of an ability to act together at a given time, and not by the Suez Crisis, but rather by forced inaction deriving from the policy of status quo and spheres of interest.

However, the Suez Crisis provided the American leadership especially with a fine excuse to explain why, after years of liberation propaganda, the United States did not, when occasion arose, give the least help to an Eastern European nation that had rebelled against Soviet rule and was waging armed combat for its freedom.

The United Nations

There remain to this day many illusions and legends in the public mind about the possible crisis-managing role of the UN and the debates in the Security Council and the General Assembly.

The 1956 revolutionary press and the programs and other statements of various revolutionary organizations often contained demands betraying that Hungarian society at the time overestimated the role that the UN could play. It was generally imagined that the UN was capable of effective mediation between the superpowers in case of a conflict, and so it was generally hoped that the Security Council or the General Assembly, supported by world public opinion, could effectively influence directing Soviet policy toward a peaceful solution to the Hungarian situation. Many expected UN observers or UN forces would intervene during the revolution itself. After November 4, almost everyone hoped that UN observers at least would arrive after the extraordinary General Assembly resolution that condemned the Soviet intervention. They expected the observers to mediate between the Kádár government and Hungarian society. Characteristic of those expectations was the way a three-person delegation of the University Revolutionary Committee sought out Imre Nagy at the Yugoslav Embassy on November 16, 1956, and suggested he "invite the UN into Hungary." According to one person's memory, Nagy replied only, "It's not that simple, guys."[14]

These expectations could have arisen because the United Nations was seen as an international conflict-resolving forum independent of both military blocs, acceptable in principle even to the Soviets. The UN framework had been already used by the United States very effectively (during the Korean War) to stop the Soviet Union expanding its sphere of influence. Many people came to the conclusion that Hungary might become a "second Korea" through UN intervention. In fact, however, up until that time, the UN had only proved itself at resolving conflicts that fell outside the conflicting interests of the superpowers. During the Korean War, the Soviet Union, for the first and last time, had withdrawn from the Security Council and so, unwittingly, made it possible for the Western military alliance to organize itself under UN auspices to fight North Korea. This campaign had proved to be a single, unrepeatable occasion, and even then, it had only made it possible to contain Communist expansion, not to push it back,[15] as an intervening nation or group of nations would have had to do in Hungary.

Connected with the UN debates was a "treachery"-type legend that arose during the days of the revolution about one of the major actors, Hungary's permanent UN representative, Péter Kós, and the statement he read in the Security Council on October 28. The legend has it that Kós's statement, which asserted that the Hungarian government protested against the UN's debate on the Hungarian situation, was a forgery, put forward by the "traitor" Péter Kós at the behest of the Soviets. To give more credibility to this myth, the revolutionary press immediately discovered that Kós's real name was Lev Konduktorov and that he was a Soviet citizen. This all seemed to be confirmed a few days after the statement was read, when Péter Kós was relieved of his post.

The matter was cleared up only in the early 1990s; however, even now, many people accept the legend as the reality, especially as the admittedly much more exciting original version resurfaces in journalism about 1956 from time to time. The truth of the matter is that Péter Kós had never been a Soviet citizen, although his name had been Konduktorov until the early 1950s, when he became a diplomat and Hungarianized it.[16] As for the ostensible treachery, it emerges from Soviet sources that the government statement in question had been initiated in Moscow, but it had proceeded through normal channels in Hungary. On October 28, the Soviets, through their Budapest ambassador, Yuri Andropov, called on the Hungarian government to issue an immediate statement saying that the events in Hungary were solely a domestic affair and the government protested against the question being placed on the General Assembly agenda.[17] The Hungarian government immediately complied with this "request." The statement was signed by Imre Nagy himself and sent out to Péter Kós by diplomatic channels before the Security Council meeting began. All this happened during the relatively "rational" phase of the revolution, when Nagy still hoped that the situation might be consolidated through cooperation with the Soviets.[18]

The real irony of history in this legend, however, is that the Hungarian mission to the UN did have a traitor. The public at the time could not know that, and the few people who have learned of it today are those who have very carefully read the footnotes in scholarly publications. The treacherous diplomat was not Péter Kós but János Szabó, the UN representative ad interim appointed by Imre Nagy, who systematically sabotaged the instructions received from the prime minister for the November 3 meeting of the Security Council, announcing the commencement of Soviet–Hungarian troop-withdrawal negotiations but failing to pass on Imre Nagy's urgent request that the great powers take a position on Hungarian neutrality, declared on November 1.[19]

The public at the time heard in the press and on the radio about the sharp debates going on in the UN Security Council. Based on what the media reported and still more on the rhetoric employed in public circles, it understandably seemed as if the main conflict in the UN forum was taking place between the Soviet Union and the Western powers. This assessment has stuck in the public mind for decades, but it is now clear from American, British, and French records that the real clashes of opposing views on the Hungarian question in the UN occurred behind the scenes, at secret three-power coordination talks between representatives of the United States, Britain, and France. For the British and French, after the attack on Egypt, did their utmost to distract attention by ensuring that the Hungarian question was transferred from the Security Council to the Emergency Session of the General Assembly convened on October 31, where they began to talk about the Middle East situation.[20] This solution was "incidentally" more favourable for the Hungarian Revolution, as it protected the issue from a Soviet veto, leaving a chance, at least in principle, that a UN resolution passed in good time—before November 4, say—might influence events in a positive way. But the Americans wanted to concentrate on the Suez Crisis and did all they could to prevent this, insisting that the two questions be handled separately. They managed to keep this up until November 4, but on hearing of the Soviet intervention, the US representative tabled the very Anglo-French proposal that the Americans had been sabotaging so successfully. American diplomacy inside and outside the UN was turned fully toward condemning the Soviet intervention in Hungary, aiming to give the impression to the world that the United States had been playing a plainly positive role from the outset in settling the Middle East crisis, as well as the Hungarian question.

This, as we know, succeeded, and it was decades before light was shed on the real role of the US leadership, based on the secret talks just mentioned.[21]

The Soviet Union

Two basic categories of myths and illusions about the Hungarian Revolution can be distinguished: one consists of those that arose at the time and persist to this day, the other of those that arose after the change of system in 1989. Those treated so far all belong to the first category, but the myths about the Soviet role include cases of both.

One of the most widespread misconceptions at the time of the revolution was that the Soviet Union would agree to restore Hungary's independence, as long as it took the form of neutrality. This idea gained special significance because it seemed realistic to many in the first couple of days of November. In the final days of October, it had become a general revolutionary demand that Hungary declare its neutrality and withdraw from the Warsaw Pact; the decision to do so was made by the Nagy government on November 1.[22] Ever since then, the rational and the irrational have mingled in people's assessments of Hungarian neutrality, which is unsurprising as the issue is extremely complex.

The general popularity of the idea of neutrality, before and during the revolution, contributed greatly to the assumption (seemingly rational but ultimately misconceived) that a neutral non-aligned Hungary would provide the Soviet Union with the same kind of security guarantee that Hungary's existing status did. Such hopes for neutrality were fuelled further by the Soviet–Yugoslav rapprochement in 1955–1956, when many drew the false conclusion that the Soviet Union was prepared to tolerate a Yugoslav-type non-aligned status in other satellite countries, as well. The Soviets certainly had made many positive gestures to revive friendship in 1955–1956, seeming to accept, for instance, the Yugoslav doctrine that there could be other roads to socialism than the one represented by the Soviet model. But the Soviet leaders—still able to think only in terms of two blocs—did not really accept the Yugoslav approach. The purpose of Soviet policy was to peacefully, steadily, and completely, and if need be, at the price of concessions, reintegrate Yugoslavia into the socialist camp, and that included ensuring Yugoslavia subscribed to the Warsaw Pact. It only became apparent to the Soviets in the spring of 1958 that the Yugoslavs were not prepared to comply at all—indeed they sought an ever more intensive international role for the movement of neutral and non-aligned countries—so that Soviet–Yugoslav relations eventually cooled again.

Another generally held opinion was that if the Soviet Union had been able to agree with the Western powers in 1955 on the status of Austria and had withdrawn its troops from its zone of occupation in the eastern part of that country, there would be hope of a similar arrangement in Hungary. But the Austrian state treaty had come about through mutual concessions as a real compromise between the great powers, whereas the West was not willing or able to offer similar compensation for the "sacrifice" of Hungary, for, to take matters to absurd extremes, the exchange value might have been the Sovietization of Denmark or the Netherlands. The concession in Austria's case had been a declaration of permanent neutrality, which meant that Austria could not join NATO, even though its independence had been restored. This was a considerable strategic gain for the Soviets; no wonder the American leaders hesitated for a long time before agreeing to it. Strangely, many people still fail to understand this relatively simple piece of political trading: they still think that the Austrian declaration of neutrality was made under pressure from the Western powers.

Meanwhile the position of the Imre Nagy government on neutrality was motivated by two considerations with opposite signs, one rational and one irrational. In the final days of October, it was still hoped that taking up this demand, which was generally supported by the revolutionary public (and at that stage would simply have meant just a promise to begin negotiations to that end), would contribute greatly to consolidating the situation. On the afternoon of October 31, Imre Nagy announced in a speech to a crowd gathered outside Parliament that "we have begun on this day negotiations on the withdrawal of Soviet troops from the country [and] on resigning the obligations placed on us under the Warsaw Pact." But he went on to "ask for a little patience from you; I think the results will be such that you can place that confidence [in us]." Answering questions from Western journalists after the rally, Nagy made an even more decisive announcement: "Hungary has the chance to withdraw from this alliance without causing a general disintegration of the Warsaw Pact and it will represent this position vigorously."[23] He must have been referring to the independent status being negotiated at direct talks with the Soviet Union, which were likely to take a long time. The public announcement was supposed to show that the political leaders had espoused these basic demands and would argue them before the Soviet Union, but they expected society to give the government its unreserved support in return.

However, the unilateral declaration of neutrality came under quite different circumstances. The government finally decided to make it on November 1 as a desperate measure, essentially because the situation could be no worse. By then, the resumed influx of Soviet troops and the behaviour of Ambassador Andropov had made it plain that the Soviets were preparing another invasion in order to overturn a Hungarian government they had hitherto recognized as legitimate.

Also part of the intricate story of Hungarian neutrality in 1956 is that the cabinet agreement in principle to declare neutrality, reached at its morning session on November 1, did not become public for decades and, more surprisingly still, did not emerge even when the main 1956 government papers were published.[24] It turned out later that two different sets of minutes were prepared intentionally, the official version omitting the paragraph on neutrality, which stated,

> For the sake of both putting an end to the armed fighting and ensuring the full and final independence of the country the Cabinet discussed the question of neutrality. The Cabinet unanimously agreed with the position that the government should declare the country's neutrality. For the time being [the Cabinet] refrains from deciding which form of neutrality should be chosen (Switzerland, Austria or Yugoslavia). This very day, Géza Losonczy will prepare a draft communiqué for public announcement, together with a simultaneous information note for the diplomatic corps, a draft telegram to the General Secretary of the UN, and finally an announcement for the press and radio.[25]

Logically, a failed revolution, in which many lose their lives, always raises the question of whether, despite defeat, the revolution may not have had some long-term effect to lend it subsequent validity and show after all that the dead did not die in vain. Although for many, including the author, the historical significance of Hungary's 1956 revolution means it suffices to find such worth in the revolution's moral content—its expression of an elemental human desire for freedom—and in the decisively positive effect it had on the nature of the Kádár system, others are left unsatisfied. This desire to find validity generated, around the time of the regime change in 1989–1990, a myth very popular to this day, namely that the Hungarian Revolution had dealt the first blow to the Soviet Union, which in the end proved fatal enough to contribute to the collapse of the Communist world system. But those espousing this view are conveniently forgetting that according to such logic, the "first blow" would actually have been the Berlin uprising of June 1953. Unsurprisingly, an East German version of this myth also reappears from time to time.[26]

In fact, one of the most important effects of the Hungarian Revolution was the clear evidence, exhibited by the passive behaviour of the Western powers, that the West acknowledged and had no wish to question the post-1945 European status quo, despite all its propaganda. That was a great relief to the Soviet leaders, who now had concrete evidence instead of tacit agreement that they need not take the Western point of view into account when settling conflicts within their empire, however drastic their methods. In that respect, the Hungarian Revolution certainly offered the Soviets an important advantage in position. The US psychological warfare about "the liberation of the enslaved nations" largely ceased after 1956, which reduced substantially the threat associated with the continual uncertainty factor over the East-central European security zone, though it had been posed only on a propaganda level. And after the Hungarian Revolution, the Soviet Union enjoyed the most dynamic ten years since its foundation, in which it managed to outdo the United States in development in some areas, such as space research. Although some people have tried to ascribe the collapse of the Soviet Union to moral factors, it actually came to pass simply because of the familiar factors of imperial overexpansion and economic uncompetitiveness.[27]

Of course, the Hungarian Revolution's moral significance and influence can hardly be overestimated, but the Westerners shaken by the Soviet intervention in Hungary were mainly people with illusions of some kind about the Soviet Union, above all left-wingers who had somehow viewed the Soviet Union as a practicable pattern or prop for a socialist model of society. They saw the

Hungarian Revolution as a test of whether it would be possible to achieve a version of socialism that combined Western political democracy with collective ownership and the principles of social equality. So the brutal suppression of the Hungarian Revolution did damage not only to the Western European Communist parties but also to the left wing of the socialist and social democratic parties. This was a big factor behind the way the New Left, emerging in the 1960s, and later the Euro-communists, distanced themselves expressly from the existing Soviet model and sought other models for the socialist system they envisaged and hoped to implement.

The biggest surprise when examining the myths and illusions to do with the Hungarian Revolution is that they include some new ones, born in the last few years. Furthermore, this new myth-making is not generated by any lack of the information necessary to make a rational judgement, or difficulty of access to it. On the contrary, it is born out of the appearance of new documents, whose very existence was not known before, which give the most reliable picture so far of the Soviet decision-making mechanism. This latest Soviet myth has arisen out of a general reappraisal of Soviet policy toward the Hungarian Revolution, prompted by examination of the so-called Malin Notes, published in the mid-1990s.

These very informative, though unofficial and sometimes fragmentary, notes made up of discussions in the Communist Party of the Soviet Union (CPSU) Presidium about the crisis in Hungary provide the first glimpse of the debates in the top Moscow leadership that resulted in the well-known decisions.[28] They confirm earlier suppositions that there were indeed very sharp policy debates in the Kremlin, but, oddly enough, the new sources have divided opinion on what was at stake.

Analysis of the notes has led some researchers to conclude that the Soviet leaders were far more open in handling the crisis than previously thought, and crushing the uprising was not the only course considered. If circumstances (not usually detailed) had developed otherwise, there might have been a chance of the revolution succeeding, or even of the 1989–1990 liberation of East-central Europe occurring thirty years earlier.[29] Researchers reaching this conclusion base it largely on a single piece of information: the CPSU Presidium agreed unanimously on October 30 (under pressure from a visiting Chinese delegation) that the Soviet troops had to be withdrawn from Hungary.[30] Although this position was altered the next day, when it was decided to suppress the revolution, the fact that the earlier decision took place is construed to mean that the Soviet Union, at that moment, had been ready to surrender Hungary.

So the problem lies in interpreting an accepted fact. Most researchers take the opposing view that the Malin Notes generally confirm, not contradict, the standard assessment of Soviet policy. Though there were serious debates in the Presidium and they may have been more heated than thought hitherto, they were not about abandoning Hungary by recognizing the success of the revolution. They concerned the degree and nature of the possible concessions to the Imre Nagy government that could be made in that situation, to consolidate it within the Communist system.[31]

The key to interpreting the often fragmented Malin Notes is to use the still valid method of evaluating every new piece of information by analyzing the whole body of information, new and old, in the context of the overall world political situation and of East–West relations in their entirety. This approach makes it quite clear that the potential decision of the Soviet leadership could never have involved "letting Hungary go." On the contrary, the withdrawal of Soviet troops from Hungary would have been the maximum possible political concession by the Soviet leadership—to avoid what they, too, saw as the bad solution of restoring order by force of arms—provided the Imre Nagy government could manage to consolidate itself while preserving the Communist system and the unity of the Soviet bloc. The Malin Notes offer plenty of concrete evidence that withdrawal could only have been considered if these two conditions had been met. The two most strongly worded and documented examples of such evidence in the Malin Notes are provided by Dmitri Shepilov and Anastas Mikoyan. Foreign Minister Dmitri Shepilov, when supporting the decision just mentioned, stated, "With the agreement of the government of Hungary, we are ready to withdraw troops. We'll have to keep up a struggle with national-Communism for a long time."[32] The expected consequence of such a decision, therefore, was not restoration of the capitalist system but rather consolidation of a situation such as Poland's: a reformed Communist system with greater internal autonomy, yet still remaining loyal to Moscow and within the Soviet bloc.

Typically, Anastas Mikoyan was the one to voice the plainest support for maintaining the status quo, although otherwise he had been the leadership member with the most liberal view on Hungary. "We simply cannot let Hungary be removed from our camp,"[33] he said at the November 1 meeting of the Presidium, a day after the decision to invade had been taken, as he tried to convince the others that the chances of a political solution were not quite exhausted, and they should wait another ten to fifteen days before intervening.

Moreover it can be imagined what effect "abandoning" Hungary would have had in Poland, where the government had managed to avert armed intervention by Soviet forces only days before. It is known now for certain that anti-Communist feelings were at least as decisive in the actions of Polish society in 1956 as they were in Hungary.[34] Władysław Gomułka could hardly have defused the discontent of the masses (as he did by pointing to the German peril) if the Hungarians had been "liberated." Abandoning Hungary under those conditions would have had a domino effect, the prospect the Soviet leadership feared most.

So, paradoxically, such newly discovered documents as the Malin Notes may sometimes provide opportunities to create new popular myths, not just realistic interpretations. However, the task of historians persistently battling the historical myths, legends, illusions, and misconceptions must be to convince their readers that Hungary's place, role, and opportunities in the world can only be gauged realistically—in history and in the present—if mythical thinking is authoritatively overcome in our approach to the recent past by realistic historical self-knowledge.

Research for this article was supported by the MTA Politikatudományi Intézete (Institute of Political Studies, Hungarian Academy of Sciences). It has recently been published in *Putere si societate: Blocul comunist sub impactul destalinizarii*, 1956 [Power and Society: The Communist Bloc under the Impact of De-stalinisation, 1956] (Bucharest, Institutul National Pentru Studiul Totalitarismulu (INST), (2006).

Notes

1. On the Eastern Europe policy of the Eisenhower administration, see: Bennett Kovrig, *Of Walls and Bridges: The United States and Eastern Europe* (New York: New York University Press, 1991); James David Marchio, *Rhetoric and Reality: The Eisenhower Administration and Unrest in Eastern Europe, 1953–1959* (Ann Arbor, MI: University Microfilms International, 1993); László Borhi, "Rollback, Liberation, Containment or Inaction? U.S. Policy and Eastern Europe in the 1950s," *Journal of Cold War Studies 1* (Fall 1999, 3): 67–110, published also as Chapter 6 in László Borhi's *Hungary in the Cold War, 1945–1956. Between the United States and the Soviet Union* (Budapest, New York, CEU Press, 2004); Békés Csaba, *Az 1956-os magyar forradalom a világpolitikában* [The 1956 Hungarian revolution in world politics](Second enlargened edition) (Budapest: 1956-os Intézet, 2006); Csaba Békés, "The 1956 Hungarian Revolution and World Politics," Working Paper No. 16, Cold War International History Project (CWIHP) (Washington, DC: Woodrow Wilson International Center for Scholars, September 1996): http://www. wilsoncenter.org/topics/pubs/ACFB4E.pdf (accessed 19 12 2009).

2. I have not tried to be exhaustive in this study. I have confined myself to 1956 myths tied in some way to the possibility of victory in the revolution. For legends tied to an assessment of the revolution and its events and participants, see György Litván, "Mítoszok és legendák 1956-ról" [Myths and legends about 1956], in Zsuzsanna Kőrösi, Éva Standeisky, and János M. Rainer, eds., *Évkönyv VIII–2000. Magyarország a jelenkorban* [Yearbook VIII—2000. Hungary in the contemporary period] (Budapest: 1956-os Intézet, 2000), 205–218.

3. Most arguments and views mentioned appeared in the huge body of journalism about 1956. No attempt has been made to give precise bibliographical references for each, which would require a separate research program. It would also mean examining articles that appeared in the West before 1989, and dozens of references would be needed for each argument before a fraction of the potential number had been considered. But references are, of course, given for arguments in historical works or in memoirs of politicians active at the time.

4. On the part Radio Free Europe played, see Gyula Borbándi, *Magyarok az angol kertben. A Szabad Európa Rádió története* [Hungarians in the English garden. History of Radio Free Europe] (Budapest: Európa, 1996); articles by Paul Henze, William E. Griffith, Jan Nowak, James G. McCargar, and Gyula Borbándi, in *Évkönyv V* [Yearbook V] *1996–1997* (Budapest: 1956-os Intézet, 1997).

5. On US propaganda directed to Eastern Europe in this period, see Marchio, *Rhetoric and Reality*.

6. *Hungary and the 1956 Uprising, Personal Interviews with 1,000 Hungarian Refugees in Austria* (International Research Associates, Inc., February 1957, Special Report No. 12, March 1957, Hoover Archives), quoted in Marchio, *Rhetoric and Reality*, 417.

7. Refer to Csaba Békés and Melinda Kalmár, "Mikor lehet belőle történelem?" [When can it turn into history?] *Népszabadság* (October 22, 1994).

8. Dwight D. Eisenhower, *The White House years:* Vol. 2. *Waging Peace.* (Garden City, NY: Doubleday, 1965), 88–89.

9. *Foreign Relations of the United States*, Vol. 25, *Eastern Europe* (Washington, DC: Government Printing Office, 1990), 274.

10. This position crops up sporadically among historians, as well, though authors cite no new evidence for it beyond the coincidence of the two events in history. One recent example is Daniel F. Calhoun's *Hungary and Suez, 1956: An Exploration of Who Makes History* (Lanham, MD: University Press of America, 1991).

11. The most thorough work about the Suez Crisis remains Keith Kyle, *Suez* (London: Weidenfeld and Nicholson, 1991). See also Denis Lefebvre's *L'Affaire de Suez* (Paris: Bruno Leprince Editeur, 1996).

12. See Miklós Molnár, *Budapest 1956: A History of the Hungarian Revolution* (London: Allen and Unwin, 1971), 203.

13. *The Diary of Ben Gurion,* in S. I. Troen and M. Shemesh, eds., *The Suez–Sinai Crisis 1956: Retrospective and Reappraisal* (London: Frank Cass, 1990), 308.

14. Contribution by Dr. Gisele Friedrichs at the international conference entitled "A Crack in the Iron Curtain or a Mortal Wound for Communism? The Impact of the Hungarian Revolution of 1956" (Washington, DC, October 25, 2001), and her personal communication with the author on that day.

15. Communist propaganda and historiography referred throughout the Communist period to the aggression of South Korea, but the latest researches show the attack came from North Korea, with the aim of occupying the south of the peninsula and uniting the two parts of the country under Communism. Despite the assumptions at the time, none of this was instigated by Stalin. In fact, Kim Il-Sung, leader of the North Korean party, spent several months trying to persuade Stalin to allow the *blitzkrieg* that was intended to free the South in a matter of days. See Kathryn Weathersby, "Soviet Aims in Korea and the Origins of the Korean War, 1945–1950: New Evidence from Russian Archives," in Cold War International History Project (CWIHP) Working Paper No. 8 (Washington, DC: Woodrow Wilson International Centre for Scholars, November 1993).

16. On the role of Péter Kós, see the 1990 interview with him by Gábor Murányi (1956 Institute Oral History Archive, No. 239) and Gábor Murányi, "A Konduktorov-ügy" (The Konduktorov affair), *Magyar Nemzet* (August 21, 1991).

17. See Csaba Békés, Malcolm Byrne, and János M. Rainer, eds., *The 1956 Hungarian Revolution: A History in Documents* (Budapest, New York: CEU Press, 2002), 270–271.

18. For Imre Nagy's policy during the revolution, see János M. Rainer, *Nagy Imre: Politikai életrajz Második kötet, 1953–1958* (Imre Nagy: Political Biography Vol. 2. 1953–1958) (Budapest: 1956-os Intézet, 1999).

19. See Csaba Békés, "A magyar semlegesség 1956-ban" [Hungarian neutrality in 1956], in *Semlegesség—Illúziók és realitás* [Neutrality—Illusion and Reality] (Budapest: Biztonságpolitikai és Honvédelmi Kutatások Központja, 1997), 121–122.

20. See Csaba Békés, "A brit kormány és az 1956-os magyar forradalom" [The British government and the 1956 Hungarian Revolution], in *Évkönyv, 1992* [Yearbook, 1992] (Budapest: 1956-os Intézet), 19–38; Csaba Békés, "The Hungarian Question on the UN Agenda: British Foreign Office Documents from 1956," *The Hungarian Quarterly* (Spring 2000): 103–122.

21. See Csaba Békés, "Az Egyesült Államok és a magyar semlegesség 1956-ban" (The US and Hungarian neutrality in 1956), in *Évkönyv 1994* (Yearbook, 1994) (Budapest: 1956-os Intézet), 165–178.

22. On Hungarian neutrality in general, see Csaba Békés, "The 1956 Hungarian Revolution and the Declaration of Neutrality," *Cold War History* 6, 4 (November 2006): 477–500.

23. *Magyar Nemzet*, November 1, 1956.

24. See Ferenc Glatz, "A kormány és a párt vezető szerveinek dokumentumaiból 1956. október 23–november 4" [Some documents of government and leading party bodies, October 23–November 4, 1956], *História* XI, 4-5 (1989): 25–52; see also "Források a Nagy Imre-kormány külpolitikájának történetéhez" (Sources on the foreign-policy history of the Imre Nagy government), in József Kiss, Zoltán Ripp, and István Vida, eds., *Társadalmi Szemle* 48:5 (1993): 78–94.

25. MOL, XX-5-h, The trial of Imre Nagy and his associates. Investigations reports, Vol. 12, Géza Losonczy's records. For the English text of the minutes see Békés, Byrne, and Rainer, *The 1956 Hungarian Revolution*, 321–323.

26. Charles S. Maier, introducing a volume of documents forming the latest source materials on the history of the Berlin uprising, calls this assumption self-evident. See Christian F. Ostermann, ed., *Uprising in East Germany, 1953: The Cold War, the German Question and the First Major Upheaval behind the Iron Curtain*, National Security Archive Cold War Readers (Budapest: Central European Press, 2001), xvii.

27. An example of the extensive literature on the collapse of the Soviet Union, with special significance for readers in East-central Europe, is Jacques Lévesque, *The Enigma of 1989: The USSR and the Liberation of Eastern Europe* (Berkeley: University of California Press, 1997).

28. For the full text of the English translation of the Malin Notes see "The 'Malin notes' on the Crises in Hungary and Poland, 1956," trans. and annotated by Mark Kramer, *CWIHP Bulletin* 8–9 (Winter, 1996–Spring, 1997): 385–410.

29. This position has been taken most firmly by Mark Kramer, "New Evidence on Soviet Decision-Making and the 1956 Polish and Hungarian Crises," *CWIHP Bulletin* 8–9 (Winter, 1996–Spring, 1997): 358–385. An essentially similar position is held by Vlad Zubok, who writes, "We can be sure that if the power setup around Khrushchev had developed differently and if a leader less given to violence than he had headed the Kremlin, Soviet tanks would not have

rolled into Budapest and the history of Eastern Europe, including the Soviet Union, would have developed otherwise." Vladislav M. Zubok, "Hatalmi harc a Kremlben és a magyar válság" [Power struggle in the Kremlin and the Hungarian crisis], in *Évkönyv 1996–7* [Yearbook, 1996–1997] (Budapest: 1956-os Intézet, 1997), 65.

30. Békés, Byrne, and Rainer, *The 1956 Hungarian Revolution*, 295–299.

31. See Csaba Békés, "Cold War, Détente and the 1956 Hungarian Revolution," in Klaus Larres and Kenneth Osgood, eds., *The Cold War after Stalin's Death: A New International History* (Lanham, MD: Rowman and Littlefield, 2006). 213–233.

32. The Malin Notes, 392.

33. Ibid., 394.

34. See Pawel Machcewicz, *Rebellious Satellite: Poland 1956* (Washington, DC: Woodrow Wilson Center Press, 2009); and Pawel Machcewicz, "Social Protest and Political Crisis in 1956," in A. Kemp-Welch, ed., *Stalinism in Poland 1944–1956: Selected Papers from the Fifth World Congress of Central and East European Studies, Warsaw, 1995* (London: Macmillan Press Ltd., 1999), 102–104.

3.

The Economic Platforms of the Re-formed Political Parties in 1956

Susan Glanz

The Great Depression and the two world wars created an atmosphere where both politicians and the public saw that direct government involvement in the economy was the only way of preventing the repetition of these destructive events. The involvement of the state in the post–World War II economy increased everywhere in Europe. For example, in both France and Great Britain, railroads, banking (both the Bank of England and the Bank of France), and domestic energy (coal in England; electricity in France) were nationalized and placed under the jurisdiction of semi-public directorships. Health care and transportation were nationalized in England. And, in France, nationalization was accompanied by state planning. The view that planning and nationalization are important for the smooth running of the economy became the accepted European norm.

Hungarians felt the same way about the role of government. A public opinion poll conducted in 1945 found that 67 percent favoured nationalization of factories and 75 percent favoured nationalization of banks.[1] The eleven years that passed between 1945 and 1956 did not change these sentiments and none of the parties in the coalition government formed in October 1956 demanded reversing the process of nationalization in post–World War II Hungary. In 1956, none of the parties—including those that were centrist—advocated for the re-privatization of industry.

Economic background

In 1992 the University of Groningen's Growth and Development Centre created a database that estimated the per capita GDP for most countries from 1950s on. See Table 3.1.

Economists measure economic well-being and economic growth by looking at the growth rate of the per capita GDP. Based on the numbers in the table, Hungary's economic growth between 1950 and 1955 was 23.8 percent. Economists also warn that conclusions reached by this process can be misleading because:

   a. when products are low quality and not durable, people will have to buy them again and again,
   b. GDP doesn't measure the sustainability of growth. A country may achieve a temporary high GDP by over-exploiting natural resources or by misallocating investment, and
   c. quality of life is determined by many other factors besides physical goods.

Today, we know that lack of choices for consumers and producers, low quality of products, and over-allocation of investments funds to heavy industry all existed in Hungary. We also know that the pervasive atmosphere of fear made life difficult and impacted negatively on the quality of life. To make the numbers in Table 3.1 meaningful, therefore, let us compare them to pre-war data. Hungary's per capita GDP in 1935 was $2,471 and Austria's was $2,926.[3] So, in 1950 Hungary reached its 1935 GDP, while Austria surpassed hers by 26.7 percent.

Table 3.1 Per Capita Real GDP between 1950 and 1956 in Selected European Countries, Expressed American Dollars c. 1950s[2]

Year	Hungary	Czechoslovakia	Poland	Austria	West Germany
1950	2,480	3,501	2,447	3,706	4,281
1951	2,695	3,524	2,510	3,959	4,651
1952	2,762	3,598	2,521	3,967	5,046
1953	2,786	3,544	2,618	4,137	5,439
1954	2,850	3,652	2,715	4,555	5,797
1955	3,070	3,922	2,794	5,053	6,431
1956	2,906	4,110	2,864	5,397	6,839

A somewhat different data set was published by Iván Pető and Sándor Szakács, and is summarized in Table 3.2.[4]

Table 3.2: Per Capita Real Income in Hungary, 1950–1956 (1949 = 100), Expressed in American Dollars c. 1950s

Year	Per capita income for workers and employees	Per capita consumption by peasants[5]
1950	102.8	112.7
1951	97.8	118.8
1952	87.5	106.6
1953	91.0	100.6
1954	115.0	111.0
1955	121.8	124.5
1956	129.3	131.2

Although both data sets in Tables 3.1 and 3.2 show 20+ percent growth between 1950 and 1955, Table 3.2 shows that this growth was not continuous. The standard of living fell between 1950 and 1952, and in 1953 it was still below the 1950 level. According to Pető and Szakács's calculations, as the following Table 3.3 shows, the real wages in Hungary fell between 1951 and 1953, and in 1955 they were only slightly above the 1949 level.

Table 3.3: Real Wages in Hungary between 1950 and 1955 (1949 = 100), Expressed in American Dollars c. 1950s[6]

Year	Real wages of workers and employees	Real wages of workers in Manufacturing
1950	101.3	107.4
1951	89.7	94.1
1952	82.3	84.5
1953	87.0	87.9
1954	102.3	103.9
1955	106.0	107.1

Iván Berend's calculations show similar results, namely that by 1953 the prices of consumer goods were nearly 100 percent higher than the 1949 price level, causing real wages to fall nearly 20 percent below the 1950 level.[7]

What do these statistics really show? Table 3.4 below shows the average monthly wages in Hungary in 1956 and 1957. According to calculations of the Trade Union Council quoted by Pető and Szakács, the minimum wages necessary to support a family of three was Ft. 1440, and for a family of four it was Ft. 1900. Thus the wages were not sufficient to provide for minimally acceptable living standards. "According to the Ministry of the Interior," again quoted by Pető and Szakács,

> a worker could afford a new winter coat (Ft 1,000) every ten and a half years, a wool suit (Ft 870) once in every two and a half years, and a pair of shoes (Ft 260) once a year; his wife a new wool suit (Ft 400) every three years and a cotton dress (Ft 150) and a pair of shoes (Ft 200) once a year and just like her husband a new winter coat (Ft 1,000) every ten years, and a pair of stockings (Ft 45) every six months. For their child they could buy clothing (Ft 150) every six months, every three and a half years a coat (Ft 400) and a pair of shoes (Ft 90) every six months.[8]

Table 3.4: Monthly Average Wages in Hungarian, Expressed in Ft[9]

sector of workforce	1956	1957
All workers and employees	1,235	1,445
Industrial workers	1,234	1,486
Construction workers	1,152	1,512
Employees of central government, healthcare, etc.	1,338	1,560
Employees of local government, healthcare, etc.	1,136	1,238

Events leading up to October 1956

The death of Stalin in 1953 began a thawing process everywhere in Central Europe. In 1955 the debate club of the Union of Working Youth (*Dolgozó Ifjúság Szövetsége [DISZ]*, the youth organization of the Communist Party) the Petőfi

Circle, was formed. The goal of the circle was to organize public discussions, first about how the decisions of the XXth Congress of the Soviet Communist Party applied to Hungary, and later discussions were organized on a range of topics from the freedom of the press, economics, history, and education to philosophy. The leadership of each circle was composed of young Communists. The Petőfi Circle's two economic forums on May 9 and June 20, 1956, focused on two problems, the lack of statistical information, both domestic and international, and lack of knowledge of the planning process. Several similar circles were formed all over the country, and their meetings were widely attended.

Khrushchev's revelations about Stalin as at the XXth Congress of the Russian Communist Party, in February 1956, caused a political earthquake that was felt everywhere in Eastern Europe. At the end of June, Polish workers in Poznan went on strike and demanded increased wages, payment for overtime work, the abolition of piecework, and the rollback of fuel and food price increases. The revolt was crushed, the workers did not achieve their goals, and many were tried, but some political changes did occur. (Wladyslaw Gomulka, Zenon Kliszko, and General Marian Spychalski were rehabilitated and readmitted into the Party.)[10] At the same time in Hungary, in March, Rákosi announced that the miscarriage of justice against László Rajk[11] would be rectified by his ceremonial reburial on October 6.[12] On July 18, 1956, the much-hated Rákosi resigned, and calls for socio-economic and political reform speeded up after the summer of 1956. Toward the end of September, the first of the Poznan trials began in Poland, and members of the Petőfi Circle called for a solidarity demonstration with the Polish workers for October 23.

On October 13, 1956, Imre Nagy was readmitted to the Hungarian Workers' Party.[13] *The Washington Post* evaluated Nagy's return as "a big step toward liquidating the remnants of Stalinism by formally announcing that ex-Premier Imre Nagy has been restored to party membership."[14]

Even before the demonstrations could be organized, on October 6, after the Rajk funeral, students marched through Budapest shouting anti-Stalinist slogans. On October 16 a meeting of about 1,600 undergraduates in Szeged founded the League of Hungarian University and College Students (*Magyar Egyetemisták és Főiskolások Szövetsége* [*MEFESZ*]), a students' organization independent of the Union of Working Youth (*DISZ*) and the HWP (Hungarian Workers' Party, or *Magyar Dolgozók Pártja*). Their action was followed in several universities and colleges. On October 22 the demands of the students at the Building Industry Technological University in Budapest were published and widely circulated.[15] Of the sixteen demands, five (points 6 through 10) dealt with economic issues. These were:

> 6. We demand a re-examination and re-adjustment of Hungarian–Soviet and Hungarian–Yugoslav political, economic and intellectual relations on the basis of complete political and economic equality and of non-intervention in each other's internal affairs.

> 7. We demand the re-organization of the entire economic life of Hungary, with the assistance of specialists. Our whole economic system based on planned economy should be re-examined with an eye to Hungarian conditions and to the vital interests of the Hungarian people.

> 8. Our foreign trade agreements and the real figures in respect of reparations that can never be paid should be made public. We demand frank and sincere information concerning the country's uranium deposits, their exploitation and the Russian concession. We demand that Hungary should have the right to sell the uranium ore freely at world market prices in exchange for hard currency.

> 9. We demand the complete revision of norms in industry and an urgent and radical adjustment of wages to meet the demands of workers and intellectuals. We demand that minimum living wages for workers should be fixed.

> 10. We demand that the delivery system should be placed on a new basis and that produce should be used rationally. We demand equal treatment of peasants farming individually.

Demand number 5 was the reestablishment of a multi-party system:

> 5. We demand general elections in this country, with universal suffrage, secret ballot and the participation of several Parties for the purpose of electing a new National Assembly. We demand that the workers should have the right to strike.

The demand for multiparty elections was a new element in the students' demands. The demands of the Writers' Union published the following day did not go as far as those of the students; it insisted on fewer economic changes, as outlined in points 3–5:

3. The country's economic position must be clearly stated. We shall not be able to recover after this crisis unless all workers, peasants and intellectuals can play their proper part in the political, social and economic administration of the country.

4. Factories must be run by workers and specialists. The present humiliating system of wages, norms, and social insurance conditions must be reformed. The trade unions must truly represent the interests of the Hungarian workers.

5. Our peasant policy must be put on a new foundation. Peasants must be given the right to decide their own future freely. Political and economic conditions must, at last, be created to allow memberships in co-operatives. The present system of deliveries to the State and of taxation must be gradually replaced by a system ensuring free socialist production and exchange of goods.[16]

That the Writers' Union memo voiced some of the demands that were just under the surface of society is shown by the report of the HWP. Document No. 21, Record of Conversation between Yurii Andropov and Ernő Gerő on October 12, 1956, reports that Gerő blames "anti-Soviet propaganda" on three economic issues.[17] These were:

b. Protests against the selling of [former] German properties as a form of Hungarian payments to the Soviet Union;

c. Protests against the alleged short selling of Hungarian uranium to the Soviet Union (even though the country received a Soviet loan before shipping [the raw materials] added comrade Gerő)

d. Complaints that Hungary is involved in unfavourable trade relations with the Soviet Union.

In the same document Andropov blames the

> economic hardships…to a great extent on the fact that our [Hungarian] friends have lately given up keeping an eye on the national economy. Several questions concerning industrial production are pending, most of them are not being taken care of at all…It is worth noting that while lately the Hungarian comrades are constantly receiving advice from the CPSU leadership on various issues, and even when they agree with these suggestions, afterwards they are too feeble when it comes to enforcing their execution.

The first Soviet armoured units entered Budapest in the early dawn hours on October 24. On the same day, during the morning hours, the HWP Central Committee confirmed Ernő Gerő in his post as first secretary and Imre Nagy as prime minister.

On October 26 a delegation of workers from Borsod County met Prime Minister Imre Nagy and presented to him a list of demands. Imre Nagy agreed with the demands and promised to fulfill them. The economic components of the demands that Nagy agreed with were

> the publication of foreign trade agreements, the use of uranium to the benefit of the Hungarians, the raising of base wages, the abolition of hidden price increases, the lowering of retirement age, the raising of family support and retirement payments, the abolition of the childlessness tax, introduction of train transportation subsidies, increased construction of apartments, and subsidization of private housing construction. The reorganization of agriculture should be voluntary, based on the interests on the peasantry.

Both the demands and Nagy's support for the demands were read on the national radio stations.[18]

On October 28, 1956, the Law Faculty of Loránd Eötvös University in Budapest founded the Revolutionary Committee of the Hungarian Intellectuals (*Magyar Értelmiség Forradalmi Bizottsága*). The economic demands listed in their appeal were published on October 28, 1956, and were similar to the demands published by the student groups and the Writers' Union, namely in the following points (2, 4–7):

2. The Government should abrogate all foreign trade agreements which are disadvantageous to the country. It should make public all foreign trade agreements concluded in the past, including those relating to uranium ore and bauxite....

4. Factories and mines should really become the property of the workers. We shall not return the factories and the land to the capitalists and to the landowners. Our factories should be managed by freely elected workers' councils. The Government should guarantee the functioning of small-scale private industry and private trade.

5. The Government should abolish the exploiting "norm" scheme. The Government should raise low wages and pensions to the limit of economic possibilities.

6. The trade unions should become genuine workers' organizations representing the workers' interests, with their leaders freely elected. The working peasants should form their own organizations to safeguard their interests.

7. The Government should ensure the freedom and security of agricultural production by supporting individual farmers and voluntary farm co-operatives. The hated delivery system, by which the peasants have been robbed, should be abolished.

As well, the demand for multiparty elections was again included in the statement: "We demand general elections with secret ballot. The people should be able to freely nominate their candidates."[19]

The *United Nations Report of the Special Committee on the Problem of Hungary* published in 1957 summarized the economic demands represented in the earliest resolutions and manifestos as a demand for openness.[20] "The demand for the publication of the facts about foreign trade and Hungary's economic difficulties, publication of the facts about uranium, reforms in connection with factory management and trade unions, the 'norm' system and other working conditions, and a revision of agrarian policy, especially in regard to agricultural co-operatives and compulsory deliveries....The economic objections showed a deep seated resentment of Hungary's dependence on the Soviet Union and the uncritical copying of the Soviet economic system."[21]

On October 28 Imre Nagy announced on radio that "the Hungarian government agreed with the Soviet government, the Soviet troops will begin immediate withdrawal from Budapest." In the same speech he promised that "the new government will work on a new broad-based program, in which we hope to solve the justified demands of workers." Nagy enumerated the "justified demands" that his government would work on, including the question of wages of work norms, the raising of minimum pay in the lowest wage brackets and the smallest pensions, and the raising of family allowances. To help resolve the housing crisis, the government promised the support all state, cooperative, and private construction of homes and apartments. He applauded the establishment of workers' councils. He also promised to work on a plan to increase production by agricultural cooperatives and by individual farms.[22]

On October 30, at 2:28 pm, Prime Minister Imre Nagy announced on national radio, "In the interest of the further democratization of the country's life, the cabinet abolishes the one-party system and places the country's government on the basis of democratic cooperation between the coalition parties, reborn in 1945. In accordance with this decision an inner cabinet has been formed within the coalition government, whose members are Imre Nagy, Zoltán Tildy, Béla Kovács, Ferenc Erdei, János Kádár, Géza Losonczy and a person to be appointed by the Social Democratic Party."[23] The four coalition parties were the Smallholders' Party (represented by Zoltán Tildy and Béla Kovács), the National Peasant Party (represented by Ferenc Erdei), the Hungarian Workers' Party (represented by János Kádár and Géza Losonczy), and the Social Democratic Party.

The multiparty democracy was short lived; it lasted for six days, from Tuesday, October 30, to Sunday, November 4, when the second Soviet invasion of Hungary began. After the initial announcement, several political parties immediately started to reorganize. Due to the short timeframe in which they were operating, the parties did not have time to develop full platforms.

The economic platforms of the coalition parties

The Smallholders' Party

On Wednesday, October 31, Radio Kossuth reported, and street posters announced, that the Smallholders' Party had been re-formed.[24] The party's much maligned Secretary-General Béla Kovács was understandably reluctant to assume a leadership role.[25] He assumed the post of president only after much convincing. The radio reporter and several papers quote him as saying "no one should dream of the old days. The days of the aristocrats, bankers and capitalists have ended forever. Those, today, who think in terms of 1939 or 1945, are not real smallholders."[26]

Due to the party's lack of time to develop an economic platform, modern scholars are forced to evaluate the publications by various local party organs and draw conclusions based on these platforms.

The recurring demands that were published by different Smallholders' Party cells did not go beyond the demands by the students in *MEFESZ* or those of the intellectuals. The poster published by the party cell of the 12th district of Budapest on October 31 asserted that "the economy of the nation cannot be run by any dogma...."[27] Some of the demands listed (13, 19, 27–28) were as follows:

13. Election of new union leadership. The right to strike.

19. Small crafts, services, students, and artists should receive subsidies from the state; and factory workers should receive a share from the profits of their factories.

27. All war indemnity payments and deliveries to the Soviet Union must be re-examined. While this re-examination is continuing, the deliveries must be stopped.

28. The just demands of the peasants should be satisfied by the Provisional Government.

A more detailed platform was published by the provisional executive committee of the Smallholders' Party of Györ-Sopron County.[28] Their circular, also published on October 31, lists eight economic demands (1–6 and 11–12), namely:

1. The acceptance of the principle of private property.

2. The unity of peasants.

3. The dissolution of state owned retail and service sector and the return of these establishments to private ownership. The acceptance of the idea of the sanctity of private property.

4. Unconditional support for private enterprise. Only self-initiated cooperatives, esp. to take advantage of large scale purchases and sales, should be allowed, and only if it is beneficial to members.

5. Full compensation to those who suffered because of forced collectivization.

6. Reopening of the denied pension applications, and the raising of all pensions to the level of providing decent living standards....

11. A new wage system that allows households with one wage earner to support a family.

12. The economic platform of the central Smallholders' Party cannot go against these demands.

Another appeal, addressed to railroad workers, in addition to the above listed demands, included the demands for a five-day, forty-hour workweek and for the abolition of the norm system. The appeal also stated that "land should belong to those who work it and the demand that the issues relating to the wage and family support systems be solved immediately."[29] István Varga, an economic advisor to the party, in an interview on November 3 added the demand of releasing economic and trade data to aid rational decision-making.[30]

The party support for a market-based system in small industry, farming, and retail trade is clear. Priority was placed on reforming the pension and wage systems and redressing past economic injustices. The termination of forced collectivization was also demanded. The party ceased its legal activities on November 4. A provisional executive committee met occasionally until the early spring of 1957.[31]

The National Peasant Party

Representatives of the National Peasant Party (*Nemzeti Parasztpárt*) met on October 31 at Vajdahunyad Castle, in Budapest's City Park. As some party leaders were viewed as Communist fellow travellers, and to indicate a break with this recent past, the party adopted a new name, the Petőfi Party, after the poet Sándor Petőfi, a leader of the March 15, 1848, revolution.[32] The formation of the National Peasant Party, and its name change to Petőfi Party, was announced on Thursday, November 1 on the radio.[33] The party did not publish a program, but a program is implied in interviews and reports written by leading members. Of the party's local organizations, the one in Szabolcs-Szatmár County reorganized the fastest, probably because this county was the party's stronghold after 1945. The most detailed program proposal was given in an interview by Sándor Varga, the secretary of this Szabolcs-Szatmár County organization. The economic program outlined by Varga was the following:

> The respect for private property is the basis of party policy, and the party will fight for free choice in production and free choice in sales....

> The 1945 land reform was legitimate and we will not return land owned by peasants. But, we find it necessary to demand the review of all those unlawful acts that were instituted against small peasant landholdings from 1948 on...Respecting the freedom of sales choices for peasants until healthy peasant cooperatives are organized, we want to maintain the cooperatives, not as monopolies but as buyers of the products at market prices that peasants cannot deliver to the cities....

> The organization of politically independent peasant interest groups.

> We demand the immediate review of the tax system, as the current system places undue burden on the peasants....

> We demand the reevaluation of the wages of peasants working on state farms and in state forests, the immediate abolition of the piece work systems, and the introduction of a progressive compensation system, where these agricultural employees receive a greater percentage of their wages in-kind and receive a small share of their income, sufficient to finance small purchases, in money twice a month.

We demand the reevaluation of the restrictions on keeping animals by the employees of state farms, the permission of keeping a cow, and the abolition of the restrictions of keeping pigs, chickens, and other small animals.

We demand the reevaluation of the social insurance and social health care system, and the provision of support for peasants identical to those of industrial workers. We demand the expansion of the social health care system to individual farmers who wish to do so.

We demand the immediate reorganization of the agricultural machine industry to permit the production of machinery that would be profitably employable on small farms, and that these machines also be made available on credit.[34]

The speech outlines the party's goal of representing peasants and achieving parity between state farm and forestry workers and industrial employees. The goal of terminating forced collectivization is listed as a priority, as is the need to include peasants in the national social insurance and healthcare system.

Ferenc Farkas, the secretary general of the Petőfi Party, emphasized on Hungarian Radio on November 3 that all parties in the coalition government wanted to maintain the socialist successes achieved to date that could be used by an independent, free, and democratic socialist country. This meant the acceptance of a nationalized industry and banking system.[35]

On the same day, in an interview published in Jász-Nagykun-Szolnok County's *People's Daily* (*A Nép Lapja*), the party representative was asked about the reorganized party's platform. His answer was "that the final program is being worked on, but our goals are already clear. We want to build strong ties with the Peasant Alliance and with the Smallholders' Party. We will continue to fight for land to be owned by those who work it."[36]

One of the most influential thinkers of the period was István Bibó. He was serving on the executive committee of the newly reconstituted Petőfi Party when he was appointed minister on November 3, one day before the second Soviet intervention. On the morning of November 4, Bibó continued typing in his office in the national Parliament while Soviet troops occupied the building, and he stayed in the Parliament building for another two days.[37] On November 9

Bibó wrote, "A suggested solution for the Hungarian problem."[38] The economic solutions listed in the memo under points c and d are:

c. Hungary's social structure is based on the principle of prohibition of exploitation (socialism) which means:

  i. to maintain the 1945 land reform with a maximum of 20 to 40 acres;

  ii. to maintain nationalization of mines, banks, and heavy industry;

  iii. to maintain the existing social ownership of factories through workers' management, workers' shares, or profit-sharing;

  iv. the possibility of free individual or cooperative enterprise, with guarantees against exploitation;

  v. freedom of private ownership within the guarantees against exploitation;

  vi. general social insurance.

d. Reparation for those economic and moral injustices that have been committed shall by no means involve restoration of the *status quo ante*. All compensations shall be made according to the principle of prohibiting exploitation and only in respect of ruined homes or loss of property earned by labour.

The Bibó plan reiterated the goals of maintaining the "achievements" of 1945, the land reform and nationalized large industry. Yet Bibó suggests that public ownership can be more "profitably" maintained by worker management, employee stock ownership plans, or by creating profit-sharing plans for workers. He advocated an all-inclusive social insurance system and reparation payments to compensate those who had lost homes or property.

At its December meeting, the provisional executive committee of the Hungarian Socialist Workers' Party (HSWP) was preparing a new government program, and on December 8 Bibó and other leaders of the Petőfi Party prepared and signed the so-called Declaration about the Fundamental Principles of the State, Social, and Economic System of Hungary and about the Ways of Overcoming the Political Crisis.[39] They asked K. P. S. Menon, India's ambassador to Moscow—who was then visiting Budapest—to convey its contents to the Soviet leaders.[40] This document reiterates the previously listed economic demands in points 2–8:

2. The country's social and economic order shall be based upon social ownership of the decisive majority of the means of production. In accordance with this, the mines, factories, banks, and other large enterprises that were in state ownership on October 23, 1956, must remain in social ownership.

3. The land ownership rights established by the 1945 land reform shall not be interfered with, but the upper limit of private ownership of land shall be determined by the area that can be cultivated by a family without regular recourse to outside labour.

4. The peasantry, craft industries, and all economic activity in general, must be guaranteed the right to form economic activities, on a voluntary basis, in order to secure the advantages of large scale production.

5. Private enterprise shall be allowed within the limits imposed by professional qualifications and planned direction of economic life. The number of persons employed by private enterprise must be restricted by law.

6. The freedom of workers and employees to form trade unions on a voluntary basis, and the right of trade unions to make collective agreements and to act in defence of their members' interests, must be secured by law. The peasantry, craft industries, small traders, and the self-employed should also have the freedom to form organizations appropriate for defending their interests.

7. The workers of state enterprises must be guaranteed in law the right to participate in the management of their enterprises through the workers' councils, and also the right to share in the material success of the enterprises's operations.

8. Compensation for economic damages resulting from the illegalities committed in the past must not lead to the restoration of the former property and income of those who suffered losses, and especially not to any possibility for the restoration of exploitation…

Goals 3–8 were not included in the new HSWP party platform. The Petőfi Party ceased to exist in January 1960.[41]

The Social Democratic Party

The Social Democratic Party (*SZDP, Szociáldemokrata Párt*) was reconstituted on October 30 in the editorial offices of the *Népszava (People's Voice)*, the party's paper.[42] The party's past president, Anna Kéthly, was re-elected as president.[43] Gyula Kelemen, the party's secretary general, summarized the recent past of the party as "hundreds of our leaders were imprisoned, and thousands were deported."[44] The following day the provisional leadership of the party was elected.[45] Initial emphasis was on party reorganization, and due to the brief time period of the party's legal existence no platform was published. Work on the platform was postponed to a date after the Socialist International meeting in Vienna, which was to begin on November 1. The party president and deputy-secretary travelled to this meeting to represent the Hungarian party.

In her editorial on the front page of the November 1 issue of *Népszava*, Anna Kéthly wrote, "We must protect the factories, mines and land as those must remain in the people's hand."[46] In an article on November 2, Gyula Kelemen, the party's secretary-general, calls on the party's peasant members to "save their strength for the fight to make it impossible to return the large estates."[47]

Most party announcements dealt with reorganizing the party, and programs were only hinted at. The county Heves poster emphasizes typical social democratic goals, such as,[48]

- Making unions true representatives of workers
- Abolishing unfair and exploitative piece-work wage systems and bonus systems
- Raising wages to the extent it is bearable by the country and immediately re-evaluating low wages
- Demanding a market-based small industry (service) and market-based retail trade

The same county party cell's November 1 proclamation stated that "our party's goal continues to be the raising of the living standard of the whole working population." Further down the poster it states the following: "The protection of peasant interests; peasants who got land grants should not suffer, but with reasonably—rational—production techniques while serving the whole nation's interests, should serve their own."[49] Another poster states that "the party welcomes the service workers and will fight for the independent functioning of the service industry."[50]

The party's president, Anna Kéthly, did not return from the Vienna meeting to Budapest after the second Soviet invasion. The party ceased functioning, several leaders left Hungary, and some left-wing members and union leaders eventually joined the Kádár regime and were rewarded with high positions.

From the Hungarian Workers' Party to the Hungarian Socialist Workers' Party

On October 24 the HWP felt that it could control the events. Imre Nagy in a radio address stated that the "peacefully demonstrating Hungarian youth were misled by enemies....The Hungarian government will not allow itself to be pushed off the road of democratization, which is in the interest of the Hungarian population, a program discussed and agreed upon with a large segment of the public."[51] But next day, Nagy was less confrontational. In his radio address he talked of "the public's despair over the serious political and economic mistakes....Shortly after the restoration of peace, Parliament will meet. I will submit a detailed and all-encompassing reform plan which will cover all important questions...."[52] On October 26 the radio anchor reading from the *Szabad Nép* [*Free People,* the party's paper] reported of the new party leadership under János Kádár, Ferenc Donáth, and Gyula Kállai, all previously imprisoned by the Rákosi regime.[53]

Nagy, in his previously mentioned radio address on October 28, stated,

> We wish to solve the old and justified demands of workers to their satisfaction; amongst them the issue of wages and norms, the raising of the lowest bracket of the minimum wages and lowest pensions by calculating them based on years worked, and raising the family subsidies. To solve the extremely grave apartment shortage, the government will support to the utmost state, cooperative and private construction of buildings. The government, to solve the desperate apartment shortage will support state, cooperative and private construction....[54]

The government applauds the workers' initiatives of expanding a factory-based democracy and approves the formation of workers' councils....

The government will immediately end the illegalities committed while forming agricultural cooperatives...[and] will develop a plan to increase agricultural productivity, to increase production by agricultural cooperatives and by individual farmers...The government will put an end to the serious illegalities which were committed in the name of agricultural cooperatives.[55]

The *New York Times* succinctly evaluated the events and statements in the following statement. "Politically, Premier Imre Nagy's concessions amount to nothing less than surrender to the will of the people. He and his Cabinet Ministers have now promised free elections and the end of the one-party dictatorship. They have announced the end of the hated collective farm system."[56]

On October 30 Hungarian radio announced that the reorganization of the Hungarian Workers' Party and its reemergence as the Hungarian Socialist Workers' Party (HSWP, *Magyar Szocialista Munkáspárt*) on November 1, 1956. János Kádár's speech on the radio indicated that his was another political party campaigning to achieve electoral victory. He stated the party's goal as "Workers, peasants and intellectuals! The new Party, the Hungarian Socialist Workers' Party, is prepared to do its share in fighting for the consolidation of independence and democracy....We turn to the newly formed democratic parties—first of all... to the Social Democratic Party—with the request that they help consolidate the government and thereby overcome the danger of menacing countries and intervention from abroad...."[57]

On November 4, in an open letter read on the radio, the formation of the new Kádár-led government was announced.[58] This new government was called the Hungarian Revolutionary Worker-Peasant Government (*Magyar Forradalmi Munkás-Paraszt Kormány*), and the party's economic platform was summarized on a poster in the following points (2, 6–10, 12):

2. The government program is to protect our popular people's democracy and socialist system from all attacks. The protection of our socialist achievements, and the continued movement on the socialist path....

6. The rapid and significant raising of the living standards of the employees—especially of the workers. More apartments for workers. We

must make it possible for factories and companies to build apartments for their workers and employees.

7. The adjustment of the five-year plan, charging the economic leaders to take into consideration the country's economic conditions in order to raise the living standard of the population as fast as possible.

8. The termination of bureaucracy and the spreading of democracy for the employees.

9. Worker management must be built on broad based democracy in factories, on shop floors and in enterprises.

10. The development of agricultural production, the termination of compulsory delivery systems, and provision of aid to individual peasants. The government will terminate all illegalities that were committed during forced collectivization.

12. Support of small industry and retail trade.

In this poster Kádár explains the need for his new government by blaming "the weakness of the Imre Nagy government and the counter-revolutionaries whose increasing influence threatened our socialist achievements, people's democracy, the worker-peasant power and the existence of our nation."[59]

On another poster, also dated November 4, a more detailed explanation is given for the takeover by the new government. It states that in addition to Nagy's weakness "on October 23rd a popular movement began whose noble goal was to correct the crimes committed by Rákosi and his cronies against the party and the public...."[60]

The HSWP's program did not go as far as the Nagy government's program. It did not include wage and pension reform or changes in the family support systems.

Other political organizations/parties

The book *1956 and the Political Parties*, edited by István Vida, reports that documents indicate that thirty-one parties or party-like organizations or attempts to organize parties existed during this period in Hungary.[61] These were

1. Hungarian Socialist Workers' Party (*Magyar Szocialista Munkáspárt*)

2. Hungarian Social Democratic Party (*Magyar Szociáldemokrata Párt*)

3. Smallholders' Party (*Független Kisgazdapárt*)

4. Petőfi Party–National Peasant Party (*Petőfi Párt–Nemzeti Parasztpárt*)

5. Hungarian Revolutionary Youth Party (*Magyar Forradalmi Ifjúsági Párt*)

6. Democratic Popular Party (*Demokrata Néppárt*)

7. Christian Democratic Party (*Keresztény Demokrata Párt*)

8. Catholic Popular Party (*Katolikus Néppárt*)

9. Christian Hungarian Party (*Keresztény Magyar Párt*)

10. Christian Front (*Keresztény Front*)

11. Hungarian Freedom Party (*Magyar Szabadság Párt*)

12. Hungarian Independence Party (*Magyar Függetlenségi Párt*)

13. Party of Justice (*Igazság Párt*)

14. Hungarian Democratic Union (*Magyar Demokratikus Unió*)

15. National Revolutionary Party (*Nemzeti Forradalmi Párt*)

16. National Organization of the Unaffiliated (*Pártonkívüliek Országos Blokkja*)

17. Christian National Party (*Keresztény Nemzeti Párt*)

18. Hungarian Life Party (*Magyar Élet Pártja*)

19. Hungarian Popular Party (*Magyar Néppárt*)

20. Hungarian Radical Party (*Magyar Radikális Párt*)

21. Party of the Nation's Defenders (*Honvédők Pártja*)

22. Christian Popular Party (*Keresztény Néppárt*)

23. Christian Socialist Party (*Keresztény Szocialista Párt*)

24. Christian Democratic Popular Party (*Keresztény Demokrata Néppárt*)

25. Party of Hungarian Unity (*Magyar Egység Párt*)

26. National Uprising Party (*Nemzeti Felkelés Pártja*)

27. Hungarian Christian National Party (*Magyar Keresztény Nemzeti Párt*)

28. National Radical Party (*Nemzeti Radikális Párt*)

29. National Camp–Independent Hungarian Socialist Party Movement (*Nemzeti Tábor–Független Magyar Szocialista Pártmozgalom*)

30. Bourgeois Democratic Party (*Polgári Demokrata Párt*)

31. Arrow Cross Party (*Nyilaskeresztes Párt*)

According to Robert Huckshorn's definition, "A political party is an autonomous group of citizens having the purpose of making nominations and contesting elections in hope of gaining control over governmental power through the capture of public offices and the organization of the government."[62] To act as a party, a party must register its name, elect temporary party officials, and have a constitution or by-laws. Several of the above listed parties had only one or two members (13–16), and some showed no activity (17–20) and thus were not real political parties. Other organizations never got off the ground (21–31).

Of the thirty-one parties, therefore, only the first twelve in the above list would meet the definition of a functioning political party. The economic platforms of the coalition parties (listed 1–4) have been discussed above. The platforms of the other eight parties are summarized in the following pages.

The economic goals or platform of other parties

The Hungarian Revolutionary Youth Party

The economic goals listed in points 3, 5–9, and 11 on the poster announcing the formation of the Hungarian Revolutionary Youth Party (*Magyar Forradalmi Ifjúsági Párt*)[63] states,

3. We want to develop an economic and political system that will eliminate the depressive feelings stemming from the uncertainties of tomorrow, and at the same time eliminate the country's economic uncertainty....

5. We want to fight for the rights of workers so that they can become the owners of factories and with that their standard of living will rise commensurate with increased production.

6. We will protect the rights of the peasants gained in the revolution.

7. We want to provide to the head of household a wage that allows him for carefree provision for his family and permits him to satisfy cultural and other demands.

8. We support the initiatives of Hungarian small industry and retail trade.

9. We will soon offer solutions to solve the housing crisis....

11. We will protect the achievements of the revolution with all our might.

On another poster the party demanded "the raising of the standard of living and the upholding of the achievements of the revolution."[64]

The Democratic Popular Party

At 10:20 pm on November 1, Dénes Farkas announced the reorganization and the platform of the Democratic Popular Party (*Demokrata Néppárt*) on radio. He positioned the party as an opposition party by stating that, "the party's program is its old program. We will support the government in maintaining order, protecting property and life....As in the past we are not willing to participate in any coalition."[65] The old party platform in 1945 was based on maintaining private property, though it "supported the nationalization of those industries that are for the public good."[66]

In the party's application for permission to function, three of the stated party goals (2, 3, and 4) are economic, namely:[67]

2. We believe that there is a unique Hungarian democratic socialism. We want to protect the socialist achievements of our nation, primarily the

land reform, including the break up of church property; and the public ownership of banks and other large enterprises.

3. We support private initiatives limited only by public goals, especially in small scale manufacturing, in retail trade and service industries.

4. We support independent unions and the right to strike.

The Christian Democratic Party

Six of the sixteen points of the Christian Democratic Party's (*Keresztény Demokrata Párt*) program dealt with economic issues.[68] These were points 5, 9, 11, and 13–15:

5. Immediate acceptance of foreign economic aid and grants without any economic and political preconditions....

9. Our whole economic policy must be reorganized with the help of the revolutionary workers, youth, peasants, service employees and intelligentsia to meet their interests. A fair tax system must be developed, so that the tax burden falls equitably on small and large economic units. Tax rates must be public.

All national—natural and intellectual—treasures must be used only to serve Hungarian national interests (uranium, bauxite).

Immediate payment of the unfairly withdrawn pensions, re-evaluation of the pension system, and compensation for those whose pensions were denied. Re-evaluation of new pensions....

11. Land-reform for the working peasants, the right to form cooperatives voluntarily; aiding of the individual peasants by a fair tax system and long-term credit. The distribution of collectively held agricultural machinery in accordance with the decisions of the peasants.

13. Independent unions...Placing the publicly held factories and wholesale outlets in the hand of workers' councils.

14. The return of the nationalized small-scale manufacturing and retail trade within reason, or as decided by the revolutionary unit.

15. Compensation for all who suffered unfair and illegal economic disadvantages between 1945 and 1956.

In another document, the party emphasized, "We are against the return of large property, but we want land reform, as the current situation is chaotic and unfair to the Hungarian peasants. We want private property! End to state-capitalism. Factories should be run by workers' councils."[69]

The Catholic People's Party

On the evening news on November 1, the radio announced the formation of the Catholic People's Party (*Katolikus Néppárt*).[70] This party also saw itself as an opposition party, which became clear when the party program was read on the radio. The statement said, "We can not work together with the government... until the compromised members of the cabinet are exposed. We insist on maintaining the social achievements of the post 1945 period, in fact we demand their expansion."[71]

The Christian Hungarian Party

The Christian Hungarian Party (*Keresztény Magyar Párt*) published its platform on November 1.[72] The economic demands were contained in the following points (3–13):

3. No government interference in agriculture, industry and trade. Abolishing all import and export duties and following the example of Switzerland of free economic life with abolishing of currency regulations.

4. Immediate return of all one family houses.

5. The return to previous owners of all small- and medium-sized trading companies and land up to 50 *hold*s (28.76 hectares or 71.05 acres)[73] from reserve land.

6. Creation of a wage level for men so women would not be required to leave the family hearth.

7. Renting those factories, not using domestic raw materials or other preconditions for profitability, to foreigners. The pay scale should match that of the home country. 20% of the output can be sold to the Hungarian state at cost and no more than 10% of employees may be foreigners.

8. All state owned enterprises should be converted to stock companies, with 75% of the shares held by employees, and 25% by the state.

9. The introduction of the maximum 40 hour work week, with 36 hours in mining. The minimum wages should be Ft. 1,500.

10. Both agriculture, and retail trade and small scale industry should have access to loans with 20 year repayment schedule; and the establishment of savings banks in villages to provide these loans.

11. A one year moratorium on all loans.

12. 80% of construction projects by the state should be building apartments, where priority should be given to young couples and homeless people.

13. The abolition of exploitative system of norms, and work competition.

The Christian Front

The leaders of the Christian Front (*Keresztény Front*) were released from prison in October 30, 1956, and immediately began organizing.[74] The poster announcing the formation of the party emphasized, "Our leaders were released from prison only 24 hours ago," and that they saw the party as an umbrella organization for all Christian parties. "There can be only one Christian Party, we do not commit to supporting individuals, but to the success of our program."[75] Their program dealt with political reorganization of the country. They advocated the restoration of the kingdom and a two-chamber Parliament. From this statement, it is clear that this party also saw itself as an opposition party. They "advocated for a class-free society…for a Christian socialist state."[76]

To achieve their goal of a "true Christian classless society they did not want to reverse the achievements of socialism, approved of previous distribution of land, the nationalization of factories, banks and mines. They advocated limited return to private property."[77]

The Hungarian Freedom Party

The Hungarian Freedom Party (*Magyar Szabadság Párt*) summarized its goals in its motto: "The dual motivators in the world are family and property."[78]

> The imposed industrialization changed the composition of employment. The majority of the population is still agricultural, and this is the backbone of the nation.

> Back to land. Let the population love the land as before. We will not let the achievements of the land reform be destroyed....

> We will help individual peasants, by providing cheap loans to rebuild destroyed buildings and machinery. Special attention will be paid to restocking the animal herds.

> We understand the goals of cooperatives....There is no need for those money losing cooperatives that must be supported by public financing.

> Hungarian industry must be proud of its past....The opening of the borders mean strong competition, which can be met by cheaper and better consumer goods.

> Our workers should be the real owners of the factories, should receive parts of the profits.... Norms should be abolished....They should have the right to organize freely.

> Small scale industry was an important pillar of the nation's independence....

> We want to support individual initiatives....

> We want to restore the chambers of commerce.

> We will abolish the unfair premium reward system, which was most often given to undeserving individuals. A satisfactory wage system will result in satisfactory work. As above, we emphasize that workers must receive a share of profits above their wages.

> We mean to provide healthcare for all.

> We must create an old-age pension system worthy of a civilized nation.

The Hungarian Independence Party

The Hungarian Independence Party's (*Magyar Függetlenségi Párt*) application for formation refers to the party's 1947 platform. Two economic concerns are listed in their platform of six issues.[79]

> 4. Sanctity of private property.

> 5. Reduction of the tax burden to a level where it is sufficient to support the public infrastructure and is bearable for an individual.

Conclusion

Of the twelve political parties outlined above, only four parties—the Hungarian Revolutionary Youth Party (*Magyar Forradalmi Ifjúsági Párt*), the Christian Democratic Party (*Keresztény Demokrata Párt*), the Christian Front (*Keresztény Front),* and the Christian Hungarian Party (*Keresztény Magyar Párt*)—were new parties. All the other parties had their start in the post-1945 period. Technically, the Hungarian Socialist Workers' Party (*Magyar Szocialista Munkáspárt*) was a new party in name only, as the Hungarian Workers' Party reorganized under this name. Only two parties—the Social Democrats and the Smallholders'—existed before the war. The Peasant Party was established before the war, but it did not function during the war. Between 1948 and 1956, only eight years had passed, so the parties and their programs were still alive in the public's mind. Based on the historic roles the parties played, Vida placed the parties on the left to right political spectrum as in the following table.[80]

Table 3.5: Political Parties in 1956

Left		Centre		Right
HSWP		Smallholders'		Catholic Popular
Social Democrats		Petőfi		Christian Hungarian
				Christian Front
			Democratic Popular	Hungarian Freedom
	Hungarian Revolutionary Youth		Christian Democratic	Hungarian Independence

However, examining the economic platforms of the parties shows that their views were more homogenous. Table 3.6 below shows the issues mentioned by the respective parties. The numbers correspond to the names of the parties in both tables, and compare it to the program of the Nagy government. The issues raised in the platform are marked by "x".

Table 3.6: Programs of Political Parties in 1956

Nagy Govt. pre–October 30		1. HSWP	2. Social Dem	3. Smallholders'	4. Petöfi	5. Revolutionary	6. Democratic Pop.	7. Christ. Democrat	8. Cath. Popular	9. Christ. Hung.	10. Christ. Front	11. Freedom	12. Independence
	Maintenance of land reform	x	x	x	X	x	x	x	X	x	x	x	
	Maintenance of public ownership of large industry	x	x	x	x	x	x	x	X		x		
	Private property in service industry and retail trade	x	x	x	x	x	x	x		x	x	x	x
X	Individual, private land ownership	x	x	x	x			x		x	x	x	
X	Abolishing of the norm system (piece work)		x	x	x					x		x	
X	Higher wages		x	x	x	x				x			
X	Pension reform		x	x				x				x	
X	Higher minimum wages		x							x			
X	Worker management	x				x		x		x		x	
X	Increased housing construction	x				x				x			
	Profit sharing		x	x						x		x	
	Healthcare reform				x							x	
	Independent unions		x	x			x	x				x	
X	Termination of forced collectivization	x		x	x			x					
X	Increasing family support payments												
X	Publication of statistical/ trade data			x									
X	Revision of tax system				x			x					x
	Compensation for damages			x	x			x					

According to Anthony Downs's rational-efficient political party model, each party's political activities are centred on "the parties' electoral activities, at the expense of virtually all other functions," as winning elections is the goal of each party. "Voters also act rationally, using the information provided by the party candidates to make selections that will benefit them personally."[81] The promise of improving the standard of living is always central to all political parties. As Tables 3.3 and 3.4 show, the majority of Hungarians lived near poverty. The slight increase in real wages from 1954 was still below what was necessary to support a family.

To improve the standard of living, the members of the coalition government, the Revolutionary Youth Party, and the Christian Hungarian Party promised to raise wages and/or to raise minimum wages. Only the Social Democrats, the Petőfi Party, the Christian Hungarian Party, and the Hungarian Freedom Party promised to abolish the hated norm system. This is interesting as all published pre-revolutionary demands, and the program of the Nagy government, included the demand to abolish this payment scheme. Until October 1956, 67 percent of workers were paid on piece work; from November on, nearly all enterprises switched to paying hourly wages.[82] Worker management and profit sharing was mentioned by the Petőfi Party, the Christian Democratic Party, the Hungarian Freedom Party, the Hungarian Revolutionary Youth Party, the Christian Hungarian Party, the Smallholders', and the HSWP. (Worker management and profit sharing were to be achieved through the Workers' Councils. The councils were terminated by the Kádár regime on November 11, 1957.)[83] Another tool some parties believed would strengthen the workers' role in the economy were independent unions, which were supported and promised by the Social Democrats, Smallholders', the Democratic Popular Party, and the Christian Democratic and Hungarian Freedom parties. The expansion of the healthcare and social insurance system was promised by the Petőfi Party—agricultural workers and peasants were excluded from the then-existing system—which specifically mentioned its constituent base, while the Hungarian Freedom Party talked of expanding benefits coverage to all.

With the exception of the Hungarian Independence Party, all parties directly or indirectly mentioned the maintenance of the land reform, public ownership of large industries, and the return to some form of private ownership of land and in the service and retail industries. The Nagy government's program did not mention land reform and nationalization of industry and banking, as these were cornerstones for building socialism. Only the Christian Hungarian Party mentioned converting state ownership into employee ownership of the factories through stock conversions.

Another issue, the need to increase housing construction, was raised by several groups before the revolution and by the Nagy government but was mentioned only in the platform of the HSWP, and Hungarian Revolutionary Youth and Christian Hungarian parties.

As mentioned previously, due to the short time that the parties were allowed to openly function, they did not have time to develop detailed platforms. Instead, to attract past and new members, they most frequently listed the most common complaints of Hungarians. For this reason, on the surface it appeared that party platforms were all quite similar.

Bibó explained the support for these similar programs the best:

> We must not forget that the aversion for an orthodox capitalist, reactionary, anti-communist restoration is the concern not only of the Soviet Union and the communists, but also of the young people, workers, and soldiers who carried out the revolution and shed their blood for its victory. The majority of them were not communists but the great majority consider themselves socialists. It is morally inadmissible and also, from the standpoint of Hungarian internal politics, impossible, that the forces of reaction should profit, thanks to the votes of the older generation, from the freedom bought by the blood of young revolutionaries.[84]

Another possible explanation for the uniformity of platforms is that the majority of the political actors spent time in Rákosi's prisons. The methods of the pre- and post-1945 and 1947 elections were fresh in their memories. They were afraid to be labelled reactionaries and probably did not know how much they could trust the Nagy government. After all, martial law was imposed on October 24, and the "uprising" was labelled counterrevolutionary until October 28. To the participants, the change in terminology to "revolution" and the opportunity to organize came suddenly, and they wanted to proceed slowly. This argument is supported by statements of the Christian Front, as well as

Catholic Popular and Democratic Popular parties, which declared themselves "opposition" parties—yet they proposed solutions that were similar to those put forward by the non-opposition parties.

The end: the second entry of the Russian army

With the second entry of the Russian army on November 4 the various political parties ceased their activities.

The January 7, 1957, issue of the *New York Times* reported, based on a Hungarian radio broadcast, "that the Government intends to conduct talks with various factions of public life, whether members of parties or not, who are willing to fight against the counter-revolution and for the maintenance of social achievements...."[85] Over a month later, on February 14, the *New York Times* reported, "based on a 'usually reliable' source," that Kádár had "forecast the 'liquidation' of the Social Democratic Party" in a speech made at Újpest on February 9, 1957. Kádár "also predicted that negotiations would begin with two other non-Communist parties, the Smallholders' and Petőfi Parties, at an unspecified future date, to broaden the present all-Communist Government."[86] The promised multi-party talks never took place.

The economic changes brought about by the Revolution

1957 was simultaneously a year of political repression and the beginning of a less rigid economic system. To prevent the repeat of the uprising, and to assuage discontent in the general population, the government introduced economic changes to improve the standard of living. The party appointed the Economic Committee (*Gazdasági Bizottság*), a group of reform-minded experts to propose ways of revising Hungary's economic system. The committee's report marked the first step on Hungary's road to economic reform. Of the many changes introduced, only a few will be listed here.

Until October 1956, 67 percent of workers were paid based on piece work; from November on, nearly all enterprises switched to paying hourly wages.[87] In 1957 companies were allowed to experiment with various wage schemes. A plan was drawn up to lease up to 6 percent of small retail outlets and restaurants to private individuals. To encourage private ownership in the service sector, tax rates were lowered.[88] The hated obligatory delivery system for peasants, which was initially abolished by the Nagy government, was never reinstituted. Over 60 percent of peasants left the cooperatives during the revolution and many started or restarted their private farms. In 1957 Kádár, to appease the party hardliners, restarted collectivization, but he allowed peasants to keep some land private. In 1957 social insurance was extended to members of agricultural cooperatives.[89]

The result of all the changes was that between 1957 and 1960 consumption grew more rapidly than national income. Per capita real income was 50 percent higher in 1960 than it had been in 1950. According to the University of Groningen data, the Hungarian per capita GDP in 1960 was $3,649, a 47 percent increase compared to the per capita GDP of $2,480 in 1950.

Hungary had begun to make its own goulash (Communism), though at this time there was little meat in the stew.

Notes

1. Robert Blumstock, "Public Opinion in Hungary," in Walter D. Connor and Zvi Gittelman, eds., *Public Opinion in European Socialist Systems* (New York: Praeger Publishers, 1977), 136–137.

2. From http://www.ggdc.net/maddison/ (accessed June 1, 2005).

3. From http://www.ggdc.net/maddison/ (accessed June 1, 2005). The Geary Khamis PPPs is an aggregation method in which category "international prices" (reflecting relative category values) and country purchasing power parities (PPPs) (depicting relative country price levels) are estimated simultaneously from a system of linear equations. From http://stats.oecd.org/glossary/detail. asp?ID=5528 (accessed June 1, 2005).

4. Iván Pető and Sándor Szakács, *A hazai gazdaság négy évtizedének története 1945–1985. 1. Az újjáépítés és a tervutasításos irányítás időszaka* [Four decades of economic history of our country, 1945–1985. 1. The period of rebuilding

and economic planning] (Budapest: Közgazdasági és Jogi Könyvkiadó, 1985), 217.

5. Without deductions and taxes (Ibid., 217).

6. Ibid., 221.

7. Iván T. Berend, *A szocialista gazdaság fejlődése Magyarországon, 1945–1975* [The development of the socialist economy in Hungary 1945–1975] (Budapest: Kossuth Könyvkiadó, 1979), 104.

8. Pető and Szakács, 232.

9. Ibid., 314.

10. *The Washington Post and Times Herald*, August 5, 1956, A1.

11. László Rajk (1909–1949), minister of the Interior, was executed as a "Titoist Fascist" on October 15, 1949.

12. The leaders of the 1848 War of Independence against Habsburg rule were executed on October 6, 1849.

13. Imre Nagy (1896–1958) served as Prime Minister from 1953 to 1955, during which he introduced the "New Course," a more liberal economic policy. Nagy was forced to resign in April 1955 and was expelled from the Communist Party in December of the same year by hardline Communists.

14. *The Washington Post and Times Herald*, October 15, 1956, page 7.

15. Lajos Izsák, József Szabó, and Róbert Szabó, eds. *1956 plakátjai és röplapjai* [The posters and flyers of 1956] (Budapest: Zrinyi Kiadó, 1991), 16. and The *United Nations Report of the Special Committee on the Problem of Hungary* (New York, 1957), at http://mek.oszk.hu/01200/01274/01274.pdf, 127 (accessed February 1, 2005).

16. From http://mek.oszk.hu/01200/01274/01274.pdf, 129 (accessed February 1, 2005).

17. Csaba Békés, Malcolm Byrne, and János M. Rainer, eds. *The 1956 Hungarian Revolution: A History in Documents* (Budapest: CEU Press, 2002), 178.

18. László Varga, *A forradalom hangja* [The Voice of the Revolution] (Budapest: Századvég Kiadó-Nyilvánosság Klub, 1989), 79.

19. Lajos Izsák, József Szabó, and Róbert Szabó, eds. *1956 vidéki sajtója* [The press from the countryside in 1956] (Budapest: Korona Kiadó, 1996), 370;

and http://mek.oszk.hu/01200/01274/01274.pdf, 142 (accessed February 1, 2006).

20. A special general meeting to discuss the Hungarian issue was called on November 4, 1956. This and the general meeting's eleventh session in November and December passed several resolutions that called on the Soviet Union to withdraw its troops and for the Kádár government to receive the UN Secretary General and other UN observers; but the Hungarian government rejected this proposal. The UN created a special committee on January 10, 1957, to draw up a report on the chronology and to evaluate the Hungarian events based on the accounts of those who had participated in the revolution and who had subsequently fled to the West, and on other available sources. The committee's members were from Australia, Ceylon, Denmark, Tunisia, and Uruguay. The report was finished in June 1957. The special general meeting of September 1957 passed the report with majority. The resolutions related to Hungary could never be enforced, so the Hungarian issue was placed on the agenda of the UN general meeting every year until 1962. See the *New York Times*, November 4, 1956, page 192; and January 2, 1957, page 10. See also http://hungaria.org/1956/index.php?projectid=2&menuid=14 (accessed May 1, 2006).

On April 4, 1960, partial amnesty was granted in Hungary. In September of that year, Kádár travelled with Khrushchev to New York and addressed the UN on October 3. The United States wanted complete amnesty for the political prisoners before it would ease its pressure on Hungary. At the 8th Party Congress, in November 1962, Kádár announced that 95 percent of the political prisoners had already been released and on December 20, 1962, the "Hungarian Question" was removed from the UN's agenda. See Andrew Felkay, *Hungary and the USSR, 1956-1988: Kadar's Political Leadership* (Westport, CT: Greenwood Press, 1989).

21. From http://mek.oszk.hu/01200/01274/01274.pdf, 131 (accessed February 1, 2006).

22. Varga, *A forradalom hangja*, 132.

23. Ibid., 226.

24. Ibid., 284; and Izsák, ed., *1956 plakátjai és röplapjai*, 189.

25. Béla Kovács was imprisoned on false charges and then taken to the Soviet Union on February 26, 1947. He was permitted to return to Hungary on November 8, 1955. Charges against him were officially dropped on May 5, 1956.

26. Varga, *A forradalom hangja*, 295; and Nagy, Ernő, eds. *1956 Sajtója* [The press from 1956] (Budapest: Tudósitások Kiadó, 1989): *Magyar Nemzet*, November 1; *Kis Ujság*, November 1; *Magyar Ifjúság*, November 1, page 2.

27. Izsák, ed., *1956 plakátjai és röplapjai*, 227.

28. István Vida, ed., *1956 és a politikai pártok, Politikai pártok az 1956-os forradalomban, 1956. október 23 – November 4* [1956 and the political parties, Political parties in the 1956 revolution. October 23 and November 4, 1956] (Budapest: MTA Jelenkor-kutató Bizottság, 1998), 313.

29. Vida, ed., *1956 és a politikai pártok*, 338.

30. Nagy, ed., *1956 Sajtója [n.p.]*, interview in *Magyar Szabadság*, November 3, page 3.

31. Tivadar Pártay, "*1956-ban a Kisgazdapárt nem készitett pártprogramot, nem volt idönk erre*" (In 1956 the Smallholders' Party did not prepare a platform, we did not have time for it), in Zsuzsanna Körösi and Péter Pál Tóth, eds., *Pártok 1956* (Budapest: 1956-os Intézet, 1997), 43.

32. Ferenc S. Szabó, "*Mindent az idő rövidsége határozott meg*," in Körösi, ed., *Pártok 1956*, 146.

33. Varga, *A forradalom hangja*, 291.

34. From Varga, *A forradalom hangja*, 478–480.

35. Ibid., 463.

36. Izsák, ed., *1956 vidéki sajtója*, 488.

37. Sándor Kopácsi, *In the Name of the Working Class* (New York: Grove Press, 1986), 187; also in Johanna Granville, "Bibó After 1956," at http://www.csseo.org/Papers/paperGranville.rtf (accessed January 2, 2006); also in *The New York Times*, November 12, 1956, page 1.

38. Bill Lomax, ed., *Hungarian Workers' Councils in 1956* (Boulder, CO: Social Science Monographs), 210–211.

39. Johanna Granville, "*István Bibó After 1956*," at http://www.csseo.org/Papers/paperGranville.rtf, 3 (accessed January 3, 2006); and Lajos Izsák, "*Az 1956-os forradalom pártjai és programjaik*" [The parties and their programs in the 1956 revolution], in *Múltunk*, 1992, 2–3; 109.

40. Lomax, *Hungarian Workers' Councils in 1956,* 223. See also, Sándor Kelemen, "*Mindenki munkát kért, szerettek volna valamit csinálni*" [Everybody asked for work, they all wanted to do something], in Zsuzsanna Körösi and Péter Pál Tóth, eds. *Pártok 1956* (Budapest: 1956-os Intézet, 1997), 131.

41. Vida, ed., *1956 és a politikai pártok,* 372.

42. Varga, *A forradalom hangja,* 241.

43. Anna Kéthly (1889–1976), a social democratic leader, opposed the merger of the Social Democratic Party and the Communist Party in 1948. As a result, she was placed under house arrest for two years and then imprisoned after a show trial in 1954. She was released in April 1956.

44. Gyula Kelemen (1897–1973) was also arrested on trumped-up charges and sentenced to life imprisonment in 1948. He was released in June 1956. Varga, *A forradalom hangja,,* 363.

45. Izsák, ed., *1956 plakátjai és röplapjai,* 220.

46. Nagy, ed., *1956 Sajtója,* 1956; *Népszava,* November 1.

47. Péter Benkő, "A szociáldemokrácia -56ban" (Social-democracy in 56), in *Múltunk* (Our Past), 1990, 3; 143–160.

48. Izsák, ed., *1956 plakátjai és röplapjai,* 439.

49. Ibid., 440.

50. Ibid., 244.

51. Varga, *A forradalom hangja,* 32.

52. Varga, *A forradalom hangja,* 72; and Izsák, ed., *1956 plakátjai és röplapjai,* 44.

53. Varga, *A forradalom hangja,* 79.

---

54. *Table 3.3: New Housing Construction*

| Year | New Construction | | | Demolitions |
	in Budapest	in the countryside	of these built by the state	
1955	7,370	24,156	13,604	9,878
1956	4,070	21,387	7,351	15,099
1957	10,050	41,263	26,214	9,527

Pető and Szakács, *A hazai gazdaság négy évtizedének története 1945–1985,* 315.

55. Varga, *A forradalom hangja*, 132.

56. *New York Times*, October 31, 1956, page 32.

57. Varga, *A forradalom hangja*, 371; and Izsák, ed., *1956 plakátjai és röplapjai*, 259.

58. Varga, *A forradalom hangja*, 489.

59. Izsák, ed., *1956 plakátjai és röplapjai*, 274.

60. Ibid., 276–277.

61. Vida, ed., *1956 és a politikai pártok*, 521.

62. Robert Huckshorn, *Political Parties in America* (Monterey, California: Brooks/Cole, 1984), 10; also found at http://www.apsanet.org/content_5221.cfm (accessed February 12, 2006).

63. Izsák, ed., *1956 plakátjai és röplapjai*, 192.

64. Ibid., 257.

65. Varga, *A forradalom hangja*, 374.

66. See Susan Glanz, "Economic Platforms of the Various Political Parties in the Elections of 1945," in Nándor Dreisziger, ed., *Hungary in the Age of Total War, 1938–1948* (East European Monographs, 1998), 169–184.

67. Vida, ed., *1956 és a politikai pártok*, 472.

68. Ibid., 451.

69. Ibid., 459.

70. Varga, *A forradalom hangja*, 359.

71. Ibid., 362–363.

72. Vida, ed., *1956 és a politikai pártok*, 462.

73. Calculations based on http://www.unc.edu/~rowlett/units/dictH.html (accessed January 13, 2006).

74. Vida, ed., *1956 és a politikai pártok*, 453; and Izsák, ed., *1956 plakátjai és röplapjai*, 212.

75. Izsák, ed., *1956 plakátjai és röplapjai*, 230.

76. Vida, ed., *1956 és a politikai pártok*, 479.

77. Lajos Izsák, "*Az 1956-os forradalom pártjai és programjaik,*" in *Múltunk* (Our Past) (1992): 2–3; 121.

78. Vida, ed., *1956 és a politikai pártok*. 516.

79. Ibid., 509.

80. Ibid., 532.

81. http://www.apsanet.org/content_5221.cfm (accessed March 1, 2006).

82. Iván T. Berend, *Gazdasági Útkeresés 1956-1965* (Looking for the road of economic solutions, 1956–1965) (Budapest: Magvetö Kiadó, 1983), 79.

83. http://www.rev.hu/sulinet56/online/szerviz/kronolog/sulikro5.htm (accessed January 12, 2006).

84. Lomax, *Hungarian Workers' Councils in 1956*, 208.

85. *The New York Times*, January 7, 1957, page 3. Also see Vince Vörös' interview http://server2001.rev.hu/oha/oha_document.asp?id=326&order=1 (accessed September 1, 2006).

86. *The New York Times*, February 14, 1957, page 8.

87. Iván T. Berend, *Gazdasági Útkeresés 1956–1965* (Budapest: Magvetö Kiadó, 1983), 79.

88. Ibid., 89; and http://www.tozsdesztori.hu/idorend.pdf (accessed March 1, 2006).

89. http://mek.oszk.hu/02100/02185/html/231.html (accessed January 12, 2006).

4.

The Role of Women in the 1956 Revolution

Mária Palasik

Looking through the historical literature, the key events of the uprising between October 23 and November 4, 1956, seem to be dominated by men, suggesting that men were the lead actors in these events. However, was this really the case? This paper attempts to characterize the role of women during the 1956 revolution on the basis of photographic records of key moments and events during the revolution, as well as a review of contemporary documents and some personal recollections.

It should be noted that a special feature of the majority of the photos used here is that they were attached to the documentation of legal actions initiated by the state. Some of the pictures were taken by participants and some by ordinary people, journalists, and the security organizations themselves. I examined four thousand photos at the Historical Archives of the Hungarian State Security (HAHSS) and at the collection of the Institute for 1956. I found women in approximately 10 percent of the photos. My selection was based primarily on being able to provide a representative sample of "real life" illustrations from among the photos I studied.

The other sources of the research are the files of proceedings initiated by organs of the Metropolitan Public Prosecutor's Office and the Metropolitan Court after the suppression of the revolution. The cases concerned people accused of participation in revolutionary activities between October 23 and December 1956. I used the rich database[1] of the Budapest City Archives (BCA), as well as the sources of BCA and the HAHSS. For comparison purposes, I looked at the memoirs of some of the surviving participants as well.

The photographs

I had no difficulty finding extensive documentation of the public demonstrations and the uprising. However, it was more complicated finding photographic documentation of the meetings of national and revolutionary committees and workers' councils. I found only one photo about these sessions—though these organisations kept operating until December 1956.

Unfortunately there is no photographic documentation of the private sphere and how individual families responded to these events. It is a matter of conjecture of how many young men and women actually stayed at home at the urging of mothers and fathers who feared for their children's lives.

Image group 1: Demonstrations on October 23 and 25

In this first group of photographs we can see women among the demonstrators.

Picture 4.1 was taken on Rakóczi Street, on the Pest side of Budapest. The demonstration set off simultaneously from Pest and Buda at 3:00 pm, increasing rapidly in numbers and becoming more radical along the way. The demonstrators were joined by students, for example from the Eötvös Loránd University (ELTE). This university traditionally has several faculties attended by female students in large numbers. These women were in the lines of the demonstrators.

Picture 4.2 was taken on Bem square on the Buda side. Here we can see the students of the Technical University of Budapest. This university had far fewer female students than Eötvös Loránd University. This is why we see fewer women in the photo. Originally the aim of both Buda and Pest demonstration groups was to express solidarity with the changes in Warsaw. However, among the demands of young people, we can find the following points: withdrawal of Soviet forces and restoration of a multi-party system.

4.1

4.2

Picture 4.3 was taken at the Parliament Building on the evening of October 23. Most of the crowd marched from Bem tér to Kossuth tér, the square before the Parliament, calling for Imre Nagy. It is interesting to note only a few women remained in the crowds by the evening.

In photo 4.4 we can see the demonstrators at the Parliament (Kossuth Square) on October 25. This day was a tragic one in the history of the revolution. There were a lot of people at the Parliament who fraternized with the Soviet soldiers. They wanted to demonstrate that the Hungarians had no ill feeling toward the Russian people themselves and that they were instead engaged in a political struggle. They felt that both Hungarian and Russian people were victims of the same oppressive political ideology. Soviet leader General Serov thought it was unacceptable for Soviet soldiers to fraternize with the enemy. That day, Serov was attending the Central Committee meeting of the Hungarian Workers' Party at the Akadémia Street party headquarters, near Parliament. After he left the meeting he gave the order to fire. Snipers started shooting at the crowd from the surrounding rooftops.

The shots rang out and caused panic among the demonstrators and among the Soviet soldiers, who also began to return the fire. They not only fired in the direction from which the shots had come, but they also fired on the young people they had been fraternizing with moments before, in the belief that they had led them into a trap. Serov's decision to order sniper fire cost a hundred lives, and three hundred were wounded.

You do not see many women in the crowd.

Image group 2: Women in armed rebel groups

4.5

On October 24 and 25, armed rebel groups organized themselves into units. One of the most important units was the "Corvin köz" group commanded by László Iván Kovács.[2] In image 4.5, two women are included among the rebels of "Corvin köz."

4.6

A rebel group at Széna tér in Buda (commanded by János Szabó) took up
position in front of Rákosi's residence. They came there to sleep and rest between
fighting. Image 4.6 shows some of these rebels.

4.7

Photo 4.7 reveals a woman between two men from the rebel group of
Vajdahunyad Street 41. The woman is the wife of the man standing on the
left side in the picture. This photo was taken by a German journalist. It is not a
spontaneous picture; the people are posing.

4.8

ÁBTL 4. 1.   A - 219/2

4.9

ÁBTL 4. 1.   A - 219/2

The 1956 Hungarian Revolution: Canadian and Hungarian Perspectives

ÁBTL 4. 1. A - 219/2

ÁBTL 4. 1. A - 219/2

While some of the images in this grouping are posed, others, such as images 4.8–4.11, seem more natural and appear to have been snapped to catch real moments in time. In these snapshot-style images, we see most of the women carrying weapons.

4.12

This photo with two women from the rebel group of Vajdahunyad Street 41 is again posed.

Image group 3: Women in traditional roles

The following images reveal women in their traditional female roles: as nurses, mourning mothers and wives, and as providers of food.

4.13   *4.14*

Images 4.13 and 4.14 show Red Cross activists and nurses carrying food and looking after the wounded.

4.16

Sír a Ferenciek terén.
Budapest, 1956. október

And in images 4.15 and 4.16, women are shown standing by the dead and paying respect at a gravesite.

**Faluról szállított libát visznek haza az asszonyok
Budapest, 1956. október vége (?)**

In the final image of this grouping, 4.17, we see women as the providers of nourishment. I found this picture at the Józsa András Museum in Nyíregyháza. Originally, the image's title was given by the museum: "Women taking geese home from the countryside, end of October 1956." But in my opinion this photo was taken after November 4. I draw this conclusion because commerce was paralyzed during the revolution, but after its defeat there was a surplus of geese that had not been sent to market while the fighting was going on. According to the oral history of the times, people had not eaten so much goose in all their lives!

Image group 4: Women in atypical gender roles

4.18

ÁBTL 3. 1. 1.   B - 86787

There is a bookshop in the background. And, in the foreground of image 4.18, a woman is setting books on fire. Burning books about Stalinism was one of the revolutionary acts during the uprising.

In image 4.19 we can see a female "collector." At this time, the West was sending a lot of foreign aid to Hungary. This picture shows an aid distribution centre. The woman in the middle of the photo is perhaps taking more than her share. She is wearing two coats. One is a winter coat and the other is a fur coat. She probably wanted to make sure she could take them all home.

4.20

4.21

ÁBTL 4. 1.   A - 219/2

4.22

ÁBTL 4. 1.   A - 219/2

I looked through several thousand photos. In half of them I saw that women preferred to remove themselves from potential conflict situations. Here are three examples.

The documents

This part of my paper is based on the review of the court documents from which I selected the photographs. These documents detail the judgements that women who took part in the uprising received. They thus expand on the photographic portrayal of events and provide some background to the variety of roles played by women in these events.

First, let us take a look at the list of women sentenced to death and executed:[3] They are:

Mrs Józsefné Angyal (d. July 21, 1959)

Mrs Gyuláné Bakos, Erzsébet Salabert (d. November 28, 1958)

Mrs Béláné Havrilla, Katalin Sticker (d. February 26, 1959)

Erzsébet Mányi (d. February 2, 1957)

Ilona Tóth (d. June 28, 1957)

The number of people sentenced to death by courts and executed is 229. Among them were 5 women, that is 2.1 percent. Two of them were sentenced to death for acts committed after November 4. However, others were executed for acts that happened during the uprising.

The number of people accused of participation in revolutionary activities between October 23 and December 1956 is approximately 34,000, of which 22,000 were sentenced. I reviewed the documents of 3,577 people from BCA's database.[4] Among the prosecuted, there were 158 women, which means that women made up just a little more than 4 percent of all people prosecuted for revolutionary activities.

I was able to draw some interesting conclusions about their activities when I examined the ages of the 158 women involved. For example, the oldest, born in 1887, was charged with calling somebody a "Jewish bitch" during the revolutionary events and had made "provocative statements before." The youngest two of this group of women were born in 1941. One of them was charged with providing nursing care to the group at Széna Square. The other was charged with preparing petrol bottles and providing weapons to fighters in Székesfehérvár.

Prosecuted women in their thirties, forties, fifties, and sixties were remanded for provocative and insulting talk aimed at politicians and the general political situation; in other words, for exercising their right to freedom of speech. Some of the quotes noted in the archival documents include:

"Kádár has started barking."

"Marosán is a drunken baker."

"The big-assed Communists have disappeared now."

"This system must change, because it can't go on like this."

"You're not a man in my eyes, snotty Communist."

"All the communists should be hanged by their legs."

"Whoever wishes Russian soldiers to stay in Hungary is not a Hungarian because the Russians have been brought in by Kádár."

The two age groups that took part in the armed clashes to the greatest extent were young women and teenagers. Most of the women in their twenties made and distributed flyers. All the prosecuted teenaged women had joined armed groups and provided first aid and food, and cooked.

Another type of activity that revolutionaries in general were accused of was participation in revolutionary organizations. In the trial documents I examined there were no women from the national committees. However, there were two women who were members of workers' councils and one woman who recorded the minutes of council meetings. Gabriella Békeffi became chairwoman of the workers' committee at the chemical works in Szolnok. Mrs. Gézáné Tóth, Valéria Steiner was a member of the workers' committee in Újpest.

There were four women charged with being members of revolutionary committees. Mária Sikos was among the leaders of the revolutionary committee of the 5th District Council founded on October 30, 1956; she was also the deputy head of the local council apparatus. Margit Bede took part in the work of the revolutionary committee of Újpest. Zsuzsanna Deckner took part in the founding of the revolutionary committee at the Technical School for Building

Engineering. Finally, Mrs. Ferencné Tóth, Zsuzsanna Bernula, was a member of the revolutionary committee of the 2nd District.

In the files of those prosecuted for founding political parties, there were three women. Erzsébet Kemenes took part in the statutory meeting of the Christian Front on November 2, 1956. Mrs. Jánosné Olaszy, Anna Meneghelló, knew about the founding of the Christian Party, but she didn't report it to the authorities. Mrs. Jenőné Moldován, Ibolya Vida, was a member of the fifteen-person board of the revolutionary youth organization that was founded at Láng Machine Factory on October 30, 1956.

Individuals were often charged with more than one offence. And there were just as many women accused of taking part in armed fights as women charged with provocation. I have summarized the types of indictments women received after 1956 in the following table for easy overview.

Table 4.1: Indictments Received by Women of the 1956 Hungarian Revolution

Charge	Number	Percentage
Participation in armed clashes	25	14.8
Red Cross activity, first aid	16	9.5
Participation in looting	19	11.2
Provocative statements	25	14.8
Editing and distributing flyers	14	8.3
Participation in workers' and revolutionary committees, party-founding	14	8.3
Other (spying on phone conversations, putting up posters)	31	18.3
Member of the national guard	1	0.6
Getting rid of neighbours, family members or enemies—denunciation	12	7.1
Hiding weapons	5	3
Participation in the women's demonstration	7	4.1

Revolutionary activities were sometimes used to resolve family conflicts. For example, Mrs. Györgyné Balázsi, Ilona Majzik (1937), was denounced by her husband for taking part in the revolutionary actions around the Eastern Railway Station. His accusation turned out not to be true.

Mrs. Lászlóné Antal, Terézia Simon (1929), appeared in the home of László Antal with members of the national guard (her sister-in-law and younger sister) on November 2 and 3, 1956, in order to enforce a custody order (*bírósági ítélet végrehajtása*) and remove the children that the courts had awarded to her. In the quarrel, she falsely accused her husband and his new family of being *ávós* (members of the hated state security).

The documents also reflect conflicts between neighbours. Mrs. Ernőné Bors, Ilona Barcsai (1918), quarrelling with her neighbours at the end of November, was quoted as saying, "There are going to be ghettos again where you'll be sent." As well, Mrs. Andrásné Bóné, Ágnes Róna (1910), called the National Guard on November 1, 1956, claiming that her joint tenant, who expelled her, was a state security officer. The armed men, seeing that it was a quarrel between neighbours, did not take sides.

The documentation of bickering neighbours goes on, and includes Mrs. Gézáné Pozsonyi, Anna Schönperger, who incited to kill one neighbour in order to get their flat because in a revolution nobody would search for the perpetrators. Mrs. Kálmánné Váczy, Alíz Krecskay, did not let in her joint tenant, Mrs. Ferencné Takács, who therefore appeared at the police claiming that the accused hadn't let her in as a result of her employment at the State Security. The revolutionaries arrested Mrs. Takács, escorted her to her flat and later arrested her sister, husband, and brother-in-law, as well.

Let me say a few words about looting during and after the revolution. It is difficult to discover whether or not women were involved in looting, though one of the photos included here shows women among the looters (see 4.24) [as numbered by Palasik when sent to Eric]. On the other hand, there are certainly some well-known photographs of women being involved in collecting money for the families of martyrs; such a collection was organized by the Hungarian Writers' Union, for instance (see 4.23). I have also seen a photo of a sign in a broken shop window saying, "The goods are in the care of the superintendant."

As for instances of looting, this will be a challenge for future researchers. In addition to asking whether both men and women were involved, they will need to consider whether or not indictments related to looting were in fact propaganda on the part of the stabilizing Kádár regime (and certainly a questioning of the myth about the "innocence" of the revolution). Perhaps such indictments were meant to give a political slant to an otherwise ordinary crime case. Or, on the contrary, perhaps including "looting" amongst charges allowed political cases to be considered ordinary crime ones? And, when considering data related to looting, as I have done during the course of research for this paper, researchers must always ask themselves: what can be regarded as a historical source, and what may be missing from this "source"? We must approach memoirs, for example, with criticism: who, after all, would claim to have taken part in looting? In the end, if we aren't careful, a hundred years after the events, the day-to-day life during the revolution might be written based only on indictments and verdicts.

Finally, here is an image revealing the silent demonstration of women on December 4, 1956. It was just one month after the Soviet invasion of Hungary. The demonstration was organized by Gyula Obersovszky and Gyula Eörsi. The women went to Heroes' Square with flowers, candles, and flags in their hands. Several thousand women placed their flowers on the tomb of the Unknown Soldier. There was also a demonstration in Szabadság Square, outside the US Embassy. The Soviet soldiers did not dare to shoot at the women. It was a brief demonstration of solidarity.

In conclusion, we might say that women's participation in the revolution was not proportional to their numbers in the overall population: 51.7 percent of the total population of Hungary (9,861,000) were women in 1956. That means there were 1,070 women for every 1,000 men—thirty more than there were before World War II. The photographic evidence shows women mostly in their traditional roles: care-giving, providing food, and in general avoiding conflict. However, even if only relatively few women participated in the armed conflicts, the very fact that any woman took up arms reveals that the revolution presented women with an opportunity to challenge their traditional roles. A parallel with some other heroic episodes from Hungarian history could perhaps be drawn, the most famous example being the women of Eger who assisted their men-folk during the siege of their town by the Turks in 1552 and whose story is told in a popular fictional work, Géza Gárdonyi's *Egri Csillagok* (Eclipse of the Crescent Moon).

Notes

1. Database of the suppression of the 1956 revolution. Introduction by Zsuzsanna Mikó. Records of the charges and verdicts were edited by Béla Sarusi Kiss and Ákos Tasnádi. The pictorial records were prepared and edited by Gabriella Csiffáry. Budapest City Archives, 2006.

   On some of the photos used in this paper, there are captions in Hungarian. These captions were prepared for the court cases in whose files they are deposited as support documentation. Therefore they have no bearing on my captions which were prepared to illustrate aspects of the participation of women in the Revolution.

2. For a brief biography of Kovacs, see the online encyclopedia of the 1956 Institute: http://www.rev.hu/history_of_56/szerviz/kislex/biograf/kovacs_uk.htm (accessed December 17, 2009)

3. Eörsi László, *1956 mártírjai* [The Martyrs of 1956] (Budapest: Rubicon-ház, 2006).

4. The names of those sentenced appear in full in the archive's database, and that is why I am allowed to use full names.

5.

The Hungarian Revolution of 1956 as Narrated by Shoah Survivors

Julia Vajda

"That summer sane people did not speak about the events of the previous fall any longer, and especially not about what the insurgents were like. They were not even mentioned any more."

Péter Nádas, *Parallel Stories*

The year is 1956, eleven years after the Soviet army liberated Hungary. Or the Russian Communists occupied it. On the one hand, the two are the same, but on the other hand they are just the opposite. Some see it this way, some the other way. As for the facts, bloody and painful World War II ended in Hungary on April 4, 1945, essentially liberating all Hungarian citizens—save for a few small groups, not to be discussed here. Over the years, however, it became clear that the Soviet troops were not going to leave Hungary after the end of the war and the peace treaties. Thus they became not only liberators but also occupiers. And they "forced" Hungary to introduce a regime that was far from being welcomed by all citizens.

Many came to interpret the end of the war as liberation and occupation at the same time; nevertheless, some still see it as only one of these—especially looking back from the present day. And the two groups are mutually exclusive. For some the feeling of being liberated after the war has been overshadowed by the history of the next forty years, while for others the experience of liberation overshadowed the events of the next forty years. Given their persecution before and during the war, Shoah survivors can never forget that sense of liberation. Not even those Shoah survivors for whom the next forty years brought renewed persecution and abuse.

There is, however, another fundamental issue related to 1956: to stay or to go. After many years of living behind the iron curtain, the revolution first opened up then closed the borders but, with some difficulty—leaving the country was still possible for a while. And while individual Hungarian reactions to the above dilemma is clearly interrelated with how those individuals interpreted the end of the war, what also needs to be taken into account is each person's life and experiences over those eleven years from liberation to 1956.

Usually a sociologist is expected to discuss her field of study in general terms. But generalizations at this level would only lead to meaningless commonplaces. For instance, one could suggest that the liberated Jews, trusting that the new regime would protect them from harm, became Communists. Indeed, some went so far in their zeal and their desire for revenge that they joined the Communist Party and made a good career as party officers, or even joined the *Államvédelmi Hatóság* (ÁVH, the state security organization) and became victims of popular wrath in 1956. We could add that the Jewish upper-middle class soon realized that Communism was just as abusive a regime as the previous one in terms of destroying their lives, and they fled the country. Looking at 1956 one can see these two basic groups—those who supported the Communists from the inside and those who recognized it as a tyrannical institution and did not—but a third group can also be readily identified. This is the group of people who trusted Communism but failed to gain high positions in the regime, and so in 1956 they simply feared that the regime, which provided their security, would be overthrown. Of course, we could continue with this kind of categorization, making ever finer distinctions and delineating ever smaller groups.

However, social status, which serves as the basis of this kind of categorization, is only one factor in any individual's behaviour and motivations. Being a psychologist, as well, I do not think this categorisation satisfactory. In order to understand a persons' behaviour, we must also try to understand the role of the individual's psyche. We have to understand how society as a whole, as well as the individual's closer environment and his/her own psychic structure, all shape the individual's life story and its narration.

My contribution to this collection of essays about the 1956 revolution is based on two of about two hundred narrative life story interviews made with Shoah survivors by our research team over a period of one and a half years.[1] In the interviews, each lasting on average three or four hours, we asked the interviewees to tell us about their whole lives. Here I would like to illustrate how differently these people experienced the Hungarian revolution in 1956, despite their common background as far as the Shoah goes, and reveal the factors that influenced these differences of experience.

Going through the bulk of the material to examine how these now rather elderly people talk about the revolution as part of their life stories, the first surprise is that the majority of the interviewees do not even mention it. In the several-hour-long interviews, in which the interviewer does not ask about events and stories not volunteered by the interviewee, the revolution does not appear at all, or if it does, it is just an insignificant event that had caused some disturbance in the interviewee's everyday life. One should not forget, of course, that they were interviewed as Shoah survivors and thereby the primary focus of the interview was necessarily the Shoah. Nevertheless, when asked to tell their whole life stories, one could have assumed that they would not bypass as shocking an episode of Hungarian history as 1956.

At the same time, in the narration of emigrant survivors, the revolution and emigration are central events—the reasons for this are obvious. Using a term by László Tengelyi, 1944 and the Shoah are "fate-altering events" in the lives of all survivors ("*sorsesemény*" in Hungarian): episodes that make the persecuted rewrite their life stories. And this can apply to 1956, too. There are many for whom 1956 has also become a "fate-altering event." For people who emigrated or were thrown into prison, the revolution became a "fate-altering event," whether they wanted it to or not; the moment rewrote their life stories. They could no longer narrate their life without that moment, in the light of which earlier events were rewritten in order to produce a coherent version.

By briefly presenting and interpreting a couple of interviews, the goal of my contribution here is to give a forceful illustration of how these people, the majority of them now over eighty years, talk about 1956 from the perspective of today's reality and how they talk about it as part of their Shoah-centred life stories—if they mention it at all. Once we comprehend the why's and how's of their narrations and the underlying motives, we may understand not only the reasons for the overall silence about the revolution on behalf of those Shoah survivors staying in Hungary but also how the Shoah and pre-Shoah experiences influenced the 1956 experience in the narration of both emigrants and those who stayed at home.

*

Klári, Mrs. Salamon—let us call her by this name[2]—was born in Budapest in 1928. Here is the summary of the facts of her life as she told us in a one-and-a-half-hour-long narration when first asked to tell her life story. Her father was born in an upper-middle-class Jewish family that owned a business, and her mother came from a poor Jewish family. Klári is their only child. Until 1944 the family's upward mobility goes unbroken. After their initial poverty, when the grandparents were trusted with raising the child, their business grows and they can afford ever bigger homes, where they bring the child to live with them. They also employ a number of assistants, servants, and gardeners in the business and at home. Klári is sent to schools, but because of the *numerus clausus* law (setting a quota for the number of Jews who can be admitted to an educational institution), she can only go to a public school (from where it was not possible to go on to higher education) instead of a secondary grammar school. After that she goes to a school to learn sewing. While in school, she is constantly a victim of anti-Semitic incidents.

In 1944 her father, using false documents, passes himself and his family off as non-Jews and helps the female family members escape from the ghetto, but bad luck drives them into the arms of an Arrow Cross troop, and they end up in Bergen-Belsen. There the father works in the kitchen and can feed his family. The two women stay together throughout their time there. Through the help of a Lagerälteste, the work they do is not too hard and earns them extra food. Not long before liberation the father is sent to another camp. The two women are liberated together, but the mother dies a few days later. Klári befriends another girl, a hairdresser, who also lost her mother in the camp. They open a hairdressers' shop in Budapest. A few months later she receives a letter from her father who has also made his way back home from the camp. She returns home and she and her father live with an uncle.

Klári soon marries a man whom her mother used to say would make a good husband; his wife and two children died in Auschwitz. First she has a son, then a daughter with him. At this time she works at TÜKER, a state-owned company, selling lumber and building material, and she enrols in various training courses and finally in the University of Economics. A few years later she and her husband divorce and Klári remarries. After 1956 her professional career continues in the Ministry of Foreign Trade, where she works until retirement. Both her children hold university degrees, and currently she has four adult grandchildren and one great-grandchild.

Let us see how Klári talks about 1956, how she experienced it back then. Quite extraordinarily, or at least unusually for our Shoah survivor interviewees, she mentions that she lived through 1956 right in the first sentence of the interview. Is she haunted by her memories of 1944? Obviously, her successful life since then is unlikely to be the reason for this mention. However, after that first sentence she does not talk about the revolution again, and all she says is that when she met her second husband she worked in the Ministry of Foreign Trade, where she had gone to work after 1956. As dictated by the rules of the narrative interview technique, however, the interviewer goes back to the first mention:

> Q: Right after you told me you were born you said that besides the Second World War you had lived through 1956, too, but in the end you did not speak about it.
>
> A: Well, yes. In 1956 I was the head of the human resources department of TÜKER in Budapest, and overnight, being a Jew, being the head of the department of human resources, and being a party member—I did not tell you that in 1947,* in 46 I joined the Hungarian Communist Party*"[3]

As she herself realizes, she failed to mention it before. While her party membership was not part of her story narrated in relation to the Shoah, now she explains it as her reaction to having gone through the Shoah—most probably she does not only think this is the reason today but this was her motivation at that time.

Basically I thought that what had happened to me once already should not happen again, and at that time I thought that it was the Communist party that could take care of my interests and my rights as a human being. I joined the party, and in 1988 or in whatever year there was this screening,[4] and I had been a party member up to then. At that time I was already elderly and I thought there was no sense in joining the party again, but I would like to emphasize that the fact that I don't have a membership card does not mean that I am not a fanatic Communist, [though] I have never been one, I always judged the situation with a cool head, but obviously, I have been on the left, right to this day.

So Klári describes herself as a fanatic Communist, or rather tries to make the relationship between fanatic Communist and leftist, at least in her case. The reason for her uneasiness may be the current political climate in Hungary in which being a Communist is not *comme il faut*, and to acknowledge one's one-time Communism is not *comme il faut*, either: in the current political discourse, being a Communist is equated with participation in the ÁVH, and party membership in the 1950s with membership in the 1980s.

Well, in 56 I was removed from my position, naturally.

What's her point with this "naturally"? That this was the fate of party members? She does not explain her meaning.

We lived right below the castle and I could not even get to work because they were shooting from the castle. And I was lucky, in the sense that I was packed to leave this country, I had had enough, friends called to say let's go, that's enough, the name-calling of Jews started again, the Arrow Cross started again, the rabble surfaced again, we should go.

Maybe "naturally" refers to this anti-Semitism that was beginning to resurface. Perhaps it was the Jews rather than the party members who were disposed of "naturally"? And she, as a Jewish woman, felt she had to flee again.

The most essential things were packed in a basket waiting for the truck the next day....

She does not elaborate on the topic of anti-Semitic attacks; instead she suddenly repeats her desire to go, not explaining her reasons for it. Why? Is what she perceives as anti-Jewish attitudes a good enough reason? Or she may have had bad experiences—of course she has—with the working of the regime but she is not telling us about them. Is there a reason why she is unwilling to talk about this?

> And the three of us, me and my two children, were to go. I asked my husband, are you coming? No. I am going, anyway.

A family drama plays itself out. Klári is prepared to go but her husband does not want to go with her. And her wording allows us to think that it is not a serious problem for Klári. We know that they divorce four or five years later. Was there a problem in their marriage as early as that? Maybe she wants to get out, not only out of the country but also out of her marriage. Anyway, she does not follow this line but continues with the emigration.

> And my child got diphtheria the day before. And that they did not come in the apartment, as I told you we lived in a basement apartment, there were a lot of people in that building who did not like us, and the reason why they did not come in, did not hurt us, was, it was because there was a red sheet of paper nailed on the door saying that there is someone with infectious disease in the apartment. And that's what saved us from suffering some serious harm once again.

Emigration thus fails because of the child's illness, but it is good for one thing: it protects them against harm, be it provoked by her party membership or by her position as head of a human resources department[5] or by her being a Jew.

> When things calmed down a little, and I could go to my workplace, I was told that I have no place there any longer. That I cannot come back there. There was one single person, a department head, who said, Klári, I always have a job for you. But the director himself, who was a Jewish boy and with whom I went to the same Jewish primary school, he told me, you are not the head of the human resources department any longer, you are a nobody here, you will go to the records office to address envelopes. There was only one person, a department head, who said, Klári, I always have a job for you. Mind you, I have to emphasize that during the over six years I was the head of the human resources department, the company was awarded the title "excellent company" several times, I was given awards, my work was recognized. Now, from one moment to the next, I became unfit.

Things seem to get mixed up. While Klári's perception of the period is that anti-Semitism had started again, it is her Jewish boss who fires her. At the same time, the department head, who always has a job for Klári, is not Jewish—at least we can presume this even if Klári does not say so, despite the fact that this would be crucial information in this part of her narration. Presumably the man who is to be thanked for saving Klári's career is not Jewish, either:

> The gist of the story is that I really was addressing envelopes when Endre Koroknay, a department head in the headquarters of the TÜKER companies learnt that I had been fired and he called me in and gave me a job, and I worked there for two years as a clerk. I was, much appreciated they were very nice to me, I learnt a lot there, and then I was transferred to the Ministry of Foreign Trade from there.

The stories Klári elaborates on thus do not back up her fear of the re-commencement of anti-Semitism, nor her feeling that she is persecuted as a Jew.

> So this was 56, so I after all did not experience it directly and I could not even go out because there was fighting everywhere in the streets, there were problems everywhere, and I had the sick child because of whom I practically could not leave the apartment, I was lucky, then too I was lucky.

In her summary she herself emphasizes how lucky she was. But what can her fear of anti-Semitism hide? What could have been her understanding of the events? As Klári does not elaborate, the interviewer asks a question:

> Q: In relation to 56 you said you had wanted to emigrate because anti-Semitism had started again.

> A: Well, **it started**, quite clearly, quite clearly*, OK, it was said that 56 wanted to topple the regime, the same people, the same fascists took centre stage again. Again, there were children coming with guns, shooting at people. I worked at TÜKER, I was the head of the human resources department. The next day they said, get out of here, they did not let me in, it was clearly anti-Semitism.

So Klári cannot imagine any other reason for her being fired than anti-Semitism, although so far she has failed to point to a concrete example. Why?

You can tell me that 56 was this and 56 was that, it was horrible, surely **it was the scum that came to the surface again**. And it was them again, who did the-, the *persecution of people in the most brutal ways, anti-Semitism started again**, the Arrow Cross came out again, the same as in 44. The situation was very difficult here, that period was very contradictory.

It is as if Klári could not find her way around in this contradictory world. The only thing she knows, because she already went through it once, is that in times of trouble the Jews are the first to get bashed.

I am sure there were people who did not want this, there were people who really wanted to bring down the regime....

Would she approve of these people who wanted to bring down the regime, though? Would this not have hurt her? She was the head of a human resources department, which in the 1950s meant that she was part of the hated regime: she had power over life and death. Could she have been frightened because of this? She may have had every reason to be afraid because a human resources department head was likely to have been removed from her job.

But for me that regime, for me that regime was good because no one dared to utter the word Jew.

Yes, Klári feared that toppling the regime would not only involve losing her position as head of a human resources department but also her personal safety. And she is unable to separate the two, even today. This is quite understandable. The Communist ideology promised the equality of all and that the Jews would not be second-class citizens. And for Klári it was not only a promise; it was reality:

And they gave me the opportunity to study, and they gave me the opportunity to develop and get ahead, basically the regime was good for me, with all its faults. With the fault that you could not travel abroad, with the fault that you could not obtain an apartment for 20 years, and there were very, very many problems, and it was very hard, but I had a secure job and *I knew that my existence was safe and not insecure, and that I would not be hurt and would not be persecuted.

Klári was frightened because with the regime toppled, she would lose her security. She could not be sure that the new regime would rectify only the earlier faults and the problems she herself experienced and not bring back the Jews' pariah status. Moreover, losing her personal safety was not merely a theoretical possibility, as she actually lost her job. She herself can see that to some extent:

> Fifty-six brought about this again. I was working in the human resources department but they did not let me enter, the man who was made the leader of the workers' council[6] clearly was a fascist, and he told me that you don't have a place here any more, I could not even go in. The head of the transportation department said, Klári you may come to my office any time and take it easy. But I was sacked from my position and the work I had successfully done for five or six years, I was put in the records office addressing envelopes, so there was I again with the insecurity under the same impossible conditions as once before, as in 44, and unfortunately those memories stay with you and, they come back again and one was scared once again.

What Klári fails to see, though, is that while all that was happening was frightening and reminded her of 1944, she herself was not persecuted for being a Jew; her main persecutor was also a Jew. Yes, we do know the myth that the Communist regime itself was a conspiracy of the Jews, the Jews created it, and the Jews benefitted from it. So Klári, the functionary of the regime, could have been identified with the regime and could have appeared as a participant of the Judeo-Bolshevik conspiracy. But we have to see that from what she told us she could have expected the same fate and the same harm even if she had not happened to be a Jew. And that the quarantine sign on her door could have just as easily protected the functionary that she was rather than the Jew.

Of course, we cannot know the opinions and experiences of those who did not like her or even hated her as a human resources head. When we ask about her party membership mentioned in relation to the events of 1956, she says,

> Q: You said that you joined the party in 1946 or 47. Would you care to say something more about it?

> A: Sure. Back then-, I worked in different party functions, I was a party liaison officer/this was my highest status (laughing), but I took part in everything I could. Marches on May 1st, I taught a basic party course, I taught, if it was possible, then I basically actively participated, in everything that went with party membership. In the ministry there were regularly

held members'– and at the other place members' meetings were held on a monthly basis. This was very good company, because there were ministers present there, I saw several ministers in and out of office while I worked there. I had very good contact with the heads of departments, some of them were very nice people, I have to admit there were one or two who were not what they should have been, but most of them were good, helpful people. And not only party members could make a career. For instance the head of the department I worked at was not a party member and still he was head of a department, and still he was also teaching at the university. So it is not true that only party members could make a career, it is not true, people could make a career according to their talents. Maybe the chances were better to get promotions because human relationships were different. Because when the minister called me in, and I walked in and he talked to me in the same human tone, and asked my opinion, most of the time he accepted my opinion, what I said to him. It was somehow different, we belonged together more, we helped each other, different, maybe not, I cannot really put it in words, but it was a much more humane, a much more informal atmosphere, it was much more helpful. And these contacts have been maintained ever since, we keep holding these friends' meetings. So* this was it, even though not all of them were Jews, and not all of them were party members, but the human relationships were better.

For Klári the party was a homelike, friendly, and protective environment. And what for outsiders appeared as the use and abuse of power and functions, and angered those who rejected the regime or did not fully identify with it, for her were nothing more than the natural concomitants of her amicable relationships. As she felt the party environment was the only refuge and safe place for her against the persecution of Jews, she did not understand, and maybe she can never understand, why it provoked others. She only felt that any attack against the regime—and this is exactly what happened in 1956—could destroy the only safe world she knew and make her a pariah again.

At the same time it is worth remembering how Klári tells the story of her aborted emigration. Her plan to leave Hungary fits with her state of mind regarding the Communist regime: she felt she had to go because the regime was about to be toppled, and, as she believed, the Jews were being persecuted. Which may indeed have been the case; I do not wish to deny it. We do know that anti-

Semitic attitudes exist in Hungary even today. Nevertheless, Klári's fear did not originate in any personal experience of anti-Semitism in 1956, but rather the riotous and insecure situation revived her old fears. She did not want to flee the regime but the toppled regime, especially if her private life was a failure and her marriage did not give her happiness anymore.

And why does she stick to this version of her life story even today? Klári remained a faithful cadre of the regime after 1956. She advanced in her career. She obviously made all the compromises the regime expected of her, and most probably she had no difficulty doing so. This is what she might have referred to when she called herself a "fanatic Communist." She hoped for and got security from this regime. Even if she had reasons to revolt against it in 1956, she could not go away, and today it is easier for her to see the hardships of the 1950s minimized in comparison with the troubles she was afraid of then and was still, seventeen years after the change of the regime, with anti-Semitism set free once again. At the same time, by emphasizing the security provided by the regime, it is easier for her to lessen the significance of her aborted emigration. She never again tried to leave Hungary. As we learn later, her aunt immigrated to Israel in 1947 but came home three years later, highlighting the fact that choosing Jewishness is not necessarily a good solution. In the 1960s this aunt immigrated to the United States and committed suicide twenty years later, proving, in Klári's mind, that she was right not to go. No matter that Communism currently is not exactly popular, Klári insists that she has always been and still is a fanatic Communist, in other words, she still thinks that she could only feel safe in the old regime, not least because it was that regime that ensured her a living standard above the average.

*

Let us now see an absolutely different story.

I will call her Magda, Mrs. Berkes. Magda comes from a family similar to Klári's, in that her parents' financial situation had also been very different. In Magda's case, it is her mother's side that was a well-to-do, upper-middle-class Jewish family, presumably much better off than the family of Klári's father. Magda's father came from a poor Jewish family. Both her mother's and father's families came from Transylvania (which has belonged to Romania since the end of World War I), and her parents and some of their brothers and sisters came to live in what is today's Hungary and settled in the city of Szeged. But they left behind many relatives so the Trianon peace treaty affected them personally.

Magda is born in 1926 as the first child of her parents, has a Jewish governess from Vienna from the age of three, and learns to speak French as fluently as her mother tongue in her early childhood. She continues her education first in a Lutheran primary school then in a well-known Catholic secondary school.

In 1944 she is eighteen, but despite being a Jew she is allowed to take the final high school exam. Right after the final exam in June she is deported to Auschwitz with her whole family from Szeged, including aunts, uncles, grandparents, and her six-month-old baby sister. Except for her, all the others are immediately sent to the gas chamber, including the baby. Most of her relatives in Transylvania had already met the same fate.

Fortunately, Magda is strong enough to be sent to work in an ammunition factory, where she is allowed to bathe daily and is fed a little better than those who remained in the camp. She is liberated there, and after a few months she goes to live with her only living relative in Transylvania. She spends two years there.

Coming home after two years, she marries immediately and joins the Communist Party. After 1956 she goes to work for a foreign trade company, travels a lot, and never renews her party membership.

This is the story she tells us in response to our first question requesting to tell her life story. In this story she only briefly touches upon Communism and the 1950s, and she does not mention the revolution except to say that after 1956 she went to work for a foreign trade company. Let us see how she talks about this era:

> Well, so with this enormous enthusiasm that there is this tenet one can hang onto, can –fight the last remnants of Nazism and **at last this is something** with which one can oppose all that was Nazism, and and this wonderful tenet, Marxism-Leninism (4)

What is this long pause? Why does Magda stop for four seconds?

> And it is very good that = one=can enthuse for something.

When Magda says this, it makes us think that in her view enthusiasm is a quality that comes upon us only in rare moments; it is not an innate ability. It must have been very hard for an upper-middle-class girl to be enthusiastic about an ideology that rejected her upper-middle-class family and upper-middle-class world. However, having her entire family killed in the Shoah, except for one Transylvanian aunt, she certainly appreciates the security promised by Communism. Still, a shadow of ambivalence seems to appear, but we have not heard anything in her personal story yet that would produce this.

> But life is as it is: and theories are just theories, and practice is practice. So, when we got this far and the relocation[7] of people started, maybe=I have=already=spoken about this, so this was the first thing that disillusioned me; because, eventually, those who were relocated, on the basis of whatever theory, you see- *

Yes, Magda knows what it means; she experienced it herself. She would not buy into the official explanations of the Communist regime. She knows that if her parents were still alive and had not lost all their wealth in the Shoah, they could have been among the deprived and relocated. It seems, however, that she does not have the same strong and undifferentiated urge for revenge—as that of many of her fellow sufferers, who see an Arrow Cross man everywhere—that would make her support these horrors.

> By 1953, by the time Stalin died, unfortunately I came to know perfectly well that* what is theory and what is practice. So much so that I got disillusioned very soon – with my **dreams**, with saving the world, ((sighs)) (4). But everyone has to go through these stages.

Magda today remembers that she was a zealous Communist for not more than five years. Why is that? Had she lost her enthusiasm merely because of the relocations?

Later, we ask about what she mentioned right at the beginning of the interview, that she lived in historical times. In response, she slowly develops the story in depth; a story that took place in the 1950s, which turns out to be the source of her disillusionment.

> Q: You mentioned that the- the historical times interfered with your life. Would you say some more about it?

A: Yes. Because one- Because times are historical even though there is no crusade, it is historical times when there is no thirty years war, and when there came the happy period after the Compromise,[8] but in **historical** times one always thinks that such times mean some great world-shaking disaster, right? When one lives one's happy childhood years for instance, and nothing happens to the child except that the child goes to school,=and comes home,=and=is=given=a disciplinary warning at school or is not=given a disciplinary warning, that is not historical times. But when you have to move into the ghetto, and are deported to Auschwitz and etcetera etcetera, your parents are taken away, or you are put in jail by ÁVH, **those** are historical times.

Here Magda is not telling her personal story but is generalizing and in her generalization calls up a historical event that has not been mentioned so far. Perhaps she herself or someone close to her had been jailed by the ÁVH?

Thus I, when I=told=you=that=history interfered= with my=life on several occasions, I was meaning this, that my first, the first loss in my life was my tutor, Rebecca who had to go home to Vienna because her mother was ill, and in Germany the Hitlerian turn had already taken place, and died there. So=this=was=the=first thing, when I felt, I had to feel that history interfered with my life. And this was repeated several times, this was repeated, then, when I was deported, and when, and then again, and then all over again: life was mocking me, when my husband was imprisoned as part of the Szebenyi trial,[9] and they made me an unskilled worker in no time.

Magda makes a long list of the already-mentioned tragedies before she comes to the ÁVH—mentioned only in general terms before—and her personal experience with it. Why is it so hard for her to get to this point?

And there I was with my communist enthusiasm you see, and then I was supposed to deal with this in my mind and in my life, for God's sake what's this again? When-when I had to realise that finally I had an inspiring theory in my life, and then it turns out that this too is absolutely worthless, and terrible, and so -. What was I so enthused about? So I felt many times in my life that, that's what I meant when I said history interf-, history always interferes in li-, in everyone's life.

Is it her disillusionment that makes it so hard for her to get to this point? That it was hard to give up her Communist faith? That she was shaken because after thinking that she finally had something to be enthusiastic about, something that promised something new and beautiful instead of the horrors, now turns out to be something she cannot believe in? Anyway, she closes the topic and for some reason does not elaborate on her own story. May there be something in her story that is difficult to tell?

Later in the interview we ask about Rebecca in response to which we listen to lots of nice stories about her marriage and grandchildren. Then we get to the point where we can return to what she said about her husband.

> Q: Could we go back a little to your husband? You mentioned that in-that in: the Szebenyi the Szebenyi trial he was put in jail and you
>
> A: That one was another husband. That was terr-, I couldn't get over it yet./ I could not get over it. ((speaking in syllables)) I don't have, I cannot, I cannot express my opinion. Simply, I am not over it yet! (5)

What other husband? Is it possible that we have not heard about a second husband in the course of several hours of narration? What skeleton has she in the closet? And why were those years so terrible that she cannot talk about them today? Was she by herself? Was she abandoned by her friends? Was the hardship of making her work as an unskilled worker that bad? That after the forced labour for the Nazis she had to do hard physical work again? Or is there something even more horrible that inhibits her? Is it related to her divorce? Or are her divorce and the imprisonment connected? After a long pause she says,

> I don't want to talk about it right now. ((sighs)).

The interviewer naturally agrees, saying, "Yes, of course." And the analysts can go on pondering what that horrible experience could have been that Magda cannot and does not want to share with us, she who talked with admirable plasticity and in detail about her Nazi camp experiences.

> Q: You said you became an unskilled worker. Could you perhaps talk about this one?
>
> A: Of course, about that I can. Under socialism, you know, it was like-was like ll-((sighs)) (3) this kind of falling from grace, and these self-

blaming trials and*, you know. I don't remember whose witty remark it was that when the Soviet Union or=or only its Communist Party wiped out all its enemies, and because it continuously needed enemies, then it started=searching=the enemy within itself. That –th er this is a bon mot but there is a lot of truth in this bon mot....

And she explains at considerable length what the regime was like, what the conditions were like back then, what the show trials were like, and she does not go over to her personal story for a good while. Then

> Something like that happened to my first husband that *he fell from grace; and- and that was only one fact which contributed to my realising what the practice of socialism in reality is, because fate was so good to me, you know, the clever learns from the mistakes of others, but no:, I had to go through it on my own

She seems to keep avoiding telling her own story. As we have already suspected there is something very hard for her to tell.

> So what happened was that I=then=was assistant head of the department=of popular education in county **Borsod**, and my husband was imprisoned, they of course did not=tell=why, and I was fired from my job and put out of my apartment within a day, * I was fired from everywhere, and I=found=myself=there again by myself.

She starts her own story, in which the part about being fired from her job and moved out of her apartment echoes her Shoah experience, though she had attended a secondary grammar school where she was not harassed.

> I must add that the family of my husband supported me by all means and wanted to help me. I did not accept because I always wanted to be able to **look after** myself....

Why does Magda say this? Why did not she accept help? Earlier she said about her mother-in-law that when in 1947 she met her husband she

> called her mummy-mummy and [I] called her mummy-mummy because she was doubly my mother. On the one hand, you see, by the right that she was my mother-in-law and on the other hand because she wanted very much to be a substitute for my own mother

Why does not she want to accept mummy-mummy's help? Did their relationship get worse? But then why do they want to help? And why does Magda, right after this quotation, say,

> I don't like to talk abo-, about the periods of my life after that.

Let us see how she continues her story about being an unskilled worker:

> that's how I became an unskilled worker in Komló. I was loading and pushing the bogie in the mine ((ironically)). And life is always ironic and a bit vexing =you see, because I worked in the mine in Komló, as an-unskilled worker

This must have been hard physically, too, and Magda, surviving and coming home from the Shoah, speaking two foreign languages fluently and two more reasonably well, was not prepared for that. This situation seems to evoke the Shoah, but she is ironical about it and talks about life's little tricks and sense of humour. What is she referring to? Similarity to the Shoah, or to something else?

> Then, and then, you see, some years later, thanks to the mine work I did, I travelled, or **started** to travel over half the world a few years later. Life is such.

This would be the humorous side life? That first she works in a mine and later travels over half the world? She talks at length about her trips, how she saved money earned from other jobs to supplement the meagre daily fee abroad in order to maximally enjoy life as a sales agent in the Far East, where the average Hungarian could not go in those times. However, she turns back to the tragedy before 1956 only several minutes later.

> Needless to say,=you see, that in 56 I did not join the party again, because I knew exactly what this party was. And after all finally, socialism did not corrupt me so much, and I thought I don't have to pretend, I will get by somehow. So that I **don't** have to be a party member since I do not agree with the party. Which- which eventually (after all) was a painful process on my part, you see, because it meant total disillusionment. And then eventually I landed this sales agency job.

She ends her story about breaking with the party, in which we can feel the dignity of the upper-middle-class girl who would not pretend for petty favours if not necessary. At the same time she makes us suspect that there is another story in the background that shook her so much, in addition to hard physical work and disillusionment, which she cannot and does not want to talk about.

In any case, the interviewer asks more questions about the story that took place in the early 1950s:

Q: You mentioned that as early as in 53-

A: Yes, sure. Yes. So now this was the one side of that thing, the other side, unskilled worker, there, I went to that higher party course; I was removed from my apartment, I was fired from my job; and I had to ask myself the question: «Good Lord, now what is this? Now what is this? What did my husband do? Why is he in prison? »

Magda's account of the events and her state of mind suggests that she felt very insecure and frightened. What should she think? Is the party right to imprison her husband? And most likely she was not allowed to talk to her husband as people carried off to prison by the ÁVH were not entitled to receive visitors. And even if he had been entitled, it could not have been any real conversation because of the severe controls. But she knew her husband as an honest man. What was the truth? At that time, the practice of show trials was not widely known yet and Magda did not know what she knows today and explained to us at length, i.e. how the party looked for enemies within itself when it ran out of enemies outside.

«And what did I do? » Me, I knew about myself exactly that I sure had not done anything apart from being stupidly enthusiastic. You see, and I wanted=to do=good=all the time because=I=wanted all the time- to save the world. It must have occurred to me to ask myself whether my husband had really done something?

She goes on explaining her uncertainty. If she is sure that she did not do anything wrong, can she be sure about her husband?

And I had to ask-, first my idea was that if the party, all in capital letters, back and forth, simply makes an official disappear, imprison him, and that person happens to b= my =husband, but I, as a convinced communist I know that he **must have done** something **awful**! That's why the party, all in capital letters, back and forth, had to imprison him! Eradicate him! Because he betrayed it! **The Party**!

Magda seems to believe what her party tells her. Her husband *betrayed* the party. Otherwise he would not have been thrown in jail.

> But I had to realise, what did I do? You see? And if they will do this to **me** and I had done nothing wrong, then did my husband do anything wrong at all?

But, she recalls, when she was removed from job and apartment, she became suspicious.

> And if he did not do-, if he did:, it's his business, why am I punished? And if he did not do anything, why are we, both of us, punished? Why?

She slowly realises that if she is punished unjustly, maybe her husband is, too. This means that there is something wrong with the party. Even if it is right to punish the husband, it also punished Magda, the woman belonging to the husband, who certainly has not done anything against the party. How does Magda feel about it? It is possible that she herself was unjust to believe her husband guilty? This may be the story she cannot tell us? That her husband was imprisoned as part of a show trial and that there was a time when she believed that the party was right? And could this be the reason why she does not go on narrating in detail her personal story but instead goes back to her not re-joining the party? Is she ashamed of trusting the party more than her husband?

> So when Stalin died I knew perfectly, I had felt on my own skin what the **practical** implementation of **Stalinism**-Leninism was. You see? Then I had no illusion >whatsoever any more. Because then I already kn- knew what the reality was<. And **this was exactly why**, when **56*** came, I did not re-join the party. I thought I would not go on with the show, no matter what.* Yes.

Yes, Magda has the guts not to re-join the party. But what happened to the marriage? What happened between the two of them, one having believed that the other was guilty, but it was only the party that was guilty? She punished the party by not re-joining it, but was that enough? Could that have been enough for the husband to restore trust between them? Or perhaps the imprisoned husband never knew about this crisis of trust? Once she understood that it was the party that was guilty, could Magda pretend that nothing had happened? We do not know when they got divorced exactly, only that they did sometime in the 1950s. Maybe the divorce was the consequence of this story? That the husband did not forgive what could not be forgiven? That Magda believed those who accused him? As the interview progresses, this increasingly becomes our impression.

How does Magda live with this burden after 1956? Interrupting her story after telling us how she got disillusioned with the party, she starts speaking about her job as a company sales agent.

> And after all finally, socialism did not corrupt me so much, and I thought I don't have to pretend, I will get by somehow. So that I **don't** have to be a party member since I do not agree with the party. Which eventually (after all) was a painful process on my part, you see, because it meant total disillusionment.

We have heard this already.

> And then I got this this foreign trade job. Which which in which, in which I did all sorts of tricks so that some small things could be done differently than it was supposed to be done by by: the masses, I got myself that little something, you know? But I I fou I discovered for myself eventually that that* in the East there are minerals, I=did=not=discover=this but that there is a Hungarian engineer, and what I discovered was that that a certain kind of support pillar in the mine that was generally made of wood before, but in the Second World War the Germans realized that it could be made of metal, so it can be made of steel, and=this is more economic, and that certain types sell well there. Well, now, what you needed there was on the one hand fluency in foreign languages,

She says proudly that she, who had been deprived of so much in life, had that skill.

> On the other hand, the Hungarian ministry of foreign trade always delegated the stupidest people as heads of mission, who paid always the lowest per diems, so the senior people never travelled there. The per diem in Tunisia was so meagre /hah hah ((laughs)) that you could not afford a roll of film. But there was this wonderful Tunisia. I saved money elsewhere so that I could afford to live there, you know, I found this world for myself. And there I was selling this good Hungarian equipment, and I demanded

and **was given** a hired driver and a rented car and had myself driven out in the desert, well=there=you=can't drive there on your own, you see. And I made some very good business. There I managed to get that little difference, that little extra, you know, that the-. Yes.

"That little difference." What can she be thinking about? A little difference that makes her feel good? Or that makes her different from the average? That makes her the daughter of the proud upper-middle-class mother, who could obtain anything she wanted before her world fell apart.

> My mother got it into her head that er that, there was this very fashionable tablecloth at that time, I do not remember its name. One day my mother thought about it, and presented her idea to my father, that we needed it for big family gatherings, when all the relatives from Transylvania came, and my father judged that it was not exactly an expenditure that necessarily needed to be made. My mother did not say a word. But she looked up in this journal, something like Burda, and went to Vienna, bought the materials and the pattern - and whatever. And my mother sat at it and I don't know, in a year and a half, or I don't= know=in=what=time she made it herself. *Yes. Because she wanted it badly, my father did not want to pay for it, and the will of both of them was fulfilled, finally./My father didn't have to pay for it ((giggling)), my mother made it.

*

Magda's and Klári's stories are alike only inasmuch as the lives of both of them were broken by the Shoah at the end of their teenage years, at the moment when they became adults. There isn't, however, much similarity in how they experienced the rest of their lives, partly under the influence of the Shoah. They both put their faith in Communism—an ideology heralding the equality of all and promising that the horrors they underwent can never happen again. Klári holds onto this ideology at all costs and wavers only for a second when she plans to emigrate. She does not see how similar this regime is to the previous one; she does not allow herself to realise that she is out of the frying pan into the fire, even though this time she is not persecuted by the regime. All her life, she has had her security and a decent standard of living from the Communist system and from her faith in it.

In contrast to Klári, probably primarily due to her different personality but also because she—but mostly her husband—was picked out by the regime as an enemy, Magda slowly realizes her mistake and recognizes that this regime is not what it pretends to be. Painfully, the only thing she can do is to break with it and reflect on it. However, this comes too late. She cannot save her private life. She needs another decade to pull herself together and find a new partner.

Nevertheless, while only these two women among all the Shoah survivors interviewed mention 1956, even they do not feel it as an essential and crucial part of their lives worth talking about. In Klári's case, one of the reasons for not feeling that 1956 was a crux was that she continued identifying with the regime for fear of losing the security it provided. Neither the revolution nor the ensuing reprisals made her waver. This could be true for many interviewees. The persecuted, such as Magda, however, would have welcomed the success of the revolution, but after its suppression they move on to establish a *modus vivendi* that allows them to benefit from the knowledge and skills they acquired earlier in the now slowly changing regime.

All this, perhaps, is specific to the generation of those interviewed. Now we can only reach those survivors who were still young during the Shoah. Once liberated, the majority of such young people found themselves on their own and for most of them the Communist Party was the only thing they could put their faith in. Their immature identities and the instability of their lives prevented them from clearly seeing their choices as one totalitarian system gave way to another. Thus, as described in Freudian mass psychology, the Communist Party and its ideology would come to replace their mothers and fathers and become the only thing they could rely on.

Notes

1. The interviews were made within the framework of the sub-program "Totalitarianism and Holocaust" (research leader Júlia Vajda) of the research program "Totalitarianism and Europe" (research leader Mihály Vajda),

sponsored by the National Research and Development Program of the Hungarian National Office for Research and Technology.

2. I have not only given false names to my interviewees, but I have also changed some data so that the core of the narrated and lived stories have not changed but the person I am talking about is no longer the same as my interviewee.

3. The text of the interview was transcribed phonetically. For the sake of legibility though, the excerpts in this paper are written in a way that is closer to regular orthography; conventional punctuation rules, however, are not observed: commas and full stops are used only at places where such stops were clearly indicated by the interviewee's tone. At the same time, only few of the transcription marks were retained: emphatically said words are in bold type; * means a short pause, while the number in parenthesis stands for the seconds of longer pauses. Marks of meta-communication are in double parentheses; / means the starting point of meta-communication, while = means that the words are spoken without any pause. The characteristics of spoken language, colloquialisms, faulty inflection, repetitions and moans are left unchanged, or are marked.

4. The interviewee refers to the 1989 transition when the old Communist party was replaced by a new one. Both the members of the old party and non-members could join the new party. A "screening," however, also took place in 1948 when the Communist and Social-Democratic parties fused and the earlier Social-Democrats were "screened out" and banned from the Communist party.

5. In the Communist-Socialist regime, especially in its early period before 1956, human resources department heads were very powerful. They could decide whether to employ someone for a certain position, and their decision was based on one's faithfulness to the party and on coming from the right social class rather than on professional considerations.

6. Beginning on the day after the revolution broke out in 1956, workers' councils were set up across the country to represent the workers' political interests. The councils managed the plants and fulfilled employers' and interest protection responsibilities. They also participated in the new local political leadership.

7. In Hungary between 1948 and 1953, persons and whole families considered politically dangerous were relocated. Their assets were confiscated and they themselves were moved to a "compulsory place of living," where they were usually made to do agricultural work.

8. After the suppression of the Hungarian revolution and fight for freedom in 1848 and 1849, Austria governed Hungary with tyrannical methods. However, lengthy negotiations led to the Compromise between Austria and Hungary in 1867 by which Hungary regained a relative degree of independence within the Habsburg Empire. This was, actually, the beginning of the Austro-Hungarian Monarchy.

9. The Szebenyi trial was linked to the trial of László Rajk, which was the most important of the show trials in Hungary. László Rajk, a former illegal Communist and the Minister of Internal Affairs between 1946 and 1948, was arrested by the ÁVH in May 1949. He was sentenced to death in September 1949 and executed.

6.

The Impact of the 1956 Hungarian Revolution in Argentina[1]

Judith Kesserű Némethy

The outbreak of the Hungarian revolution on October 23, 1956, brought forth solidarity movements from Hungarian émigrés and their environment all over the world. It has justifiably been called "the cleanest revolution," for Hungarians were probably never as united as they were during those days, and during the long months and years of retribution that followed. Émigrés saw only one mission for themselves: to help the fighting nation.

In Argentina, the response was overwhelming. Among the émigrés of 1948, differences between left and right disappeared as churches, associations, clubs, and youth groups worked together to help the freedom fighters, and later the refugees, as well as those who couldn't escape. Through marches, protests, masses, donations, petitions, publications, and exhibitions, all of émigré society was mobilized.[2]

On October 25, 1956, leaders of the Hungarian émigré organizations sent telegrams to Argentina President Pedro Eugenio Aramburu, US President Dwight Eisenhower, UN Secretary General Dag Hammarskjöld, as well as, among others, to the Argentine, Cuban, and Peruvian ambassadors to the UN, to the Austrian chancellor, to the president of Yugoslavia, and to the International Red Cross.[3] They urged authorities to voice their support in protecting the people of Hungary against the reprisal of the Soviet-led Communist government and to speak out on behalf of their human rights.

On October 27, more than 10,000 people gathered at the Metropolitan Cathedral in Buenos Aires for prayers and the celebration of a mass in Hungarian and Spanish. From there, the crowd marched in silence through the city streets to place a wreath at the foot of the statue of José de San Martín, the hero of Argentina's independence. Composed of Hungarians, members of sister emigrations from behind the Iron Curtain, and Argentines, the formation was a kilometre long, in lines of four, dotted with flags and enormous placards.[4]

On October 30, leaders of the Centro Húngaro (Argentina's most important Hungarian club) invited the heads of all Hungarian émigré organizations to form the Committee of Assistance for a Free Hungary, in order to coordinate the strategies and actions aimed at providing support for the revolution. It acted through subcommittees—press and publicity, monetary, social services and activities, foreign affairs, transportation and youth—all coordinated by a central secretariat.

The movement had two main elements. One branch focused on the moral and material support of the fighting nation through an extensive collection of donations in money and kind to be categorized, packed, and shipped. The second branch managed the reception and assistance of the refugees, arranging for housing and assisting with job searches. The club's facilities were crowded with dozens of volunteers working in shifts from 8 am to midnight, collecting, sorting, classifying, and packaging the mounds of food, clothing, blankets, and medicines. Over 2,500 bags and crates were shipped to Hungary during those days. Citizens formed long lines to donate money and goods. Others signed up to donate blood. During its four weeks of work in the Centro, the assistance committee received a total of 1,200,000 pesos and shipped by air and sea over 80,000 kilograms of clothing, food, and medication.[5]

These numbers reflect the solidarity of the Argentine people, who throughout the upheaval showed their generosity and support. The memories of the bloody 1955 Argentine revolution that ousted Perón were still fresh, and they followed with sympathy the events in Hungary. They gave immeasurable proof of this through anonymous donations of money, jewellery, and goods. The Argentine Red Cross made 2,000 units of blood available to the Viennese Red Cross, at which point university students en masse offered to replenish the supply.

The Secretary of Aviation, upon learning that more than two hundred exiles enlisted to join the freedom fighters, offered the assistance of the Argentine Air Force to transport them to Hungary. (The revolution was crushed before this action could materialize.[6]) When word went out that orphans were fleeing Hungary in great numbers, over 11,000 Argentines volunteered to adopt them, while the Argentine government offered homes to 3,000 children. The country appropriated the declaration made by President Aramburu: "In every Argentine heart there must live a small Hungary." Thousands of letters of support and solidarity arrived from every corner of the nation.[7]

In order to facilitate immigration procedures for refugees, the Argentine government created, on November 19, a National Commission of Aid to Hungary, presided over by the Foreign Minister. The Asociación Cultural Argentina pro Hungría, formed by prominent members of Argentine society before the revolution, mobilized all of its connections to help the cause of the revolution. The Hungarian émigré Catholic school provided full scholarships to twenty-six refugee children. These efforts were broadcast to Hungary by the *Voice of America*.[8]

The newspaper *Délamerikai Magyarság* (Hungarians in South America) made an enormous effort to propagate the Hungarian fight for freedom. Within hours after the outbreak of the revolution, this paper, through the Associated Press, broadcast Argentine-Hungarians' protests against the use of Soviet troops in Hungary. It provided the thrust behind a series of press conferences, communiqués, articles, and radio and TV publicity that were disseminated around South America.[9]

The paper also carried out considerable political action, and high-ranking leaders from all Argentine political parties except the Communists took an active part. After the crush of the revolution and the retribution that followed, a series of mass demonstrations and protests were organized in front of both the Hungarian and Soviet embassies, in which crowds of Argentine sympathizers also took part. Some of these demonstrations became violent, with cars being burned in front of the Soviet embassy.[10]

Throughout 1957, demonstrations, protests, masses, prayer groups, and conferences continued. On the first anniversary of the revolution a huge exhibition was organized in the Casa de Mendoza in Buenos Aires. More than 150,000 people visited it in two weeks, and 25,000 signatures were collected and sent to the United Nations, demanding that Soviet troops leave Hungary. The exhibition was then taken to several Argentine cities, as well as to Montevideo and Santiago de Chile.[11]

Of special importance is the literary and journalistic output in Argentina following the revolution. Numerous books, journals, and periodicals documenting the events were published in Spanish and distributed among Argentine officials, as well as government agencies of all Spanish-speaking countries, embassies, and UN delegations. For years to come, Hungarian journalists in Argentina were dedicated to keeping alive the spirit of the revolution through news, photographs, poems, and manifestos. They reported on Cardinal Mindszenty's radio messages, on the refugees, and on other émigré groups' activities of support. They also built strong ties with the Argentine press, writing articles and editorials in Spanish for the public at large. *Frente Común*, Argentina's forceful anti-Communist paper, printed news from Hungary in each of its weekly issues. Hundreds of articles and radio broadcasts appeared for months in all main newspapers and radio stations, as well.

For two years, *Délamerikai Magyarság* dealt almost exclusively with the revolution. Its 1957 almanac published the content of all Hungarian radio broadcasts—the free, revolutionary ones, as well as those under Soviet occupation—from October 23 to November 4, hour to hour, minute to minute. It was translated into Spanish that same year 1957 as *S.O.S. El drama de Hungría*, with illustrations by Lajos Szalay.[12] Although the drawings were made thousands of kilometres away from Hungary, few artistic creations could convey more vividly the tragedy of the revolution and its suppression. The iconography is at once realistic and apocalyptic in its description of the violence and the feelings of violation and defeat. The publication and wide distribution of this book in Spanish, together with *¡Hungría no se rinde!* (Hungary does not surrender), with 10,000 copies printed of each, are the paper's most meaningful and lasting contributions to the cause of the revolution.

From 1957 to 1966, more than twenty-five Spanish-language books and brochures on the revolution were published in Argentina. Examples include, among others, *Hungría en sangre* (Hungary in Blood), *La revolución popular húngara. Hechos y documentos* (The Hungarian Popular Revolution: Facts and Documents), reports by the UN Special Commission and the Commission of International Jurists on Hungary, the Spanish translation of the White Book on the Hungarian Revolution (based on actual documents),[13] poetry anthologies, and novels. Most informative was Elemér Vácz's bibliography in Spanish covering about 350 publications from the Western world, all dealing with the 1956 revolution.

The embassy of the People's Republic of Hungary and the 1956 revolution

The events that broke out in Hungary and their echo in Argentina provoked fear and denial among the personnel at the embassy of the People's Republic of Hungary. The fact that both the Argentine authorities and most of the population at large sided openly with the revolution, together with the marches, the protests, the series of articles, the exhibitions, the outward expressions of outrage—all of this sowed uncertainty among the embassy's employees. In their reports to the Hungarian Foreign Ministry, they emphasized that the Argentine media were spreading "the wildest news about the events in Hungary" and that the fierce attacks on the Soviet Union, the Communist movement, and the Kádár-régime were done with the full support of the Argentine government. Undoubtedly, they said, the events provided ammunition for the enemy camp and mobilized all the "reactionary forces." On November 10, 1956, Ambassador Sándor Nagy sent the following report to the Hungarian Foreign Ministry:

> [Courtesy visit to Vice-president Rojas] I inform Comrade Minister that the Argentine Vice-president Rojas received me on November 8…. It surprised me that he would do it right now, when the Argentine press, radio, television, and propaganda spread the wildest news about the events in Hungary. It is evident that with support of official organisms a strong attack is being directed first against the Soviet Union, but also against the whole Communist movement. Apart from an attack initiated against the Kádár administration, we [the embassy] are not being attacked, but at the same time, unfortunately, our "fame" has grown among reactionary

elements. The Hungarian events armed the enemy camp and mobilized all reactionary forces. It seems probable to me that Rojas was prompted by this situation when he received me right now. I was prepared that he would put provocative questions to me, as he did to the Czechoslovakian ambassador Pavlicek, when receiving him....I set forth that the present moment was not appropriate for the visit, I would have preferred it to occur in a calmer atmosphere. He answered that it didn't matter that there was unrest in Hungary, they understood it, and that their feelings were with the Hungarian people. (He probably was thinking of something different than I).[14]

On December 10, 1956, the Hungarian Foreign Ministry issued strict instructions to the embassy in Argentina (regarding the observation of the lives of the Hungarians who arrived in Argentina and neighbouring countries). In view of the fact that as a consequence of the events more than a hundred thousand Hungarians immigrated to the West, many of whom wanted to settle in Argentina, Chile, Bolivia, and Uruguay, the ministry felt that the work among Hungarians had to be intensified. Therefore, the embassy was to observe closely the lives and numbers of the Hungarians recently arrived in those countries. It was to monitor the immigration process and investigate the kinds of activities the so-called 'reactionary' Hungarian institutions organized for the newcomers, what help these were getting, and through which organizations.[15]

The situation of the Communist foreign representatives became critical, not only *vis-à-vis* the Argentine authorities and people but within their own camp, as well. A number of members of the Hungarian embassy defected. The Budapest Office of Hungarians Abroad was especially concerned by the fact that a large number of members of supposedly "loyal groups" changed their political allegiance and withdrew from their clubs. The office saw it as its primary responsibility to intensify activity in the so-called "progressive and loyal" émigré organizations, in order to be able to rely on them to increase propaganda material in the press.[16]

A year later, in December 1957, the Foreign Ministry detailed the guidelines regarding the embassy's role among the right-wing émigré organizations in Argentina. It ordered the embassy to closely watch and report on the organizations, their leaders, and their press. The goal was infiltration and the creation of animosity among these groups. A favoured strategy was to lure prominent but less "reactionary" personalities back to Hungary, as a way to further undermine émigré morale:

> ..We find it especially important to observe from now on the activity of international émigré organizations, such as the League of Captive Nations, the International Anti-Bolshevist Organization, the Free Europe Commission, that are the common international organizations of right-wing émigrés of the Soviet Union and of the other popular democracies, such as the National Committee, the Community of Camaraderie of Hungarian Ex-Fighters, the Revolutionary Council of Strasbourg (Kéthly, Király, Kővágó), the Freedom Fighters' Association organized by Béla Király, the Social-Democrats' activities in different countries, as well as the organizations of writers and other intellectuals. Moreover, we want to receive information permanently from our embassies on the fascist organizations of the right-wing émigrés in each country.

> The right-wing Hungarian émigré organizations and its members carry out significant activity that is harmful to the Argentine masses as well. Even before the counterrevolution, émigré organizations of considerable influence operated in Argentina (for example the Centro Húngaro, the Community of Camaraderie of Hungarian Ex-Fighters, etc.). During and after the counterrevolution, their activities intensified. Their temporary strengthening was due primarily to the fact that keeping the so-called Hungarian issue alive was in the interest of Western imperialist circles. The activities of these right-wing organizations and personalities are in many instances supported politically, economically and morally by official Argentine circles.[17]

Clearly, of major concern for the Hungarian Foreign Ministry was not only the actual political mobilization of the émigrés but also its perception that their efforts were actively supported by the Argentine government. Thus, after the 1956 revolution, Bolshevist propaganda became very intense in Argentina, as well. Every effort was made to tarnish the reputation of the revolution. The book *Tormenta en Hungría* (Storm in Hungary) exalted János Kádár—a party leader who betrayed the revolution—as the personification of the heroes who defended "the building of Socialism in Hungary."[18] In 1957 the Hungarian

Foreign Ministry planned an exhibition for October 23, documenting the counterrevolutionary character of the uprising. However, these documents never arrived in Argentina, and the exhibition organized in August of 1958 in the left-wing club Törekvés had little impact, with only about 150 attendees.[19] Diplomatic relations between the Hungarian People's Republic and Argentina did not improve after the revolution. In fact, they worsened during the left-wing government of Arturo Frondizi as a consequence of the execution of Imre Nagy, Hungary's Communist prime minister who had sided with the revolution.

As for relations between émigré organizations in Argentina and the Hungarian government, these ranged from nonexistent to strained at best, until the eventual lifting of the Iron Curtain in 1990.

Notes

1. This contribution was excerpted and translated from Chapter 4 of the author's book *"Szabadságom lett a börtönöm." Az argentínai magyar emigráció története. 1948–1968* ["My freedom became my prison." History of the Hungarian Emigrés to Argentina. 1948–1968] (Budapest: *A Magyar Nyelv és Kultúra Nemzetközi Társasága*, 2003).

2. In contrast, Gyula Borbándi wrote the following in his book *A magyar emigráció életrajza 1945–1985* [Biography of the Hungarian emigration 1945–1985], Vol. 1 (Budapest: Európa Könyvkiadó, 1989), 401: "The outbreak of the revolution did not provoke any special activity among the Hungarian émigrés in the West. Since nobody counted with its possibility in the near future, no preparations were made for the event of an eventual outbreak. Politicians, journal publishers, heads of the associations, editors and journalists listened to the radio transmissions and read the news, analyzing and commenting on the events in Hungary and around the world during the 14 days of the popular uprising and of the freedom fight."

3. Antal Sorg, *Beszámoló a "Szabad Magyarország Segítő Bizottsága" megalakulásáról és működéséről* [Report on the Establishment and Activities of the Free Hungary Aid Committee] (Buenos Aires: SN, 1957).

4. See *Embassy of the Hungarian People's Republic*. 10.30.1956. Hungarian National Archives (MOL) XIX-J-1-j-00495-332/56, 5. box, Ambassador Sándor Nagy to Imre Horváth Minister of External Affairs. "Situation of our embassy with regard to the latest events in Hungary. I inform Comrade Minister that the latest events in our homeland activated the fascist groups residing in Argentina: Hungarians as well as of other nationalities. During the observation of their activities, we found out through our friends that they are preparing a large-scale manifestation against our embassy for October 27....They prepared the meeting of the multitudes organizing a large-scale Mass...."

5. Their motto was: "*Kétszer ad, aki gyorsan ad*" (He who gives fast gives twice), *Magyar Ház Értesítője*, December 1956, page 1.

6. According to Domonkos Ladányi and Zsigmond Endre's letters to Zsuzsánna Kesserű de Haynal, September 2006.

7. Zsuzsánna Kesserű de Haynal, "1956. *október – Buenos Airesben*," *Krónika*, Toronto (October 1986): 6–9.

8. *Embassy of the People's Republic of Hungary*. 9.14.57. MOL XIX-J-1-j, 11.d. Activity of the right-wing émigrés in Argentina. "On September 7 the Association of European Captive Nations held an assembly in Buenos Aires with relation to the General Assembly of the United Nations of September 10. Next day the press informed in long articles about this assembly, in which 'representatives' of the following 9 countries took part: Albania, Bulgaria, Czechoslovakia, Estonia, Latvia, Lithuania, Hungary, Poland, and Rumania. On behalf of Argentina, Dr. Rodolfo Medina, president of the Asociación Cultural Argentina pro Hungría Libre, took part and also gave a speech. In the assembly there were 10 speakers of different nationalities, who praised the 'heroic acts' of the October counterrevolution. Stanislaw Sliwinski, president of the Association of European Captive Nations, in the name of the 'delegations' of the 9 countries expressed the hope that the UN Extraordinary Assembly, which met on September 10, finds a remedy to resolve the Hungarian problem. He demanded 'freedom' for the 9 nations and declared the participants' solidarity with the Hungarian nation – and here he obviously referred to the counterrevolutionaries..."

9. *Embassy of the People's Republic of Hungary.* 1.17.1957. MOL XIX-J-1-j-00480/38/1957, 5.d. "Press summary: How does Argentina react to the events in Hungary. The events in Hungary were at the centre of the Argentine press's attention for the past months. The tone of the news about the events is based on the influence of Western press agencies on Latin America. From the start, the news, information and comments had the following three principal characteristics: 1. Huge volume of false news. 2. Attempt at creating panic with its hysterical tone. 3. Argentines also took part in this press campaign and centralized propaganda, in which national and foreign fascist elements also participated very actively."

10. de Haynal, "1956. *október – Buenos Airesben,*" 7.

11. *Embassy of the People's Republic of Hungary.* 12.31.1960. [MOL XIX-J-1-j. 20/b 10. d.] "Diary of events of the Hungarian emigraton in Latin-America during 1960.... March 16, 1960. The right-wing newspaper D.M.C. [*sic*] organized in the Argentine sea-side resort city of Mar del Plata an exhibition on the counterrevolution, under the title "Hungría no se rinde" [Hungary does not surrender]. The exhibition was previously held in Buenos Aires, Córdoba and Mendoza."

12. Lajos Szalay, the world-famous graphic artist, lived in Argentina between 1948 and 1960. He was a professor at the National University of Tucumán and at the Escuela Superior de Bellas Artes of Buenos Aires. He immigrated to New York as a consequence of his drawings on 1956: "In South America, as in many other parts of the world in those days, the active leaders of the cultural life were communists, and I naturally moved in intellectual circles at university level. Thus my situation became difficult as soon as I spoke up on behalf of the suffering of the Hungarian people.... The situation in Argentina became unsustainable, my daughter received death threats from strangers, so I had to move away with panicky speed." Lajos Szalay, *Végtelen a tenyérben* [The infinite in the palm of the hand], interviews with Péter Bakonyi (Budapest: *Múzsák*, 1987), 42.

13. *People's Republic of Hungary.* 6.5.1959 MOL XIX-J-1-k. Arg.4/j.3.d. Sándor Nagy. "Publication of book dealing with Hungary. The May 21 issue of the Délamerikai Magyarság informs that the largest Argentine publisher,

Editorial Kraft, will soon publish the white book of the counterrevolution in Spanish. Actually this book already appeared in bookstores in Buenos Aires; its author is Melvin J. Lasky. The original edition is by Martin Secker, ·Vanburg, Ltd. London. The book is a collection of documents on the echo of the counterrevolution abroad, illustrated with some of the photos already known in Hungary. The price is 250 pesos. Should you find it necessary to acquire it, please let us know as soon as possible."

14. 11.10.1956 MOL XIX-J-1-j. Arg. 4/j. MNK 334/szig.titk./56 KÜM 007987-335/56, 5.d.

15. 12.10.1956 MOL XIX-J/1/j. 20/a 10. d. KÜM-007923

16. 12.9.1957 MOL XIX-J-1-j-Argentina 005471/1957, 20/a, 10. d.

17. 12.9.1957 MOL XIX-J-1-j- Argentína 005471/1957, 20/a, 10.d. Sándor Nagy "Tasks regarding the emigration in Argentina."

18. 7.2.1957. MOL XIX-J-K-Arg-4/j-1957, 3.d.

19. 3.28.1957 MOL XIX J-1-j-001747/57 TÜK 4/j, 5.d.

7.

1956 in the Republic of Hungary since 1989

Heino Nyyssönen

Riots and demonstrations took place in Hungary during the autumn of 2006. Flags with a hole in the middle flew in front of international audiences in September. Some felt that the protesters had revolution in mind, while others felt the events did in no way compare to those that took place in 1956. Nevertheless, 1956 has occasionally appeared as a reference point for current events. For example, during the first session of national round table talks in 1989, a representative of independent lawyers argued that three topics should be put into practice from now on: free elections, workers' councils, and the right to travel. In other words, some wished to follow the precepts of 1956, to "continue" and fulfil the demands of an earlier historical moment, as those moments appeared from the perspective of 1989.

Hungary can be seen not only in the context of its early political reforms but also in terms of several symbolic political actions that have recently taken place, such as a new interpretation of 1956, the reburial of Prime Minister Imre Nagy, and the declaration of the republic on October 23, 1989. However, according to the statements of current eye-witnesses and veterans, 1956 has not received the dignity and attention it deserves. In spite of political resurrection, bitter debates and confrontation have shadowed the legacy of 1956 in Hungary.[1]

The purpose of this paper is to study the content of these allegations and political debates, focusing particularly on how 1956 has become a political matter and politicized since October 1989. There are a couple of studies that deal with the systemic change in Hungary up to the first free elections and the first years of the new democracy.[2] Here, I would like to take a step ahead and examine how the historic 1956 and its commemoration have been present from the autumn of 1989 until now in public debates conducted by different political actors, such as politicians, the media, and even professional historians. 1956 was not only of secondary importance to Hungary's democratic transition, but it is now at the core of contemporary Hungarian political culture.

I have approached this study knowing that the past is not mere history but is ever present and influences contemporary views.[3] According to my argument there are two factors that have had an influence on the contemporary politicization of the 1956 revolution and its memory. The first one if that the Kádár regime did not permit any open discussion of the 1956 revolution: there was no critical debate of the 1956 revolution in the public sphere. During the Kádár era, the recent past was monopolized by the ruling Hungarian Socialist Workers' Party, which also manipulated events from the recent past for political legitimization. In the new democracy, however, we can also find traces of political legitimization based on history. However, claiming the "truth of 1956" begs for political activity, which, in addition to requiring research work, also stresses the role of the new parties. We could then stress the second factor—or how new political parties formed in 1989 using the memory and legacy of 1956, as well as prior, short-lived experiments with democracy to build their own political identities—and surmise that critical debate and research work began at the same time, when political parties and social movements started to discover their historical roots in order to build their individual identities. As a consequence 1956, the historic event, had to compete for validation with other historical pasts and political identifications. Those who opposed political use of history and party statements remained voices in the wilderness.

In fact 1956 and the memory of the revolutionary attempt play such a crucial role in current Hungarian political culture that I cannot give the whole picture in one article.[4] Nevertheless, I would first like to take a look at the free elected Parliaments and essential political debates, which concerned 1956, as well: symbols, national holidays, debates concerning punishment, and commemorations. (Particularly, October 23 has been celebrated and commemorated since 1989.) Finally, I would like to speculate with a rhetorical question: Would the status of 1956 be different if October 23 had not become a national holiday? In fact, the third Republic of Hungary does not have a day of its own, as 1989 is inextricably linked to earlier history. The third republic chose October 23, 1956, as a day to commemorate, instead of the celebration days honoured by the former republics of 1918 and 1946.

History in Parliament

In 1990 the new Parliament became the most essential forum in Hungary; it also dealt with the topic of 1956. Several ministers in the new government had themselves participated in the 1956 uprising, such as the historians, Prime Minister József Antall and Minister of Defence Lajos Für. Also the new president of the republic, Árpád Göncz, had a 1956 background, as did the former prime minister Gyula Horn (1994–1998) who had joined the Budapest armed police forces in mid-December 1956. In spite of these influential names, the proper 1956 "group" in Parliament consisted of around ten former activists. Included in this group were prominent persons, such as Miklós Vásárhelyi, Béla Király, and Imre Mécs, all of whom represented the liberal Alliance of Free Democrats. In addition, the governing parties had some veterans in their ranks—naturally the number of those who had personal memories and experiences from 1956 was essentially larger in the Parliament.

In the first session, the freely elected Parliament enacted a law, which commemorated the memory of 1956 and its historical significance. In the first paragraph, the memory of the event was codified into law, and the second paragraph declared October 23 as a national holiday. At that time the new speaker at Parliament, György Szabad, a historian by profession, considered 1956 to be the most important connection the new republic had to the historical past, as well as the most important basis for the creation of the third Hungarian Republic, formed on October 23, 1959.[5] The law and the speech could be interpreted not only as a tribute to 1956 but also as an attempt for new historical legitimization of the third republic, even after free parliamentary elections. However, less than two months later, the majority in Parliament was ready to choose the old crown of Hungary as the new coat of arms and thus give up the Kossuth emblem, one of the most important republican symbols and a clear political symbol of 1956.

What happened? In 1989 the image of the Kossuth emblem had frequently been present in public discourse. For example, György Litván, historian and a free democrat candidate in the 1990 elections, wrote in October 1989 that the choice of a coat of arms was not merely heraldic but also posed a political question. According to Litván, the government needed to choose amongst historical, imperial, or republican traditions. Litván included himself in the republican tradition, in which he also included great historical figures, such as Kossuth, Petőfi, Károlyi, Jászi, and Bibó.[6] After the parliamentary elections of 1990, this "revolutionary" moment had already "passed," and the "crown party" had won a majority over "the Kossuth party." In Parliament, liberals made a counter-proposition, which finally failed in the vote: in certain sites and occasions the Kossuth emblem could be used, however "the crown" would be used on more solemn occasions.

In addition to these symbolic actions, Parliament dealt with other topics. Imre Nagy and his companions had been rehabilitated in the summer of 1989 by the Supreme Court. In February 1990, the old Parliament enacted a law and rehabilitated more than 100,000 persons who had been illegally sentenced between 1945 and 1963. By 2000 four rehabilitation laws were completed. The last one, CXXX/2000—nicknamed the "Ilona Tóth law" after a medical student who had committed manslaughter in 1956 and was hanged—went further than any of the others. The law nullified sentences given on the tasks and identification of the ideas of the revolution and fight for freedom as acts committed in action. The law concerned verdicts sentenced by ad hoc courts and processes that came to being after 1956 as sentences coming out of people's courts.[7]

Since 1990, compensation has also become a topic in public discourse, and several compensation laws have been enacted, beginning in June 1991. The third compensation bill deals with 1956, with law XXXII/1992 concerning compensation for those who lost their lives or freedom for political reasons. As well, in 1992 the government proposed an initiative of "taking care of the nation" (*nemzeti gondozásról*). Compensation varied from 500,000 to 1 million Ft and was paid out to those who suffered personal or material loss between 1939 and

1989. As such, compensation was offered to both the victims of the Communist regime and the victims of Nazism and the war. The law defined several categories, such as national resistance during World War II, and participation in the 1956 revolution. Moreover, in cases of serious physical injury, or 67 percent loss of full working capacity, a monthly compensation was to be given.

However, one of the most controversial debates in the first Parliament dealt with punishment of past crimes (*igazságtétel*, "making justice"). In the summer of 1991, the leading party in government, the Hungarian Democratic Forum (MDF), undertook to include quite an extensive political reckoning with the past on its agenda. It seems plausible that the debate sparked by the MDF's agenda and its consequences resulted in radicalizing and polarizing both veterans and the Hungarian public, a polarization that has continued until this day. According to the plan, it was time to speed up the systemic change and carry out prisons terms for those who committed political crimes during the previous regime, regardless of whether they were supported by the majority.[8] As such, the plan did not materialize, but one of its consequences was a retroactive bill that would have punished homicide, treason, and disloyalty between 1944 and 1990. Open voting in Parliament took place in 1991 precisely on the anniversary of the second intervention by the Soviet troops in 1956. The topic of punishments and the use of the retroactive bill divided Parliament, as the government was ready to use this undemocratic retroactive law as a means to deal with the past, while the opposition either voted against it or abstained from voting. Members in the opposition and a few relatives of the deceased preferred to name the perpetrators in public, feeling that the real criminals should be named with the full extent of their actions made known within the framework of the rule of law.[9]

After the vote, President Árpád Göncz made the decision to turn to the Constitutional Court to clarify the content of the law. In March 1992 the court found all paragraphs of the law against the Constitution. According to the decision, the paragraphs were not clearly defined, and a law must already be enacted before a crime can be said to have been committed. After a few other proposals and political struggles, the Constitutional Court made its final statement in 1993. On the basis of the Geneva Convention of 1949, the court declared that crimes committed in 1956 were not considered war crimes but crimes against humanity. Over seventy "volley fires" (*sórtűz*) were counted, from them over thirty led to an investigation, but finally less than ten led to juridical proceedings. However, only in two cases, in Salgótarján (1997) and Tata (2001), was a perpetrator sentenced to five years in prison.[10] Although a few other processes led to sentences, they were not carried out, as the amnesty law of 1990 released men over sixty years old and sentenced to less than three years in prison. Some trials were extremely complicated, raising political emotions and also historians' testimonies, as in the case of Mosonmagyaróvár. In fact the last cases were closed in 2003, more than forty-six years after the crimes were committed and twelve years after the first debate about them in Parliament.

The second controversy dealt with lustration and its scope. In fact, lustration has become a political topic in many other former Communist-ruled countries, but hereafter the point in Hungary is that it involved 1956, as well. Nicknamed as the little brother of *igazságtétel*, the law was finally enacted in March 1994, after several debates and proposals. The law entered into force on July 1, 1994, and therefore did not concern the first Parliament at all. The bill, XXIII/94 "for controlling persons chosen to particular important positions," deals with officials and secret members of the former counter-intelligence (III-III). However, it also concerns persons in the armed forces (for example, people who collaborated with the Soviet forces in order to suppress the uprising) and members of the Fascist Arrow Cross Party in 1944.[11] Occasionally a few public scandals have taken place, such as the one concerning film director István Szabó. Szabó defended his collaboration with the secret police by arguing that he had saved the life of his friend, who had been present at Republic Square (*Köztársaság tér*), when the party headquarters siege took place on October 30, 1956.12

According to the lustration bill, the files of the security services would not be made available to the public until July 1, 2030—thirty years after the lustration process would have ended. However, according to András Domány (1998), the law had not achieved its original goal, not even in its restricted form from 1996, which was to reveal former political secret service professionals, secret officers, and agents. In 2000–2001 Fidesz prolonged the law again for the next four years and broadened it to concern around 15,000 persons, including the media, 2,500 judges, and 1,400 lawyers. After 2002, the Hungarian Socialist Party preferred to restrict the screening again but then its small coalition partner, the Alliance of Free Democrats, was eager to broaden its scope again. Finally, in 2005, the government was ready to open files and publish the names of former informants. At that time, because of the polarization, the majority could not agree with the opposition, as it needed a two-thirds majority in the Parliament to proceed.

In addition to rehabilitation, compensation, lustration, and punishment, Parliament itself has played a role of lieu de mémoire. In October 1990 Parliament held an honourary session at which relatives of the 1956 martyrs and heroes of the revolution were present. On that occasion, President Árpád Gönz and Prime Minister József Antall raised historical parallels between the likes of 1848 and 1956 in their speeches. Particularly Antall stressed the significance of 1956 as an essential part of Hungarian national mythology, a mythology that could help Hungarians to overcome present difficulties.[13] In 2002 the biggest opposition party, Fidesz, did not participate in the main commemorative event in Parliament. They demanded that a 1956 veteran should make a speech at the commemoration, but when the idea did not come to fruition, the party withdrew from the whole event. Instead, a representative of the smaller opposition party MDF read a greeting at the occasion, which was signed by the association of political prisoners (*Pofosz*), Committee of Historical Justice (TIB), and two other 1956 organizations.[14]

On the one hand we can criticize the whole idea of commemorations in Parliament. These rituals deteriorate a legislative organ and silence the most valuable forum of political debate. On the other hand we must stress the fact that the Hungarian Parliament is already a *lieu* concerning 1956. Parliament played a role during the revolutionary days and the state minister, István Bibo, was the last man to remain there when the Soviets launched their second invasion.

Finally I would like to discuss the political legacy of Imre Nagy in Parliament; his memory and name were present in a few proposals since 1990. When a general amnesty was declared, Nagy's name was symbolically used to name that law. Secondly, when the MPs discussed withdrawing from the Warsaw Pact, they renewed Nagy's declaration from 1956. For Prime Minister Antall, the decision to renew Nagy's declaration was historical as Antall's father would have participated in the delegation that was supposed to negotiate the topic in Moscow in 1956. In a certain way Parliament finally "continued" the work interrupted in November 1956.

However, Imre Nagy soon became a contested person. A political controversy had taken place already before the first session in May 1990, when his name was ousted from the commemorative law just before the opening session. Partly with this and partly with other political incidents in mind, the socialist-liberal government returned to the issue in 1996 to commemorate the 100th anniversary of Nagy's birth.[15] Hungary has a certain "tradition" with commemorative laws; up until now this has been the second last to deal with the memory of a person, as Saint Stephen was also codified into Hungarian legislation in 1999 as the founder of the first Hungarian state, the first Christian king of Hungary, as a result of which his crown was ceremoniously transported to the parliament in Budapest and put on display.

Regarding decorations, Nagy also plays a role. In 2002 the socialist-liberal coalition created a particular Imre Nagy decoration. The medal is delivered on the basis of "patriotic and exemplary activity concerning Hungary's independency, social dialogue as the unity of the nation and peaceful systemic change."[16] The decoration has a flag with a hole in the middle. In present-day Hungary, this symbol has been hoisted to represent a broader utterance of dissatisfaction on several other occasions, as well, from remembrances of 1956 to farmers' demonstrations, from commemorations of Trianon to violent riots in the autumn of 2006. However, the Imre Nagy decoration was not the first of its kind to do so. From the autumn of 1991, on the initiative of the prime minister, the president granted decorations in Parliament for services rendered in the name of the nation and in the defence of the fatherland during the 1956 revolution and fight for freedom. Among the first honoured persons were, posthumously, about thirty prominent revolutionaries from Imre Nagy to Péter Mansfeld, who had been hanged on his eighteenth birthday in 1959.

Debates regarding national holidays

In the summer of 1989, the Budapest Committee of the Hungarian Socialist Workers' Party (MSZMP) introduced an initiative that October 23 be celebrated as "a day of reconciliation." In September it became public that the opposition had established an October 23 committee to prepare for that day's celebrations. Symbolic power struggles continued when the committee made a statement that the day should be a "day of national celebration," not a "commemoration." As a compromise, current Speaker of the Parliament Mátyás Szűrös noted that the day of the 1956 uprising should be "a common celebration for national reconciliation." Despite a proposal by an independent MP, Parliament did not have time—if not lack of political will—to prepare a national holiday during the busy autumn of 1989. The reform Communist government declared the day as a national holiday just before the elections in March 1990.[17]

Another proper discussion of holidays reached Parliament in March 1991. A total of three alternatives, March 15, August 20, and October 23, were suggested as possible holiday dates. Parliament was forced to decide which of the three would be promoted to state (*állami*) holiday, while the two other would remain national (*nemzeti*) holidays. In the final vote, the winner, August 20—referring to Saint Stephen, the first medieval king of Hungary, who made Roman Catholicism the country's official religion—was supported in the ranks of the centre-right government, and March 15—referring to 1848—by the opposition.

Representatives of the leading party in the government, MDF, argued that Saint Stephen's Day best expressed the ideas of the Hungarian state and Constitution. Moreover, Christian Democrats reminded those present about the Christian character of the day. Parties in the opposition, The League of the Free Democrats (SZDSZ) and young democrats (*Fidesz*), preferred March 15. According to Miklós Szabó (SZDSZ), August 20 reflects the ideas of a one-thousand-year-old continuity, while the March and October dates represent new beginnings. Zsolt Német (*Fidesz*) surmised that October 23 is still very close and not fully understood by everybody. Both speakers preferred March 15 and argued that the day represented the unity and ideas of democracy. The standpoint of the third party in the opposition, the Hungarian Socialist Party, was not united, although their speaker estimated that plausibly March 15 would be the mostly supported.

October 23 had also support and was favoured by many MPs: "Without 1956 there would not have been 1990"; the day was "celebrated all around the world" and the whole "world paid attention to Hungary" at that time. The ranks of the MDF suggested that October 23 should be the day the republic should choose to represent the new form of government. In the end, October 23 was defined with two meanings as "the day of the beginning of the 1956 Revolution and the fight for freedom, and as the day on which the Hungarian Republic was declared in 1989."[18]

All in all, the debate in Parliament closed a longer discussion: the underlying symbolism of the official state holiday became that of a more traditional and conservative day, of St. Stephen. In addition to the emblem question, the holiday question also strengthened the prejudices of the opposition regarding the basic historical ideals of the new republic, which seemed more and more not to be related to 1956 and 1947 but prior to 1945. In spite of these political differences, Hungarians celebrate all three of these national holidays. Nevertheless, as one opinion poll from 2000 showed, the most popular holiday, August 20, had a serious concurrent in March. In the inquiry 45 percent of those asked mentioned August 20 as the most important, while 39 percent found March to be the most appropriate national holiday. The poll shows that October 23 was the least popular, with only 6 percent of those polled considering it as the most relevant national holiday.[19]

Organizations, spaces, memorials

In the previous sections I have concentrated on debates and questions brought forth in Parliament. However, streets, graveyards, and other locations have also played political roles and have become realms of memory. Of course not only MPs in Parliament dealt with the past but many other organizations have, too. Even the members of the small Party of the Hungarian October (Magyar Október Párt) emerged to paint over the street signs of Ferenc Münnich Street in the summer of 1989. They had a clear 1956 "agenda" in mind and included the revolutionaries and freedom fighters in their ranks.[20]

The most important of the 1956 organizations, Történelmi Igazsságtétel Bizottság (The Committee for Historical Justice), TIB, was founded in June of 1988 to demand rehabilitations and lobby for the interests of former veterans. Following the elections, activity was transferred partly to the parliamentary level, because six members of the original TIB became members of the new Parliament. Members of TIB maintained the memory of 1956 in the fore and, on the other hand, promoted the interests of those "calumniated by the dictatorship but who have yet to receive their sedatives."[21] However, a controversy between radicals and moderates led to a split in the spring of 1992. Controversies arising in veteran organizations are not rare, as such, but here they concerned the future of the whole systemic change, as well. Some argued that the leaders of TIB were on the side of the "brakemen of the systemic change." The chairman, Miklós Vásárhelyi, refused to run as a candidate in the Hungarian parliamentary elections and explained his decision by stating that he supported reconciliation but passions had been let loose, public life radicalized, and politics moved to the right. On March 23, 1992, a declaration, "This is Not the TIB that We Founded," came into being. The document was signed by twenty-three original members of the TIB and included current and present (opposition) politicians, researchers, and relatives of the victims. According to critics, national consensus had faded away; there existed a political tendency to reduce the significance of 1956 and the government found continuity instead in Miklós Horthy and Prime Minister István Bethlen. A few weeks after the failure of the retroactive law in March 1992, a new leadership was chosen for the TIB, and they favoured "compensation for victims of the past system as desirable as the punishment of the criminals."[22] Moreover, Pofosz, the Association of Political Prisoners, belongs to the most influential interest groups. In February of 1991, Pofosz had the opinion that the real systemic change had yet to take place as there were no compensations and legal proceedings. In addition to these two there were many other groups supporting such statements; in 1995 a weekly magazine, HVG, listed altogether nineteen organizations and four parties that had something to do with 1956.[23] The majority of them had emerged between 1990 and 1992, mainly trying to organize themselves as interest groups and tending to be concerned with compensation.

Veterans, parties, and other organizations were also active in numerous cases of memorials and statues. In Kádár's Hungary, official commemoration had focused only on the winners. At that time a total of 128 memorials were erected, of which twenty-five were in Budapest, and of which more than half, seventy-two, were memorial tablets. Other official memorials of 1956 simply did not exist—they were instead erected abroad by emigrants, in countries from America to Australia. After the Kádár era and by 1997, more than four hundred memorials dealing with 1956 had been unveiled. Of these, *kopjafa*, a wooden monument resembling a totem pole, is the most typical. Other common themes are crosses, various stones, the flag with the hole, and memorial tablets. Géza Boros (1997) referred also to the existence of combined memorials, because some parts of the statues or tablets were built in connection with older memorials. Close to the fiftieth anniversary of 1956, sixty-six new memorials will be built in different parts of the country. All graveyards in which fallen 1956ers were buried have been promised a memory wall, on the initiative of *Pofosz*.[24]

In general, memorials are hot topics and raise political ambitions as they unite and separate citizens; they canonize historical events and help to occupy political space. In Hungary, political debates regarding statues and memorials could be divided into three categories: unveiled statues, removed statues, and memorials that were debated on but not built. The group of debates regarding unveiled statues include, for example, the 1992 debate about the two memorials at the graveyard of Rákoskeresztúr, the avant-garde artwork by György Jovánovics and its "competitor," a *székler* gate erected next to it by the extreme right next. An example of a debate that raged about the second and third category of memorials was about a particular reconciliation statue foundation (*Megbékélés Emlékmü Alapítvány*) that planned a memorial to commemorate both fighting sides of 1956 at Republic Square. The original idea was to build another memorial for the martyrs, which would be located beside the existing statue of the victims. The joint monument did not materialize, however, and the old memorial was abolished in 1992. In November the memorial issue even reached the Parliament floor, when the chairman of the radicalized TIB condemned the idea. According to Tibor Zimányi, nowhere in the world was it possible for the fallen of both sides to be included in the same memorial.[25]

In 1991 the old statues depicting Communist and left-wing heroes, such as the leaders of the 1919 Communist Revolution, continued to occupy public spaces, and in October Minister of the Interior Péter Boross reminded mayors of this fact. The minister demanded the removal of certain statues and changes in street names throughout the country. One of his arguments suggested the forthcoming thirty-fifth anniversary of 1956 as a deadline for the actions. The day was a valuable tool for political actors; according to the information provided in *Népszabadság*, the extreme right planned violent removals on October 23. Their list included the memorials of Béla Kun, Mihály Károlyi, and a few Soviet memorials, for example. Although these actions were never completed, on October 23, 1991, the statue of Béla Kun was covered by a cloth—someone painted a Star of David on it, thus encouraging the discussion of anti-Semitism in Hungary. Later, Kun and many other statues were transferred to a particular statue park, which was finally opened in 1993.[26]

On the fortieth anniversary the Conservative Hungarian Democratic Forum government, elected in 1990, and allied mayors raised a general memorial for the revolution and located it in the park of Tabán in Buda. Four years later an initiative emerged to build another big monument dedicated to 1956, aiming to be unveiled on the fiftieth anniversary of the revolution. Three architects—all born after 1956—won an international competition that attracted seventy-eight applications. In the winning proposal there are 2,006 metal cylinders two to eight metres tall forming a fifty-six-degree angle. A veteran and a member of *Pofosz*, who participated in the jury, agreed and gave a statement that in the first place the memorial is directed for the future and future generations, not particularly for the veterans.[27] However, as is common regarding statue issues and significant historical events, criticism and protests were soon raised about the memorial. Already in the autumn of 2005, a flag with a hole was added to the model. Next in January 2006, Peter Boross, representing the foundations for freedom fighters, revealed an idea for another memorial representing "1956ers own values" and a contemporary flavour. This plan also received financial support from the government, and five artists were asked to participate in the competition. Since then two monuments were in the process of being made, the former already described as "official" and "central" and the latter as "alternative" in the newspapers. The "alternative" is made up of a faceless crowd, from which a figure of a woman is rising to symbolize freedom. The memorial was to be unveiled in front of the Technical University on October 21 and the "official" at György Dózsa úton October, 23, 2006—finally in the presence of whistling demonstrators.[28]

Street naming after political persons or events is a form of commemoration, as well. In general, most changes to streets emerged after the elections of 1990. Up until 1994, 350 names had been changed in the capital, and by the beginning of 2003, almost nine hundred streets were renamed. In the summer of 1989, the establishment of a particular Imre Nagy street was demanded in several districts of Budapest. For example, the small Hungarian Independence Party suggested that *Népköztársaság útja* should be renamed Imre Nagy Road and *Lenin körút* to Pál Maléter Ring. Also the Budapest Committee of the MSZMP proposed an initiative, which stated that the as-yet-unnamed square inhabited by the Batthyány Memorial Light should be named after Imre Nagy. However, in the end, Imre Nagy did not have a street named after him in the centre of Pest—a more conservative Austrian-Hungarian tradition was restored there, as well, with the name Andrássy. Nagy's Square, however, has been in front of the Ministry of Foreign Affairs since October 1991; his statue was unveiled on the centenary of his birthday. The statue was built next to Parliament on Martyr's Square, which was named after a Communist martyr, Endre Ságvári, before the change. In addition to Imre Nagy Square, two new names were established in the centre of Budapest: Square of 56ers (*Ötvenhatosok tere*) and Street of 23rd October (*Október huszonharmadika utca*). Prominent individuals like Cardinal József Mindszenty, István Bibó, and Pál Maléter, who were involved in 1956, did not have streets named for them in the capital. In the case of Bibó, the time limit has been one difficulty until recently: in Budapest a street could be named after a person only twenty-five years after his death.[29]

Commemoration of the anniversaries

János Kádár was superseded in May 1988, but still in October First Secretary Károly Grósz stated that the government would not allow the commemoration of the memory of a counter-revolution. Instead he had the view that sources must be restudied and that this research would likely benefit both society and all political leaders.[30] A year later tables had turned and the new president of the republic, Mátyás Szűrös, declared Hungary a republic precisely on the same balcony of Parliament from where Imre Nagy had spoken on the evening of October 23. In his speech, Szűrös used historical examples to clarify the present situation: Hungary was following in the footsteps of the previous republics, which he connected with the names of Lajos Kossuth (1848), Mihály Károlyi (1918), and Zoltán Tildy (1946). He specifically mentioned the uprising of 1956 and the national movement on which the republic would be based. At this stage Hungary was the first country to change its political system in the former Eastern Europe. Timing of the "Rubicon" "politicized" a political anniversary.

Since 1990 the main celebration of the 1956 revolution has usually been held at Budapest Technical University, in which the students had gathered in 1956 to demand political freedoms. Other commemorations have taken place in the graveyards and the contemporary battlefields of the city. A procession takes its departure from the university to the statue of Polish General Bem, who in 1848 helped Hungarians and in 1956 served as a symbolic *lieu*. The procession continues toward Parliament. On the fortieth anniversary of 1956, the main commemorative event was moved to the front of Parliament, at which location the statue with the flame of the revolution was built.[31] These realms of memory have become the most typical places to commemorate the anniversaries, much like receptions at the opera.

Some critical voices were raised regarding the commemorations, particularly during socialist-liberal governments between 1994 and 1998 and then again since 2002. Also a few political incidents have taken place every now and then: in 1990, for example, a number of right-wingers and skinheads marched to the radio building and introduced their own twelve points. The following year "national radio," thus, "without Communists" was the issue, and in 1992 groups of neo-Nazis whistled down President Árpád Göncz's speech. In 1994 socialists and free democrats represented the government at the official ceremonies, and for the first time, Gyula Horn (prime minister), Zoltán Gál (chairman of the parliament), and Árpád Göncz (president of the republic) laid a wreath together. In general, socialists and liberals have stressed the need for national unity in their commemorative speeches. It is also striking that socialists have emphasized their identification with and the legacy of Imre Nagy.[32]

However, Imre Nagy—or more precisely his commemoration by the socialists and liberals—was challenged by the Hungarian right in the early 1990s. For some Hungarians, socialists (and liberals) appeared to be the heirs of those who suppressed the revolution. Representatives of the right have argued that the unity in 1956 had been of a temporal nature. In 1994, one of them, Viktor Orbán, started to cultivate the concept of *polgári Magyarország*, citizens' ("bourgeois") Hungary, for his vision for the future. He politicized the past and argued that Hungarian people had demanded their *polgári* traditions back in 1956. In Orbán's view, Hungarians were condemned to peaceful coexistence instead of reconciliation. As new prime minister in 1998, he continued to develop these ideas in the opening speech at Parliament as the party on the October anniversary. Two years later, *Fidesz* argued that the aim in 1956 was a systemic change, not renewal of socialism.[33] The revolution, however, was interrupted and we do not know the final result. In the light of current sources, Orbán's view is questionable.

At the graveyard in 1999, politicians did not lay a wreath together but as private individuals, one after another. In 2002 the new socialist-liberal government planned a private action at the cemetery, which did not materialize because of the whistling audience.[34] In public, this "political theatre," as well as the issue of who lays a wreath with whom on June 16, October 23, or November 4, has led to an annual discussion of memory and comments in newspapers. In 2003 an opinion poll reflected views that Hungarians should commemorate together. These incidents and the strong commemorative nature of the anniversary might be the reasons why the October anniversary has not been that popular—particularly among younger generations—compared to the two other national holidays. With this in mind, the new prime minister, Ferenc Gyurcsány, and the leader of the Socialist Party, István Hiller, both born in the 1960s, took a new stand in defining their own meaning and the content of the day. In 2004 both emphasized the nature of 1956 as a revolution of youngsters. Gyurcsány and Hiller surmised that the day could be a common denominator and a model for Hungarian progressive thought and could be "the autumn March 15" at its best.[35]

Having all this in mind, expectations for the fiftieth anniversary were high as how the day is celebrated reflects on the image of Hungary in the international eye. Therefore academic Domokos Kosáry, the chairman of the 1956 Remembrance Committee, invited parliamentary party leaders for a meeting in October 2005. His message was that 1956 was a national topic that should not be tainted by party politics but celebrated in a decent way. In between the lines there was the idea that party leaders were also in charge of the final outcome. The government reserved Ft 3.7 million for the celebrations, as leaders from more than fifty countries were expected to participate in the main celebrations. According to the newspaper *Népszabadság* the government had supported over 500 productions: for example, 8 movies and documentary films, 31 plays in theatres, 44 exhibitions, and 26 conferences. Journalist Zsolt Gréczy also criticized political views of the opposition by comparing expenses to the celebrations of the millennium by the Fidesz-led government. According to the journalist, the present costs were less than the sum spent in the millennium, "but it is already evident that the memory of 1956 has aroused greater interest around the world." [36] In 2006 the presidents of the United States and Russia had already visited the country before October and both also commented on 1956 in their speeches.

Conclusion

In 1989 the memory of 1956 was present particularly in three political issues. First, in February the central committee of the HSWP accepted the principle of a multi-party system at the same time as it re-evaluated 1956 as a people's uprising. Second, Imre Nagy's reburial served both as a uniting rite and a moment of national mourning, which also redefined and strengthened the informal status of the opposition. Third, 1956 was highlighted on October 23, when Hungary was declared a republic on the anniversary of the great demonstration of 1956.

However, the purpose of this paper was to suggest that "history did not end" in 1989; debates have continued and consequences are present in many ways in the new democracy, as well. In general, a national day is a strong form of historical representation as it repeats annually, people prepare for it, and expectations vary concerning the why and how the national holiday should be celebrated. According to the law VIII/1991, October 23 has two meanings: 1956 revolution and the fight for freedom as the day on which the Hungarian Republic was declared in 1989. Hungary has not a particular day for independence, Constitution, or republic like many nations. Instead, the republic is linked to another earlier political event.

In principle, politicians had three alternatives to time the declaration of the new republic: first, they could have ignored all commemorations and the holiday status of October 23, which would, however, have been unrealistic during the current power struggles. Second, they could have chosen a new symbolic start and found a new day for the 1989 republic. However, a third alternative was realized, and the present was rooted in another historic topic. Establishing this kind of historical basis for the republic happened at a time when postmodernism in the West had already put different "foundations" into question.

It is notable that a separate day for the republic exists neither in Hungary nor in a few other former Communist-ruled countries. Moreover, it is notable that the current Republic of Hungary's predecessors, the republics of 1918 and 1946, are not celebrated officially, nor was there any significant public discussion concerning them in 1990–1991. Taking into account the revolutionary atmosphere of the autumn of 1989, the anniversary of the 1946 republic, in February, would have been too far away to be expedient; instead the anniversary of the first republic in mid-November was already on the horizon. However, these republics were also politically contested, and 1956 represented something new in the late 1980s. It had become the common denominator for different oppositional groups until 1990, when it had to compete with József Antall's republic with monarchist decorations. Had 1956 not received the status of a national day, it is plausible that there would have been at least one, or probably more, political groups that would have based their identity on that demand.

How do Hungarians celebrate October 23? Do they celebrate 1989 or commemorate 1956? The answer seems to be clear. On the basis of newspapers and other documents studied here, 1989 is not forgotten but it clearly remains in the shadow of 1956 and the debates of what 1956 finally was and to whom, and whose 1956 we talk about. New political identities and the image of the nation were constructed at the same time through the attempt to thoroughly research the problematic past.

Afterword: February 2007

Instead of commemorations, international television channels reported about riots in Budapest on October 23, 2006. When I left Hungary for Finland on October 24, Hungarian politicians were in the middle of a debate: who was responsible for the demonstrations and their violent suppression. October had witnessed the second clash in Budapest since September, when the attack on the television building took place. The earlier incident had occurred in the middle of a municipal election campaign, which led to a landslide victory for *Fidesz* in the opposition.

However, the forces that gathered in front of Parliament did not give up their demonstrations after the elections. Viktor Orbán launched an ultimatum to demand the resignation of Prime Minister Ferenc Gyurcsány. As a counter measure, Gyurcsány tested his popularity in a confidence vote and continued his premiership. The next step became clear in October, when *Fidesz* announced that it would not participate in the commemoration ceremony planned in Parliament on October 23 if the prime minister was going to give a speech on the occasion. Instead *Fidesz* preferred and carried out a mass gathering at Astoria Square in Pest.

Early on October 23, police emptied Kossuth Square; they argued that only by doing so could they guarantee the security of foreign state leaders participating in official ceremonies. First clashes took place in early afternoon, when the demonstrators returned toward Parliament and turned down a security barrier. During the course of the afternoon, police and demonstrators moved toward Astoria Square, where *Fidesz* supporters were holding a meeting. There were activities at several sites in the city; I personally saw trucks and vans driving on the streets, with people onboard waving flags. Instead of shouting out the slogans of 1956, people were demanding the resignation of Prime Minister Gyurcsány. In the evening, the demonstrators built a barricade near Elisabeth Bridge and held their positions until the early-morning hours.

The next day, *Magyar Nemzet* stressed "police terror" in its headline, while *Népszabadság* commented that Hungarians "could not celebrate in a decent way"; later, the historian Domokos Kosáry joined his voice to these views. All of this reflected on the international image of Hungary. For example, on Finnish television, commentators first asked how Hungarians celebrate their uprising, then they answered: they make a new one. To be more serious, demonstrators and their henchmen started a massive e-mail campaign. In Finland—which was the chairholder of the EU in the latter half of the year—they blamed the state leadership in supporting "the criminal Gyurcsány government."

When I arrived back in Budapest in February, one of the first news items I saw revealed that *Fidesz* had reserved Elisabeth Bridge for a mass meeting on March 15. According to *Népszabadság* these were "places well known" on October 23, as the police had pushed the demonstrators from Kossuth-Rákóczi Street to the bridge. On the basis of an idea of a script, *forgatókönyv* (frequently used metaphor in Hungarian politics), we know that March 15 matters. This is not only the case because the day has been used several times for political demonstrations and, particularly in 1957, there were rumours and leaflets to start the rising again on March 15. Nothing very serious happened in 1957, but the uprising led to arrests and careful political preparations in the Hungarian Socialist Workers' Party. Thus, expectations constitute politics; they did then and they do now. A further reading of recent *Népszabadság* reveals several articles, that concern expectations of the forthcoming March 15. It seems that politics as a romantic spectacle is becoming full of absurd features.

Notes

1. Litván 1995, 5–12; Népszabadság (NSZ) 16 Jun 2005; Gati 2006.
2. Cf., for example Nyyssönen 1999; Rainer 2000 and 2001.
3. With regards to my method of studying the past in the present and history discussions in the public, see Nyyssönen 1999.
4. For different traditions see for example Ripp 2002, 269–273.
5. 1990 országgyülési..., 22; Magyar Nemzet (MN) 3 May 1990; The Hungarian Revolution ... 1996, x.
6. MN 30 Oct 1989.
7. Törvények és rendeletek hivatalos gyűjteménye...2001, 1001.
8. Népszava 5 Sep 1991; Nyyssönen 2002, 187–188.
9. 1991. országgyülési..., 11132–11187; Juhász 1993; NSZ 19 Nov 1991.
10. NSZ 4 Nov 2003.
11. Welsh 1996, 418; Nyyssönen 2002, 178–179.
12. Nyyssönen 1999, 279–280; NSZ 26 Jul 2000, 6 Jul 2002, 26 May 2005, 30 Jan 2006; HVG 4 & 5/2006.
13. 1990. országgyülési..., 312; Antall József Orzsággyulési... 1994, 112–116.
14. 2000 Az Országgyűlés..., 3557–70; NSZ 24 Oct 2002; MN 24 Oct 2002.
15. Az Orszaggyűlés... 4326–4332, 23074–23080, 16273–16278; Küpper 1997, 684–691.
16. Törvények és rendeletek hivatalos gyűjteménye... 2003, 264.
17. NSZ 19 Jul 1989, 18 Oct 1989, 19 Oct 1989; Nyyssönen 1999, 193.
18. 1991 országgyűlési... 6521–6526, 6533–6537; Magyar Hírlap (MH) 6 Mar 1991; Törvények...1992.
19. MH & NSZ Sep 3 1990; NSZ 19 Aug 2000.
20. 168 óra 4 Jul 1989.
21. MH 2 Jan 1991.
22. NSZ 11 Jan 1991, 23 Mar 1992, 30 Mar 1992, 15 Jun 1992; MH 9 Dec 1991; MN 23 Mar 1992.
23. HVG 42/1995.
24. Boros 1997, 10, 141–152; NSZ Jul 15 2006.
25. NSZ 28 May 1992; MH 13 Jun 1992; 1992. országgyülési..., 21059–21063; NSZ 23 Feb 1995; MN 20 Jun 1995.

26. NSZ 10 Oct, 26 Oct 1991; MH 6 Dec 1991.

27. NSZ 21 Jun 2005.

28. MN 10 Feb 2006; NSZ 18 Oct 2005, 13 Jun, 19 Jun, 21 Jul 2006, 24 Oct 2006.

29. NSZ 22 Jan 2003; MH 16 Aug 1989; MN 31 Jul 1989; MPÉ 1990, 291; Nyyssönen 1999, 213–217.

30. MH 28 Oct 1988.

31. MH 19 Oct 1996; NSZ 24 Oct 1996.

32. MN 22 Oct 1994; NSZ 17 Jun 1995, 24 Oct 1998, 21 Oct 2003, 24 Oct 1999, 24 Oct 2000, 22 Oct 2001, 17 Jun 2006; MH 24 Oct 1995, 24 Oct 1997; Halmesvirta and Nyyssönen 2006, 256–261.

33. MH 16 Jun 1992, MN 24 Oct, 29 Oct 1994; NSZ 24 Oct 1996, 8 Jul 1998, MN 24 Oct 2000; cf. Litván 2002.

34. NSZ 24 Oct 1999, 24 Oct 2002, 24 Oct 2004; MN 24 Oct 2003.

35. MN 24 Oct 2002, 20 Oct 2003; NSZ 22 Oct 2003, 22 Oct 2004, 21 Oct 2004, 25 Oct 2004.

36. NSZ 28 Feb, 19 Jun, 15 Jul 2006.

Sources:

Minutes of the Parliament:
1990–94 Országgyűlési Értesítő
1994–2003 Az Országgyűlés hiteles jegyzőkönyve

Books of Law:
Törvények és rendeletek hivatalos gyűjteménye 1990. 1 kötet. Közzéteszi az Igazságügyi Minisztérium és a Minisztertanács Hivatala. Budapest: Közgazdasági és Jogi Könyvkiadó 1991.
Törvények és rendeletek hivatalos gyűjteménye 1991. 1 kötet. Közzéteszi az Igazságügyi Minisztérium és a Miniszterelnöki Hivatal. Budapest: Közgazdasági és Jogi Könyvkiadó 1992.

Törvények és rendeletek hivatalos gyűteménye 1992. 1 kötet. Közzéteszi az Igazságügyi Minisztérium és a Miniszterelnöki Hivatal. Budapest: Közgazdasági és Jogi Könyvkiadó 1993.

Törvények és rendeletek hivatalos gyűjteménye 1993. 1 kötet. Közzéteszi az Igazságügyi Minisztérium és a Miniszterelnöki Hivatal. Budapest: Közgazdasági és Jogi Könyvkiadó 1994.

Törvények és rendeletek hivatalos gyűjteménye 1994. 1 kötet. Közzéteszi az Igazságügyi Minisztérium és a Miniszterelnöki Hivatal. Budapest: Közgazdasági és Jogi Könyvkiadó 1995.

Törvények és rendeletek hivatalos gyűjteménye 1996. 1 kötet. Közzéteszi az Igazságügyi Minisztérium és a Miniszterelnöki Hivatal. Budapest: Magyar Hivatalos Közlönykiadó 1996.

Törvények és rendeletek hivatalos gyűjteménye 2000. 1 kötet. Közzéteszi az Igazságügyi Minisztérium és a Miniszterelnöki Hivatal. Budapest: Magyar hivatalos közlöny kiadó 2001.

Törvények és rendeletek hivatalos gyűjteménye 2003. 1 kötet. Közzéteszi az Igazságügyi Minisztérium és a Miniszterelnöki Hivatal. Budapest: Magyar hivatalos közlöny kiadó 2004.

Newspapers and periodicals:
168 óra, 1989 April–1994 December.
HVG 42/1995; 4 and 5/2006.
Magyar Hírlap (MH) 1 May 1988–31. December 1994; 18 October–24 October 1995–2005.
Magyar Nemzet (MN) 1 May 1988–31 December 1994; 18 October–24. October 1995–2005; 10 February 2006.
Népszabadság (NSZ) 1 May 1988–25 February 2007.
Népszava 5 September 1991.

Literature:
Antall József (1994) *Orzsággyűlési beszédei 1990–1993*. Budapest: Athenaeum nyomda.
Boros, Géza (1997): *Emlékművek '56-nak*. Budapest: 1956-os Intézet

Gati, Charles (2006): "Fifty Years Later". *The Hungarian Quarterly*. Vol 47 (Summer).

Halmesvirta, Anssi and Nyyssönen, Heino (2006): *Unkarin kansannousu 1956*. Helsinki: WSOY.

Juhász, Gábor (1993): "A megnevezéstől a háborús bűnösségig. Igazságtételi törvényhozás Magyarországon 1990. február - 1993. február." *Mozgó Világ* 4/1993.

Küpper, Herbert (1997): "'Personenkult" in der ungarishen Gezetsgebung?" *Osteuropa* 7/1997.

Litván, György (1995): "Research and Discussion on 1956 in present-day Hungary." In: Paula Hihnala & Olli Vehviläinen (eds.). *Hungary 1956*. Tampere: Tampereen yliopiston jäljennepalvelu 1995.

Litván, György (2002): "Politikai beszéd 1956-ról – 1989 után," *Évkönyv 2002*. Budapest: 1956-os Intézet.

Magyarország Politikai Évkönyve 1990, (eds.) Sándor Kurtán, Péter Sándor, László Vass. Budapest: AULA-OMIKK. (MPÉ)

Nyyssönen, Heino (1999): *The Presence of the Past in Politics. '1956' after 1956 in Hungary*. Jyväskylä: SoPhi.

Nyyssönen, Heino (2002): "History in the First Parliament," *The Politics of Memory in Hungary 1990–1994*. Hungarologische Beiträge 14. Jyväskylä: Universität Jyväskylä.

Rainer, János M. (2000): "A rendszerváltozás és az ötvenhatos hagyomány," In: Bozóki András (szerk.): *A rendszerváltás forgatókönyve. Kerekasztaltárgyalások 1989-ben*. 7. köt. Alkotmányos forradalom. Tanulmányok. Budapest: Új Mandátum, 2000.

Rainer, János M. (2001): "Nagy Imre újratemetése – a magyar demokratikus átalakulás szimbolikus aktusa," In: *A magyar forradalom eszméi. Eltiprásuk és győzelmük* (1956–1999). Szerk. Király Béla és Lee W. Congdon. Budapest: Atlanti Kutató és Kiadó Társulat-Alapítvány.

Ripp, Zoltán (2002): *1956 Forradalom és szabadságharc Magyarországon*. Budapest: Korona kiadó.

Litván, György (ed.) (2000) *The Hungarian Revolution of 1956. Reform, Revolt and Repression 1953–1963*. London & New York: Longman 1996.

Welsh, Helga A. (1996): "Dealing with the Communist Past: Central and East European Experiences after 1990". *Europe-Asia Studies* 48, 3/1996.

Part II

The Canadian Context

8.

Canada and Hungarian Refugees: The Historical Context

Harold Troper

Fifty years after the event, the Canadian program of refugee intake following the abortive Hungarian uprising of 1956 is recalled as a pivotal moment in Canadian immigration history. And it was pivotal. But why? What makes it so notable an event? According to the popularly received narrative, Canada and Canadians, acting out of selfless concern for those fleeing the iron fist of Soviet repression, opened their hearts and borders to those in distress. Before the influx of Hungarian refugees was over, more than 37,000 settled in Canada. It was a proud moment in the history of Canadian immigration and one that set the stage for later humanitarian outreach to refugees—the Czech and Vietnamese episodes immediately come to mind.

There is more than a little truth in this storied account—but there is also far more to it than that. To understand the watershed nature of the Hungarian refugees movement one must see it in the context of the larger Canadian immigration narrative and especially the construct of Canadian immigration and refugee policy of the preceding decade. By placing the Hungarian refugee episode in its historical setting, one soon understands the intake of almost 40,000 Hungarian refugees was at once an integral part of the Canadian immigration story and a telling exception in the checkered history of Canadian immigration and refugee policy. What is more, imbedded in the Hungarian resettlement effort are important issues of Canada's Cold War politics, of the growing power of non-print media, especially television, to both shape the popular imagination and influence public policy, and, finally, of the ability of government with political will, in this case working in cooperation with non-governmental agencies (NGOs), to overcome the bureaucratic inertia that so often haunts organizational structures.

Anyone examining the Canadian immigration narrative in the years leading up to the 1956 Hungarian uprising and the resulting Hungarian refugee crisis cannot help but be struck by what a difference a decade can make. If we could turn back the historical clock ten years, from 1956 to1946, immediately following the end of World War II, we would be hard pressed to find any hint that a decade later Canada would be a major immigrant-receiving society let alone lead the world in Hungarian refugee intake. Just the opposite. In the immediate wake of World War II, the Canadian government was possessed by issues of post-war domestic reconstruction. Immigrant intake was not on the government's radar. In the eyes of many government policy planners of the day, reopening immigration would be counterproductive to economic stability. It was widely conceded among government officials that it had been the war, with the concurrent massive government spending, rapid industrial expansion, and insatiable demand for labour, that pulled Canada out of the economic depression of the 1930s. The war now over and government spending reduced, there was fear of a fall off in industrial production and corresponding rise in unemployment just as job-hungry armed service personnel were being released back into the economy. Given their fears that a major economic slowdown threatened, and that perhaps there would even be a return to the depression-like conditions of the 1930s, the last thing government planners wanted was for Canada to reopen its doors to employment-seeking immigrants.

There is a Yiddish expression, which translates roughly as "Men think and God laughs." The heavens must have been rolling with laughter as Canadian policy planners were quickly proved wrong. After a lumbering start, the post-war Canadian economy made a smoother than expected transition from wartime to peacetime conditions. And, against expectations, the economy expanded rapidly, exports leading the way. Markets for Canadian raw materials and manufactured goods were strong in Britain and war-ravaged Europe. Demand only became stronger as the Marshall Plan poured millions of dollars into shoring up Europe's post-war economic infrastructure in an effort to hasten European reconstruction and forestall Communist expansion. And so long as the United States was intent upon beating back the threat of Soviet imperial design with American dollars, Canadian raw materials, foodstuffs, and manufactured goods found ready markets.

Nor was the export market the only source of Canadian economic strength. During the war Canadians had earned good wages but rationing, forced savings, and social sanctions against ostentatious consumption kept a lid on spending. At war's end, delayed gratification gave way to consumer spending on goods and services beyond the reach of most since not just the onset of the war but the Great Depression that preceded it. As the economy heated up, the problem soon became a shortage of goods not money, a shortage of labour not jobs.

For the first time in thirty years Canada faced a peacetime shortfall in job-ready workers. And where would those workers come from? By late 1946, labour-intensive industries, especially in the core economic sectors of agriculture, mining, lumbering, and manufacturing, were lobbying Ottawa for a relaxation of tight immigration restrictions, restrictions cemented into place during the job-hungry depression era of the 1930s, which were grounded in overt racial and ethnic selectivity. Under these immigration restrictions Asians and, in effect, all others of non-European origin were barred entry to Canada. So, too, were southern Europeans and all Jews, irrespective of country of origin, except those holding British or American citizenship. Regulations at the end of World War II only gave very limited immigration access to Central and Eastern Europeans. While regulatory provisions allowed for reunification of persons abroad with family in Canada, those who tried to bring family to Canada often found immigration officials unresponsive or exceedingly adept at hiding behind the regulatory fine print of the regulations to forestall any entry.

What about industry's need for labour? As jobs in Canada went begging, big business, lobbying for a loosening of immigration restrictions, warned that if business was denied access to a pool of immigrant labour, the economy would grind down. Many government officials, however, remained sceptical. They feared the economic boom would prove a bubble. They warned that Canada's economic problems would only end up worsening if, in a moment of optimism, it opened the door to immigration only to have the bubble suddenly burst. In addition to these economic naysayers, immigration officials, who since the 1930s had made their careers guarding the Canadian gate against all comers, remained largely unsympathetic to any liberalization of immigration. Even if the immigration door were only opened to Europeans, they cautioned their political masters that the Canadian public would be unforgiving of any government that approved the admission of those long regarded to be ethnically and racial different if not inferior. This was especially true when it came to the possible immigration of those in the Displaced Persons (DP) camps of Germany and Austria. These camps then housed Central and Eastern European groups, including Jews, the very European groups against whom Canada erected strictly enforced and racially drawn immigration barriers before World War II. Immigration officials, who could not see beyond their hierarchy of ethnic preferences, warned it was shortsighted to fill what was likely a temporary labour shortfall by allowing a permanent immigration of Jews and Slavs—those who then stood first in Europe's exit line.[1] The public seemed to agree. Only a year after the guns fell quiet in Europe, a public opinion poll found that, should Canada reopen its door to immigrants, Canadians indicated a sharp preference for the admission of recently defeated Germans over Slavic peoples—Ukrainians, Poles, Russians. The suggestion of immigration by Jews was even less popular. Only the Japanese fared worse than Jews in the poll.[2]

But, for all the warnings of trouble, the anti-immigration camp was outflanked. Immigration was reopened. The labour-intensive industries demanding imported workers and backed up by Canadian ethnic lobbying won important political allies, especially Canada's influential wartime economic czar, C. D. Howe, minister of Reconstruction and, following the war, minister of Trade and Commerce. Howe, perhaps only second in influence in Ottawa to the prime minister, was bullish on the economy. Brushing aside warnings that the economy could weaken, he argued the only thing likely to imperil the economy was a continued labour shortage.

Pressed by business and encouraged by Howe, in spring of 1947, Prime Minister Mackenzie King informed Parliament of his government's decision to reopen Canada's door to immigration. But, ever cautious of possible voter backlash, the prime minister advised it was to be a qualified opening. Canada, he promised, would not be flooded by undesirable immigrants. Rather, "it is of the utmost importance to relate immigration to absorptive capacity." And, in King's mind, Canada's capacity to absorb immigrants was as much tied to their ethnic or racial origins as it was to their employability. He was only reflecting the national mood when he observed that "the people of Canada do not wish to make a fundamental alteration in the character of their population through mass immigration." Discrimination and ethnic selectivity in immigration would remain. "Canada," he continued, "is perfectly within her rights in selecting the persons whom we regard as desirable future citizens. It is not a 'fundamental human right' of any alien to enter Canada. It is a privilege. It is a matter of domestic policy."[3]

Accordingly, Ottawa promised Canadians that immigration priority would centre on those groups with a proven track record for assimilation, particularly Northern and Western Europeans. Thus, the renewal of immigration in late 1947 was something of a throwback to the ethnic and racial immigration priorities of the 1920s. British, American, and Northern Europeans were actively courted. Legislated bars against Asians remained in place, and administrative tinkering assured that Southern, Central, and Eastern Europeans would find it at best difficult getting into Canada. Ontario was so concerned to get the "right" type of immigrant that it flexed its jurisdictional muscle in immigration matters and inaugurated a highly publicized airlift of British settlers into the province. When British currency regulations threatened to choke off the flow of applicants, special transportation tariffs were negotiated to stimulate the inflow.[4] When currency regulations similarly hobbled the immigration of other desirable Western European groups, particularly the Dutch, the federal government intervened. In 1948 a three-year bilateral agreement was signed with the Netherlands to ensure the smooth transplant of approximately 15,000 Dutch farmers and farm workers to Canada.[5]

Labour-intensive industry was pleased by the government's building commitment to renewed immigration, but it was less than pleased with continuing stumbling blocks placed in the way of importing cheap labour from outside the government's narrow ethnic circle of acceptability. Repeatedly warned that a continued economic boom hinged on increasing the number of immigrant admissions, industry pressed for access to imported labour willing to assume low-wage and low-status positions rejected by preferred immigrants and native-born Canadians alike. Specifically, industry wanted Ottawa to skim off the cream of the labour pool languishing in the Displaced Persons camps of Europe. As the economy continued to expand, with C. D. Howe very much onside and supported by pro-immigration Jewish and Eastern European polities in Canada, the federal government gradually started giving industry, working in conjunction with federal immigration and labour officials, permission to troll the DP camps of Europe for workers ready to come to Canada. All the while the public mood was monitored for any upsurge in anti-immigration sentiment, especially with regards to the arrival of Slavic and Jewish settlers.

Complementing the increased flow of labour out of European DP camps was a liberalization of family reunification provisions of the immigration regulations that opened the door to still more immigration by those who might previously have been defined as belonging to non-preferred groups. But whether they were accepted as part of the family reunification or labour immigration streams, the arrival of these settlers was first and foremost a concession to the business lobby. There can be little doubt that if there were no labour shortages few from outside of British and Western Europe would have come to Canada. And even so, in those heady post-war years Ottawa was still not entirely ready to yield on the issue of ethnic preference, or not yet. In selection of labour immigration, immigration authorities covertly applied a hierarchy of ethnic selectivity, as much as possible giving preference, for example, to those from the Baltic nations, seen by many as hard-working "Nordic types," over those from middle Europe, or Slavic and Jewish settlers.[6]

For all this, as the job market in Canada remained strong and the Canadian public more and more began to accept immigration as intrinsic to national prosperity, immigration numbers of those previously regarded as less desirable grew steadily. In fact, these numbers increased further as Canada found itself in competition for immigrant workers with other labour-short countries, including the United States and Australia. Canadian officials still had to scramble to ensure their share of a shrinking European pool. And it was not just competition for immigrants that was causing Canada problems. The pool of immigration candidates was declining. With a line of demarcation separating Soviet and Western Europe, as a matter of policy and practise, iron curtain countries foreclosed the option of out migration to the West, taking millions out of the possible immigration pool. What is more, the gradual improvement in the economies in Northern and Western Europe provided domestic employment opportunities to many who might previously have considered immigration. With industry still clamouring for labour, Canadian immigration officials began scouting out possible new sources of available European immigration—even if it again meant that traditional, ethically based barriers to immigrants had to be reconsidered.[7]

Canadians seemed ready to accept a broadening of immigration sources to include those who might previously not have been considered, in the parlance of the day, "white" or "white" enough. By the time the DP admission program had run its course, hundreds of thousands of new immigrants had found homes in Canada and largely without inflating domestic racial concerns. Instead of dealing with inflamed racial tensions as a result of immigration, provincial governments were beginning to move toward legal recognition of this new spirit of openness by enacting human rights legislation protecting individuals from discrimination—legislation long sought by immigrant and ethnic communities.[8] What is more, within the federal immigration bureaucracy, the old school of restrictionist immigration officers was being replaced by a new breed of pro-immigration personnel ready to work hand-in-glove with employers. In order to reinforce the importance Ottawa now accorded increased immigration numbers, in 1950 the old backwash of Ottawa immigration bureaucracy, the Immigration Branch, within the Department of Mines and Resources was upgraded to ministerial level within a new Department of Citizenship and Immigration. While in June 1950 the government regulations reaffirmed continued preference for British, Irish, French, and American immigrants—all believed to be suited to Canada's climatic, educational, social, industrial, and labour environment— at the same time regulatory provision was made to widen admissible classes of other European immigrants. Provisions for residents of Canada (excluding most Asians) to sponsor relatives were also widened. All these steps enabled an increasing diversity of semi-skilled and skilled immigrants, including domestics, agriculturalists, entrepreneurs, professionals, and any other workers sponsored by a Canadian employer or family member to come to Canada.

Of course tinkering with immigration regulations and administration was one thing. An overhaul of Canadian immigration legislation was another. The immigration legislation in place at the end of World War II had been set in place in the mid-1920s and was widely regarded as no longer suitable to meet the needs of a new Canada. In 1952, four years before the Hungarian uprising, the government put forward new immigration legislation designed to ensure a continuing stream of immigrants and, as far as Europeans were concerned, loosening but not entirely foregoing its traditional ethnic or racial immigration barriers. In that, the 1952 act echoed the prime minister's 1947 caution against immigration undermining the existing social structure of Canadian society. At the street level the 1952 act allowed the minister of Immigration and his officials sweeping powers to set such regulations as they felt necessary to enforce the act. At the discretion of the minister, individuals or groups might be rejected on account of nationality, geographic origin, peculiarity of custom, unsuitability to the climate, and the omnibus provision that any individual or group demonstrated an inability "to become assimilated." In effect this meant most Europeans were in. Most Asians and other people of colour were still out. But the act also granted the minister the right to waive regulations in favour of a specific group or class of immigrants if it was felt to be in the national interest. We would see this provision of the law come into play during the Hungarian refugee movement a few years later.[9]

In keeping with the deepening Cold War climate of the day, the act also called for strict security checks of would-be immigrants. In this regard, security personnel, working under the umbrella of the RCMP, functioned as something of a separate estate. A cone of secrecy was drawn over their activities and procedures. Individuals barred from Canada on security grounds had few avenues of appeal and often were seldom if ever told the true cause of their rejection. Canada's Cold War gatekeepers were especially focused on the Communist threat. Much to Canada's shame, while standing guard against Communists, others whose

World War II records should have set off alarms in Ottawa didn't. A number of Nazis or Nazi collaborators slipped into Canada, and Canadian authorities did nothing to remove those brought to their attention.[10]

With the 1952 legislation in place, the wall of restriction against people of colour developed small cracks. Responding to a changing British Commonwealth, as former British colonial holdings declared their independence, and hoping to gain an economic toe hold in the developing world, Canada took a first step toward a more racially open immigration policy by setting a small but nonetheless symbolically important immigrant quota for its non-white Commonwealth partners, India, Pakistan, and Ceylon. If the numbers of non-whites admitted to Canada was small, the precedent of government-sanctioned admissions of any non-white immigrants should not be minimized.[11]

Of course immigration is not simply policy and legislation. It is people, and as the 1950s wore on and the Canadian economy generally remained buoyant, so did demand for immigrant labour. By the late 1950s, with DP camps a thing of the past, Eastern Europe closed off to immigration, and numbers declining from Northern and Western Europe, the pool of those applying to emigrate to enter Canada from Northern and Western Europe in decline, and business interests still insistent that continued prosperity was at stake if the import of labour did not continue, immigration authorities shifted their eye farther and farther afield. Italy and other areas of southern Europe, not yet nearly as impacted by the European post-war recovery as were the countries of Northern and Western Europe, found itself on the Canadian immigration radar screen. To expand the Canadian immigration catchment basin, the federal cabinet lifted restrictions against the admission of Italians, previously barred as former enemy aliens. Even as Canadian security personnel cautioned that the powerful Communist Party in Italy might use Canadian immigration as a way to infiltrate spies into Canada, Canadian immigration offices were opened in Italy. Still anxious that any increase in the number of Southern Europeans might set off a racial backlash in Canada, immigration officials first hoped to concentrate their efforts among more "Germanic" northern Italians. Things did not go as planned. Almost immediately immigration from poorer and less developed southern Italy dominated the immigrant flow. And with virtually no public backlash in Canada, it was not long before Italian immigration climbed into the tens of thousands.[12] In the industrial heartland of southern Ontario and urban Canada more generally, Italian labour soon became a mainstay of the thriving construction industry much as Eastern European Jews had been to the needle trades and Ukrainians to the breaking of the prairie sod. Italians were soon followed by Greeks, Portuguese, and peoples of the Balkan Peninsula.

What all this historical background added up to was that during the decade leading up to the Hungarian uprising, Canadian immigration remained at heart economically self-serving, even as it was, to a declining degree, still ethnically and racially selective. As a result when it came to immigration, the government was forever balancing the needs of the economy against any social and political costs. But this was also an era of Cold War anxiety, and immigration played out against the Cold War backdrop. Issues of security and immigrations sources stand out as Cold War related. All these factors impacted on the Canadian response to the Hungarian uprising. But there were other important factors that also shaped the Canadian response. And, if truth be told, the Hungarian episode was not the first post-war European uprising against Soviet domination to set off a flow of population westward. In June of 1953, three years before the Hungarian uprising, a revolt erupted in East Germany when a strike by East Berlin construction and healthcare workers turned into a countywide uprising against the East German government of the day. There were demonstrations in more than five hundred towns and villages. The uprising was eventually suppressed by Soviet troops stationed in Germany working with East German police, but their task was not easy. In spite of the intervention of Soviet troops, the wave of strikes and protests lasted a month and hostility to Soviet authority continued to run deep. Many, fearing Soviet retaliation escaped into West Germany or into West Berlin by simply taking the then still-functioning subway connecting eastern and western zones of Berlin.[13]

In retrospect the Western response to the East German uprising was cautious. There was, for example, little or no wholesale effort made to ease the plight of East German escapees by affording them the opportunity to relocate to Western receiving countries like Canada. Why was that? Perhaps because the 1953 uprising and consequent dislocation of population from East to West

Germany was seen by West Germany as an internal German matter. As a result, West Germany neither required nor requested international assistance in relocating escapees from East Germany. What is more, Western nations were particularly cautious in doing anything that might lead to a change in the German status quo, especially with regards to igniting hopes of German reunification—a prospect less than agreeable to the French and British.

There were also other reasons why the dislocation of Germans following the 1953 revolt created little humanitarian outpouring of popular sympathy in the West, and certainly nothing to compare with that which flowed to Hungarians just a few years later. For one thing, there was still residual antipathy for those whom many still regarded as a defeated enemy. But there was more than that separating the response to the German and Hungarian revolts. The 1953 German uprising, dramatic as it was, did not have the kind of Western media and especially television attention that accompanied the Hungarian uprising three years later—even though the 1956 Hungarian uprising had to compete for media attention with the Sinai War and the British and French invasion of Suez. In large part this reflected the difference three years made in the spread of television. Taking Canada as an example, in 1953, when the East German revolt broke out, domestic Canadian television broadcasting was barely a year old and only one quarter of Canadians had a television in their homes. Three years later, in 1956, nearly eight out of every ten Canadian households owned a television set and CBC television programming was available to the vast majority of Canadians. With television becoming a ubiquitous part of Canadian life, newsreel footage of daily events, once reserved to movie theatres, became a regular part of the daily Canadian television diet.[14] And Canadian television coverage of the 1956 Hungarian uprising and the subsequent outpouring of some 200,000 refugees into Austria received intense coverage, but not just as a matter of numbers. Newsreel footage, some gathered from British and American networks, gave the outflow of refugees from Hungary a human face.[15] Not to be outdone, the daily press in Canada also gave the Hungarian uprising and the flight of refugees into Austria in-depth front-page coverage.[16]

If it is impossible to accurately measure the exact impact of all the media coverage and the images that backed up that coverage to which Canadians were exposed, there can be no doubt but that the impact on the Canadian public imagination was real and immediate. It tugged at the heart. On December 4, Russell Jones, who covered the uprising for United Press from Russian-held Budapest, offered street-level images of ruthless Soviet repression of the Hungarian people. In a December 4 story widely reprinted in Canadian newspapers, Jones offered an eyewitness account of the more than 30,000 women who assembled in Heroes Square in Budapest to lay wreathes and flags at the tomb of the Unknown Soldier. Regarding this as a provocation, Soviet soldiers surrounding the square were described as jumping from their vehicles weapons drawn and charging into the crowd of women. Jones reported that the women bravely held their ground and the soldiers, taken aback by the cold determination of the women, held their fire. The day after he filed this report Jones was expelled from Hungary. But he continued to report on the uprising. A few days after being expelled, he wrote that across Hungary "the fiercest fighters were the workers." And why did they rise up against Communist domination? "It was for these simple, basic things that the Hungarian people fought...the right to speak and think freely, to elect men of their own choice, and to raise their children in their own way. They will go on fighting for them."[17]

Blanket media coverage was made even more gripping by the coining of a collective noun to designate those who challenged the might of the Soviet Union—"Hungarian Freedom Fighters." The term "Freedom Fighter" is today a contested term, but in 1956 the term "Freedom Fighter" had a singularly heroic ring and quickly gained media and popular currency elevating the Hungarians, Hungarian Freedom Fighters, to iconic status, at least in the West. Their struggle was accorded the stature of crusade. On January 7, *Time* magazine awarded its annual "Man of the Year" honour to the nameless Hungarian Freedom Fighter who had "shaken history's greatest despotism to its foundations." This Freedom Fighter may in the end have been laid low by eighty Soviet military divisions but, in the word of *Time*, "his greatest triumph was moral: he demonstrated the profound and needful truth that humanity is not necessarily forever bound and gagged by modern terrorist political techniques. Thus he gave to millions, and specifically to the youth of Eastern Europe, the hope for a foreseeable end to the long night of Communist dictatorship." The magazine cover offered a rough portrait of an anonymous Hungarian Freedom Fighter, a battle-torn red, white, and green Hungarian flag unfurled behind him.[18]

As the uprising was being crushed under the Soviet heel, 200,000 refugees escaped westward into Austria and to a lesser extent Yugoslavia. While designated refugees, in the popular mind they collectively retained the honorific title Hungarian Freedom Fighters. Of course, these refugees were hardly all of a kind. But together they constituted the most major European refugee crisis since the end of World War II and arguably the dominant European refugee crisis of the Cold War.[19]

What about Canadian response to the plight of those now collectively referred to as Freedom Fighters and particularly its readiness to open Canada's door to Hungarian refugee admission? It is clear that the Canadian public was far ahead of their government. Ottawa was at first cautious. If the Canadian public was moved by what it saw as a humanitarian crisis and one befalling those who suffered for freedom's cause, the government initially saw problems. To begin with, as they did in the case of other immigration initiatives, Canadian security personnel again warned government that the Communists might attempt to infiltrate this refugee movement in order to place secret agents into unsuspecting Western countries, including Canada. While not dismissing this warning, cabinet, for its part, seemed less concerned with Communists than with costs.[20] Unlike the post-war DP movement in which labour-intensive industry, ethnic communities, and families shouldered much of the resettlement burden, some in government at first questioned how much of the cost of any wholesale Hungarian resettlement program would fall on Canadian taxpayers. Faced with a humanitarian crisis, they asked if Canada was to get involved might it not be possible to work out some kind of pay-as-you-go refugee movement? And as immigration officials weighed the possibility of a Hungarian intake program, they cautioned that Canada's immigrant absorption capacity was already likely to be strained by a huge jump in British immigration applicants in consequence of the Suez Crisis. Perhaps it was best to go slow when it came to Hungarians.

So what finally shook the government into action? In large part it was Canadian public reaction. As Ottawa appeared to dither, with public officials unable or unwilling to think or respond outside their regulatory box in response to a refugee crisis of the first order, the government found itself castigated by a media and public demanding their political leaders to be bold in taking in refugees. The public reminded Ottawa that these were not ordinary refugees in the camps in Austria. They were Freedom Fighters. They had bravely carried democracy's banner. And if there was some unspoken guilt that in their struggle against Soviet oppression, these heroes had been let down by the Western democracies, there was a determination that the democracies, including Canada, could not let them down a second time. They had earned a place among us. With television images of Freedom Fighters imprinted on the popular mind, support for the plight of Hungarian refugees, for Hungarian Freedom Fighters, grew stronger.

The press on both sides of the political spectrum continued to savage the government for its inaction. In an editorial entitled "For Shame" the *Globe and Mail* castigated the government for not acting quickly to open Canada's door to Hungarian refugees.[21] As the political heat continued to rise, with a federal election in the offing and government backbenchers nervous, a cabinet afraid of being found wanting embraced the public will. With sudden boldness, a path was cut through the logjam of doubts. In a sudden rush to show results, routine immigration red tape was snipped away. Normal immigration procedures, including some medical and security checks, were waved or postponed until after arrival in Canada. Federal money was also made available to cover the cost of removal of Hungarian refugees to Canada. Cooperative agreements covering immigrant resettlement were worked out with provincial governments and NGOs. Even as the details for starting the movement still remained to be set out, the minister of immigration, Jack Pickersgill, hurried off to Vienna to take a personal hand in overseeing the removal of Hungarians to Canada. Hard on the minister's heels came immigration teams assigned to make the program happen and happen fast.[22]

Sadly, the Hungarian refugee movement was not without its cloud of racial prejudice. In 1957, as the movement of Hungarians was getting started, the director of immigration cautioned that a number of the refugees were rumoured to not be "bona fide ones but persons who had taken advantage of the situation." In a throwback to an earlier day of racial and religious prejudice in immigration selection, he stated, "These were all of the Hebrew race and were in possession of a considerable amount of funds." Orders were given immigration officers to be watchful of any spurious refugee cases, especially those of "the Hebrew race."[23] In spite of these instructions, in the mad rush to process refugees for Canada approximately 4,500 Jews were admitted to Canada, about 15 percent of the total refugee intake. Many of them were assisted by the Jewish Immigrant Aid Society, which was a key player in the federal, provincial, and volunteer sector partnership that assisted in refugee settlement.[24]

In the end, the Hungarian refugee resettlement program can be judged to have run remarkably smoothly in spite of its uneasy beginnings, lurching start, and ethnic concerns. In short order fully 37,000 Hungarian refugees were brought to Canada, most to urban Canada, which was increasingly the destination of preference for most new immigrants. But if immigration officials would later pride themselves on the success of the program, at the time many saw it as a onetime effort—a singular exception to the routine immigration process. And there was much that was exceptional about the program including the degree of government hands-on effort and financial commitment. So, too, was the foreign and domestic political context. For example, it was driven not so much by domestic Canadian labour needs but, in a remarkable turn of events, by awakened public compassion. Of course, Canada did do well by doing good—and of course Cold War considerations played heavily into the Canadian response—but this does not tarnish this episode as an exercise in humanitarian outreach. What is more, if immigration officials at first regarded this kind of refugee indicative as a one-time thing, a "one-off" exception to the procedural routines immigration officials guarded, it is noteworthy that time would prove them wrong.[25] Howard Adelman, York University professor of philosophy and refugee activist, argued that at the time "what drove the Hungarian refugee policy in Canada was humanitarianism as the pursuit of Virtue supplemented by concern with reinforcing a national self-identity as European, our economic prosperity and our interests of state both in terms of helping our friends and embarrassing our enemies."[26] But in retrospect it was also more than that. The Hungarian refugee movement, a humanitarian refugee resettlement effort, was but the first and in many ways the model for a series of Canadian refugee initiates during the next twenty years. It was also a critical step along the road to passage of the Canadian immigration legislation in 1976, which, for the first time, officially committed Canada, through its routine immigration procedures, to work to ease the distress of refugees, the displaced, and the persecuted. The Hungarian refugee movement, affirming as it was for the more than 37,000 who took up new lives in Canada, was truly a watershed event in Canadian immigration history. And its legacy continues.

Notes

1. Irving Abella and Harold Troper, *None Is Too Many: Canada and the Jews of Europe, 1933–1945* (Toronto: Lester and Orphen Dennys, 1982),190–279; Lubomyr Luciuk, "Searching for Place: Ukrainian Refugee Migration to Canada After World War II," unpublished Ph.D. dissertation, University of Alberta, 1984.
2. Canadian Institute of Public Opinion, Public Opinion News Service Release, October 30, 1946.
3. *House of Commons Debates*, May 1, 1947, 2644–2647.
4. Anthony H. Richmond, *Post-war Immigrants in Canada* (Toronto: University of Toronto Press, 1967), 9.
5. William Petersen, *Planned Migration: The Social Determinants of the Dutch–Canadian Movement* (Berkeley: University of California Press, 1955).
6. Abella and Troper, *None Is Too Many*, 238–279.
7. Luciuk, "Searching for Place"; Abella and Troper, *None Is Too Many*, 238–279; Milda Danys, *DP: Lithuanian Immigration to Canada after the Second World War* (Toronto: Multicultural History Society of Ontario, 1986); Karl Aun, *The Political Refugees: A History of the Estonians in Canada* (Toronto: McClelland & Stewart, 1985), 20–28.
8. James Walker, "The 'Jewish Phase' in the Movement for Racial Equality in Canada," *Canadian Ethnic Studies* 34 (2002): 1–29; Ruth Frager and Carmela Patrias, "'This Is Our Country, These Are Our Rights': Minorities and the Origins of Ontario's Human Rights Campaigns," *Canadian Historical Review*

82 (2001): 1–35; Ross Lambertson, "The Dresden Story: Racism, Human Rights, and the Jewish Labour Committee of Canada," *Labour/Le Travail* 47 (2001): 43–83.

9. For a discussion of the 1952 act and its application see Freda Hawkins, *Canada and Immigration: Public Policy and Public Concern* (Montreal: McGill-Queen's University Press, 1972), 101–110.

10. Reginald Whitaker, *Double Standard: The Secret History of Canadian Immigration* (Toronto: Lester and Orpen Dennys, 1987). For a discussion of the issue of Nazi war criminals in Canada see, David Matas and Susan Charendoff, *Justice Delayed: Nazi War Criminals in Canada* (Toronto: Summerhill Press, 1987); Harold Troper and Morton Weinfeld, *Old Wounds: Jews, Ukrainians, and the Hunt for Nazi War Criminals in Canada* (Chapel Hill: University of North Carolina Press, 1989); and Commission of Inquiry on War Criminals, *Report, Part I: Public* (Ottawa, 1986).

11. Hawkins, *Canada and Immigration*, 99.

12. Franca Iacovetta, "Ordering in Bulk: Canada's Post-war Immigration Policy and Recruitment of Contract Workers from Italy," *Journal of American Ethnic History* 11 (1992): 50–80.

13. Christian F. Ostermann, ed., *Uprising in East Germany, 1953: The Cold War, the German Question, and the First Major Upheaval behind the Iron Curtain* (Budapest: Central European University Press, 2003).

14. Paul Rutherford, *When Television Was Young: Primetime Canada, 1952-1967* (Toronto: University of Toronto Press, 1990).

15. Even with the Suez Crisis on the 1956 revolution's doorstep, one analysis of news coverage at the time concluded that the BBC did a better and more extensive job of covering the Hungarian revolution than of the Suez Crisis. Gary David Rawnsley, "Cold War Radio in Crisis: The BBC Overseas Services, the Suez Crisis and the 1956 Hungarian Uprising - British Broadcasting Corporation Ltd," *Historical Journal of Film, Radio and Television* 16 (June 1996): 197–220.

16. Hurdon Arthur Hooper, "The Canadian Perspective: Canadian Newspaper Coverage of the Hungarian 1956, the Czechoslovak 1968 and the Polish

1980-81 Crises," unpublished MA thesis, University of New Brunswick, 1983.

17. Russell Jones, as quoted in Nathaniel Lande, *Dispatches from the Front: A History of the American War Correspondent* (New York: Oxford University Press, 1998), 294–295.

18. *Time* magazine, January 7, 1957, page 18.

19. For a short discussion of the different camps of refugees see N. F. Dreisziger, "The Refugee Experience in Canada and the Evolution of the Hungarian-Canadian Community," in Robert H. Keyserlingk, ed., *Breaking Ground: The 1956 Hungarian Refugee Movement to Canada* (Toronto: York Lanes Press, 1993), ft.9, 83.

20. Whitaker, *Double Standard*, 84–85.

21. *Globe and Mail* as quoted in Ninette Kelley and Michael Trebilcock, *The Making of the Mosaic: A History of Canadian Immigration Policy* (Toronto: University of Toronto Press, 1998), 340.

22. For the minister's take on the Hungarian refugee program see J. W. Pickersgill, "The Minister and the Hungarian Refugees," in Keyserlingk, ed., *Breaking Ground*, 47–51.

23. Whitaker, *Double Standard*, 67.

24. Joseph Kage, "The Settlement of Hungarian Refugees in Canada." In Keyserlingk, ed., *Breaking Ground*, 100.

25. N. F. Dreisziger, *Struggle and Hope: The Hungarian Canadian Experience* (Toronto: McClelland & Stewart, 1982), 195–219; Gerald Dirks, *Canada's Refugee Policy* (Montreal: McGill-Queen's University Press, 1977), 190–213.

26. Howard Adelman, "An Immigration Dream: Hungarian Refugees Come to Canada—An Analysis," in Keyserlingk, ed., *Breaking Ground*, 41.

9.

The 1956–1957 Refugee Movement in the Context of Hungarian Immigration to Canada since the Late 19th Century

Nándor Dreisziger

The movement of the refugees of the 1956 Hungarian Revolution to Canada, remarked Professor Gerald E. Dirks thirty-three years after the event, "was unprecedented in the long history of immigration to Canada."[1] If the coming of the Hungarian refugees in 1956–1957 was a unique event in the annals of Canadian immigration history then it is not surprising that it was also a unique happening in the history of Hungarian immigration to this land.

The refugee movement was unprecedented above all because never before or since have so many Hungarians come to Canada in such a short time. It was also very special in that it had a profound impact on the existing Hungarian-Canadian community. The way the 1956 refugees were perceived by the Canadian public at large was also extraordinary. At the same time, when we survey the course of Hungarian-Canadian history, it also becomes evident that the coming of the refugees was not always and not in all respects a unique experience as many aspects of pre-1956 Hungarian-Canadian immigration history foreshadowed the movement of 1956–1957. The main purpose of this paper is to examine the 1956 refugee experience, place it in the context of a century and a half of Hungarian immigration to Canada, and establish to what extent and in what regard the coming of the refugees in 1956–1957 was a unique development in the annals of Hungarian immigration to Canada and in the evolution of this country's Hungarian community.

*

Hungarians have been coming to the shores of the northern half of North America since the earliest days of European settlement in this land. Compared to Western Europeans, however, they came infrequently and in very small numbers, and mainly as visitors.[2] It was not until the second half of the nineteenth century that they began showing up in Canada in numbers that might attract the attention of immigration historians. Even in this period, it wasn't until the very end of the century that we can talk about the rise of enduring Hungarian immigrant communities in this country.[3]

As is well known, the Hungarians who had come to Canada since the closing years of the nineteenth century came in waves or, as immigration historians call them, "streams." Perhaps somewhat arbitrarily, five such streams can be distinguished. The first is the pre-1914 stream of immigration. The second is the immigration that started in 1924 and lasted until the onset of the Great Depression. The third is the movement of the post-World War II "displaced persons." The fourth constitutes the 1956–1957 refugees, and the last comprises the Hungarian newcomers who have arrived since the end of the 1950s. In this paper, I will focus on the experiences of the "56 wave" of Hungarian arrivals and compare the circumstances of their coming to Canada and their settlement here with those of the previous three waves. The post-1959 wave will not be analyzed in detail, partly because it was more of a trickle than a wave and partly because it was a complex phenomenon that defies easy characterization.

More important, however, than the analysis of this largely chronological division of the Hungarian immigrant experience will be a classification of the subject at hand into a number of themes or dimensions. This categorization will facilitate the discussion of the history of each wave of Hungarian immigrants in a systematic manner and will allow us to establish the differences—as well as the similarities—in the nature and experiences of each wave.

The first of these dimensions concerns the motivation of the members of each wave in leaving their Hungarian homeland. This dimension reveals the extent to which the members of each particular wave were political refugees as opposed to economic migrants. The next dimension deals with the basic demographic characteristics of each wave. This will be followed by an examination of the social and religious make-up of each stream of Hungarian immigration. This in turn will lead into an analysis of what might best be called the psychological dimension of the departure from Hungary and arrival in Canada of the members of each immigrant wave. This discussion will include an examination of the adjustment to and integration in Canadian society of the various waves of Hungarian immigrants. Next will follow a look at what might be called an "external dimension" of the Hungarian immigration experience: the different ways that newcomers to this country from Hungary were perceived and received by the Canadian public at large. In the penultimate section the paper will look at still another dimension of the story, the impact each wave had on the existing Hungarian-Canadian society, its demography, social make-up, and its institutions. Finally, I will briefly compare the contributions that the members of each wave made to Canada as a whole. This analysis of the historical context of the coming of the refugees of 1956 will unfortunately be restricted in scope and breath by the limitations of space in a short study of this kind, as well as by the fact that some aspects of the Hungarian-Canadian experience have not been adequately explored to date.[4]

Political refugees vs. economic migrants, 1885–1956

The question whether or not or to what extent members of the pre-1956 streams of Hungarian immigrants to Canada were political refugees cannot be answered with a simple statement. The answer often depends on the definitions of these terms used by social scientists trying to classify newcomers into certain, often rather artificial, categories. It could be said that refugees are motivated by political considerations in their migration to another country, while economic migrants want to improve their material circumstances. But human motivations often defy simple categorization. When people make decisions about their future, they often have a variety of motives. Despite this, historians have been classifying immigrants into economic migrants and political refugees and this has certainly been the case in their treatment of the Hungarians who have come to Canada throughout modern times.

In this connection it might be asked: Who were the first Hungarian arrivals in Canada who have been deemed refugees by historians? This question is not easy to answer. Wars and revolutions in Hungary have been sending refugees to other parts of the world ever since the dawn of the modern age. In the age of the Ottoman wars of conquest, refugees from the affected parts of Hungary usually had the option of retreating to Northern or Western Hungary that was in Habsburg hands, or to Transylvania, which was nominally a part of the Ottoman Empire but usually enjoyed a large degree of autonomy. All this changed at the end of the seventeenth century when the Ottomans were driven from Hungary and the entire country came under Habsburg rule.

Habsburg hegemony resulted in periodic wars of independence in Hungary, each of which sent political refugees to many parts of Europe. The best known of these conflicts was the 1848–1849 War of Independence. Hungary's defeat by Austrian and Russian forces resulted in the scattering of thousands of the war's participants to all corners of the world, including Australia and even Oceania. It is interesting to note that only a handful of these refugees seem to have come to British North America. The most prominent of these was Márk Szalatnay, an early advocate of socialism and a lobbyist for workingmen's causes. In the late 1860s he showed up in Montreal and got involved in trade union activities. Later, he moved to Toronto where in 1869 he led a strike of workers employed in cigar factories. Szalatnay, however, was soon deported to the United States and ended up fighting for workers' causes there.[5]

Two other refugees of the 1848–1849 Hungarian War of Independence who played roles in Hungarian-Canadian history were Géza de Dőry and Paul Oscar Esterhazy. Both of them had gone to the United States in the 1850s, and they are best known in Canada as immigration agents who were the first to bring Hungarian settlers to the newly opened Canadian prairies in the mid-1880s. In fact, in 1885 de Dőry established the very first settlement of Hungarian pioneers in what for some time was known as Hun's Valley near Minnedosa, Manitoba.[6] Esterhazy never settled in Canada. Nevertheless he was more successful than de Dőry in establishing Hungarian "ethnic islands" on the prairies. The first of these came into being in what is now the Kaposvar Creek area of Saskatchewan. This colony had a slow and uncertain start, but by the turn of the century it had become a stable and growing community.[7]

De Dőry and Esterhazy were not the only refugees of the Hungarian War of Independence active in the Canadian West in the 1880s. There is a record of an interpreter who had helped the Magyar newcomers of 1886 in dealing with agents of the Canadian government. There can be little doubt that such a man must have been a Hungarian and probably a member of the exodus that had left Hungary in the wake of 1849. And, while we do not know the name of this man, we know that another Hungarian refugee of the war ended up in Fort Garry (today's Winnipeg). This man's name is known; he was Péter Nagy.[8]

Unlike de Dőry and Nagy, the vast majority of the Hungarian pioneer settlers who ended up in Western Canada during the last decades of the 19th century were economic migrants. Many of them were trans-migrants from the United States who were attracted by the prospect of returning to the land by getting a land-grant in Canada. Others were landless peasants who came directly from Hungary. Some of them intended to save some money here and then return with it to Hungary to buy land and become landed peasants. There was also a handful, mainly ministers of the faith, who felt that God and country had called them to serve their compatriots in their social and geographic isolation in Canada.

Those who came with the intention of returning had their plans postponed or dashed by World War I. Travel to and from Hungary was interrupted by the conflict. The war caused many changes in Hungary. Above all, it served to impoverish much of Hungarian society.[9] The post-war political turmoil culminated in a veritable civil war in the country in which first the Communists terrorized their opponents and then, after the collapse of the Republic of Councils, the latter, often referred to as "Whites," tormented the Communists and their real and alleged sympathizers. Communist rule was brief and not too many people left the country because of their rule of terror. The subsequent "White Terror" lasted longer and it drove tens of thousands of people, most of them associated with one or the other of the 1918–1919 revolutionary regimes, into exile. Some of them ended up in Canada and became spokesmen for leftist causes among Hungarian Canadians during the interwar years and even after. Probably the most noteworthy among them, and certainly the first Hungarian refugee intellectual to have come to Canada, was Ambrosius Czakó, theologian, educator, art lover, journalist, and political activist.[10]

The impoverishment of Hungary's population that started during the war proceeded further as a result of the post-war peace settlement. Known as the Treaty of Trianon, this peace was patterned on the Versailles Treaty that the Entente Powers had imposed on Germany. In fact, the vast majority of its clauses were the same or very similar. Hungary's armed forces, for example, were restricted to a tiny fraction of what they had been before 1914. But it was the treaty's territorial provisions that were the harshest. They deprived the old multi-ethnic Kingdom of Hungary 71.4 percent of her territory and 63.6 percent of her population, to the benefit of the country's neighbours, above all Rumania, which received a larger share of the kingdom's territory than was left to Hungary.[11]

Added to the territorial losses was the loss of resources and infrastructure. As a result of Hungary's dismemberment, the country lost 89 percent of its iron-production capacity, 84 percent of its forests, and 62 percent of its railway lines. Although Hungary retained most of its food-producing capacity, it had to depend on greatly disrupted export markets to gain any income from exported produce that she needed to pay for the imports that became essential for the economy. Especially hard hit were Hungary's food producers. Poverty became worse in the country's already impoverished villages.[12]

A further disruptive impact of the Treaty of Trianon was the mass migrations that it caused. Even though living standards in Hungary had plummeted as a result of the war, the post-war revolutions, and the economic disruptions caused by the country's dismemberment, Trianon Hungary was still a more attractive place than its neighbour states for many Hungarians whose native communities the peace settlement had left in foreign-controlled lands. As a result, some 426,000 refugees left the successor states and settled in Hungary, often swelling the ranks of the unemployed. In the interwar years there would be a further out-migration of Hungarians from the successor states, this time mainly overseas, as many ordinary Magyars found life in these countries—and, especially, service in their armed forces—unpleasant and readily exchanged it for the relative economic and political security of a country such as Canada.[13]

The immigration of Hungarians to Canada resumed in 1924 when the country's gates were re-opened to newcomers from Central and Eastern Europe. People were still leaving Hungary for the same reasons their predecessors left before 1914: poverty, rural overpopulation, uneven economic development—but all these had been exacerbated by the economic consequences of the war, revolutions and the peace settlement. Still, immigration historians usually describe the newcomers from post-Trianon Hungary as economic migrants.[14] The same can be said, with some reservations, of newcomers from Hungary's neighbours. Only perhaps those among the new arrivals who had fled from the successor states to Hungary for predominantly political reasons and then immigrated to Canada might be called outright political refugees. But they were few in number.[15]

Canada's gates to immigrants closed during the early 1930s when it became evident that the economic downturn that started in 1929 (and in some parts of the country even earlier) was not a temporary recession but a full-blown depression. From that time to almost the end of the 1940s migration from Hungary was reduced to a trickle, in some years not even that.[16]

At the end of the 1940s the next wave of Hungarian immigrants to Canada began, the so-called displaced persons, or DPs. These people, much more so than the members of the previous wave, can be categorized as political refugees. Most of them fled Hungary as the Red Army began its occupation of that country in the late summer of 1944. They were joined by Hungarian citizens who had been removed from Hungary that year and the early part of the next. They were true refugees as their abandonment of their homeland was brought about by political and military events. In fact, the majority of these people had probably never entertained the idea of emigration until the events associated with the war forced them to do so, events such as the occupation of the country first by Nazi Germany in the early spring of 1944 and then by Soviet Russia staring five months later. Nevertheless, it is possible to consider many members of this group as economic migrants, as well, in particular those who immigrated to countries other than Canada right after the war and for mainly economic reasons sought admission to this country when it became evident to them that their first choice had been ill advised.[17]

Around 1950 another group of Hungarian refugees began joining this wave. The members of this stream were people who fled post-war Hungary especially at the start of the country's "socialist transformation" under the Communist Party that was increasingly controlling all aspects of life in the country. Most of these people were political refugees although they had an economic motive, as well: by the early 1950s, the standard of living in Hungary had started a downward spiral due to the Communists' over-concentration on heavy industry and other forms of mismanagement of the economy.

As the decade progressed, the exodus from Hungary declined to a trickle after the country's borders, especially with non-Communist Austria, were sealed with barbed-wire fences surrounded with mine-fields. Crossing to the other side of the Iron Curtain became nearly impossible, and those who were caught trying to escape often paid for their act with long prison terms or their lives. It was under these circumstances that 1956 arrived in Hungary.

Interestingly, the first two-thirds of that year had brought some relaxation of Communist rule. Most important, from the point of view of those who late in the year wanted to escape from Hungary, was the continued dismantling of the most inhuman aspects of border with Austria (the mine-fields, etc.). In internal politics the removal of the Stalinist dictator Mátyás Rákosi from power, and the re-burial of Communist leader László Rajk, a victim of earlier purges, indicated to the people of Hungary the process of de-Stalinization would continue not only in other members of the Soviet bloc but also in their country. It was under these circumstances that the crisis of October broke out. Unlike in Poland, where a similar crisis was resolved peacefully, in Hungary it resulted in an armed uprising that lead to the total collapse of Communist authority. In the end Soviet leaders, after some indecision, decided to crush the revolution and restore Communist rule under a puppet-government lead by János Kádár. Next, the Kádár regime embarked on a program of intimidation and retribution.

The return of Soviet forces to the streets of Budapest and other cities and the start of the persecution of the revolution's participants and sympathizers was not lost on Hungary's population. A veritable exodus started across the Austrian border and, when crossing there became dangerous, across the Yugoslav border. It should be mentioned that Yugoslavia, while a Communist country, was not part of the Soviet bloc and decided to give temporary refuge to people fleeing Hungary.

The great majority of the people who fled Hungary in the late fall of 1956 and during the winter were real political refugees. Thousands left because they had taken part in the demonstrations and fighting that had occurred in the country. They would have risked their freedom or even their lives had they stayed in Hungary. Some had not participated in the revolution yet they feared being swept up in the process of mass retaliation that seemed to be descending on the country soon after the revolution was crushed. They never found out if their fears were realistic. Many among these people, as well as others, no doubt loathed the limitations on personal freedoms in the totalitarian system that had prevailed in their country ever since the Communist takeover. Certain members of this group wanted to restart their lives in a country where they could freely practise their religion. Still others among the refugees might have been greatly dissatisfied with the low living standards that they experienced since the beginning of Hungary's socialist transformation. Many had been waiting for years for the opportunity to leave. Others had still other motives for fleeing. There were no doubt a few who wanted to see the world outside the Soviet camp, something that was impossible for the vast majority of the people who lived there. And, some refugees probably had no clear idea why they were fleeing their homeland. A few apparently left because their friends and neighbours were leaving. To some extent, heading for the Austrian border in late November and early December 1956 resembled mass hysteria in some cities and towns of Hungary. In other words, not all the fifty-sixers were true political refugees.[18]

The demographic characteristics of the four waves

When it comes to comparing the size of the five waves of Hungarian immigration to Canada, we have to admit that the "56 wave" has no rival. From December of 1956 to the end of the following year over 37,000 Hungarian refugees arrived in the country. Never before or since had so many Magyars come in a single year. However, the stream that came during the mid and late 1920s, is not very far behind. From 1924 to the end of the decade some 30,000 came.[19]

While in sheer magnitude the influx of 1956–1957 was unique, in some of its other demographic characteristics it was hardly such. In terms of age and sex distribution, the two earliest Hungarian migrations to Canada were composed mainly of young males. Wives and girlfriends were supposed to join the emigrants after they established themselves. In the late 1920s there was also a migration from Hungary of female domestics, but it did not involve large numbers. The movement of wives joining their husbands, or of "picture brides" coming to marry single Hungarian men living in Canada, was somewhat more important in augmenting the country's Hungarian population. It began in the late 1920s and continued on a much reduced scale even during the Great Depression.[20] The DPs who came from 1948 to 1952 were also mainly (57 percent) adult males, but there were more women (30 percent) and children among them than had been the case with the two earlier waves of Magyar immigrants.

In this respect the refugees of 1956 were not much different from their predecessors. Nearly half the refugees were under twenty-nine years of age; but, there were some middle-aged and older people among them, as well: 30 percent were over forty-five. As far as sex distribution was concerned, refugee men outnumbered women three to two. In effect, however, women were much more numerous in the new wave than they had been in the earlier streams.[21]

Social and religious characteristics

The two earliest waves of Hungarian immigration to Canada were made up predominantly of poor peasants or landless agricultural workers. Most of them had come from the economically rather backward north-eastern counties of Hungary. The wave of the DPs was very different in this respect. Many of its members were of middle- or even upper-class background. Such people were numerous among Hungary's bureaucratic and military elite that dominated the exodus that left Hungary at the end of World War II. The refugees resembled more the early immigrants than the displaced persons. Most of them hailed from Hungary's working and peasant classes. Where the refugees differed from the earliest two waves of Hungarian immigrants was in their educational attainments. Most of them had technical training. There were also many professionals among the refugees; and as we know, college and university students made up a large portion of the refugees. This fact made the 1956 refugee wave unique in Hungarian-Canadian history.[22]

Among the early agricultural immigrants, Roman Catholics predominated, as they did in the population of the Hungarian countryside. Among the very early immigrants, and to some extent among the newcomers of the 1920s, as well, there were many Catholics of the Greek rite, as well as Calvinists, since the counties they had come from, those in Eastern Hungary, had a larger portion of the members of these faiths than counties in Western Hungary. On the whole, however, Protestants were under-represented among early Hungarian immigrants, just as they were under-represented among Hungary's poor, especially the landless country folk. The same could be said about Jews. In the later waves, the proportion of Protestants and Jews was somewhat larger, as people of such religious backgrounds were more numerous among the middle and upper middle classes of Hungary, and especially among professionals. Jews were especially numerous among the refugees; in fact, they were quite over-represented among them.[23]

Circumstances of emigration from Hungary and settlement in Canada

Where the "56 refugees" differed from earlier (and later) arrivals was in the circumstances of their emigration. In fact, almost everything was different about the way the fifty-sixers came to and got started in Canada. The "old timers," those who came before World War II, had a chance to contemplate their immigration to Canada, usually for years. They had the opportunity to make up their minds and change them again and again, before they had to make a final decision to leave Hungary. The displaced persons had less time to decide to leave Hungary, but they usually had weeks or even months to do so. And, their decision to come to Canada was usually made in a refugee camp where they might have spent many months or even years. Most fifty-sixers, in contrast, had to make the decision to escape from Hungary in a few short days or even hours. Thanks to the attention the 1956 Hungarian exodus received internationally, they rarely had to spend much time in camps. The "average" Hungarian refugee might have still been in Hungary in early December 1956 and in a Canadian city two or three months later.[24]

The shortness of the emigration process solved some problems but caused others. In particular it prevented people from pondering the wisdom of leaving their homeland both in their own mind and through consulting with family and friends. The decision to leave was often made in a state of emotional turmoil or in an actual moment of panic. It is not surprising that some of the refugees regretted their decision. The conclusion that some refugees arrived at weeks or months after their departure, that they should not have left, especially that they should not have abandoned loved ones in the process, caused psychological crises for them that in turn increased their problems with adjustment to their new lives in the new homeland. Despite the risks involved, some of them returned to Hungary.[25]

The refugees also had more problems with expectations about what conditions awaited them in Canada than members of the previous waves of Hungarian immigrants. While some of the early agricultural "pioneers" lacked full awareness of the harshness of the climatic and other physical conditions on the prairies, most of them did have a fair amount of information on what to expect from friends and relatives already in Canada, or at least from immigration pamphlets. The same was true, probably to an even larger extent, for the newcomers of the 1920s. The displaced persons, too, had time to gain some knowledge of Canada from friends, as well as from media reports and literature they could acquire while they waited for admission in the refugee camps. In any case, after years of chafing in these camps, Canada did not appear to be a bad place to live.

In contrast to most earlier arrivals, many of the 1956 refugees were poorly informed about Canada and Canadian conditions. First of all the vast majority of them had not been gathering information on this country in the months and years before their departure from Hungary. Even if they had dreamed of leaving Hungary long before the autumn of 1956, they probably thought of going to the United States or to one or another of the Western European countries. For some of them coming to Canada was a last-minute choice, sometimes made on the news or rumour that other Western democracies were not taking any more refugees in those chaotic months of the late fall and early winter of 1956–1957. Whatever information they had, it was derived from the Communist media and it depicted Canada in negative terms. Since most Hungarians considered information derived from Communist sources as untrustworthy, they concluded that Canada must be a good place to live in—in fact, a virtual paradise. The same conclusion was suggested to Hungarians by Western broadcasts, such as the *Voice of America* and *Radio Free Europe*. These painted a rosy picture of life in the West.

Some conditions the refugees found in the Canada of the 1950s disappointed them. One of these was the lack of a comprehensive social safety net. Especially disturbing to many of them was the lack of job security. The state in Canada—that is municipal, provincial, and federal agencies—not only did not help individuals to get jobs but did little or nothing to make sure that jobs once found lasted, or that unemployment insurance was provided, and on a long-term basis, for those who were laid off. Other unpleasant surprises for some refugees included the discovery that medical and dental services were not free in Canada, that post-secondary education involved the payment of tuition fees, that jobs relevant to their future profession were not provided for students during the summers, and the list could go on. In socialist Hungary all this, and even state-paid vacations, was available to everyone favoured by the authorities.[26]

Another factor that helped to create unreasonable expectations in some refugees was the rousing welcome they got on arrival. Such an enthusiastic reception convinced them that starting a new life would be easy. When months later the enthusiasm waned and it became evident that staring a new life would be difficult and long-term public help would be limited, many refugees became even more disappointed than they had been soon after arrival. In summing up it might be said that for many fifty-sixers, adjustment to Canadian conditions, the overcoming of the culture-shock in a new country, was difficult partly because of the suddenness of the change in their lives, as well as the fact that they came not only to a different country but to a society with a very different socio-political order. Previous newcomers had left a capitalist system behind while the refugees exchanged a socialist order for a capitalist one.

Further difficulties were experienced by professional people, and there were more of these among the refugees than among any of the previous waves of Hungarian immigrants. This was the specific problem of different professional standards and practices in Hungary and Canada. The first complication surfaced soon after arrival. Professional people found that their qualifications were not accepted in Canada. Even if they overcame this obstacle, by going back to school and/or passing further exams, they discovered that professional practices were often very different in Canada and Hungary. Not surprisingly, Canadian employers did not want to hire people without "Canadian experience." Many professionals among the refugees had to start at a lower level of expertise and only after they gained Canadian experience in that manner could they really re-enter their professions and find meaningful employment. Adjustment to the new country was difficult, for different reasons, whether the refugee was a labourer or a highly skilled professional.[27]

Canadian attitudes toward Hungarian newcomers— the external dimension

Another great difference between the "refugee experience" and the experience of the previous waves of Hungarian newcomers was the manner they were received by the Canadian public at large. That reception had a lot to do with the image of

Hungary and Hungarians in Canada in the 20th century. And that image had been largely negative.

There was a time in North America when Hungary and the Magyars had a positive image. This was after the 1848–1849 War of Independence, when the Hungarians, and especially their gallant leader Louis (Lajos) Kossuth, were seen as people who had fought for freedom against a "despotic" monarchical regime headed by the Habsburgs aided by the even more despotic tsar of Russia. The refugees of that war were men of soldierly bearing often with a good knowledge of English and even some aristocratic charisma. Alas, for Hungarians, this image barely survived the 19th century. By the turn of the new century, the Hungarian image in the United States, but soon afterwards also in Canada, was of simple peasants who had come to the New World to take jobs from North Americans, often in the capacity of strike-breakers. Instead of dashing gentlemen-officers, the new immigrants came to be seen as illiterate and backward labourers, "bohunks" as they were often called, especially south of the border.[28]

Nativism and even xenophobia was rampant in the Canada of the times. Anti-foreigner sentiments were proclaimed even by politicians. Such attitudes got a boost in wartime as a result of anti-enemy propaganda. They began abating in Canada in the late 1940s, but it was not till decades later that multiculturalism became accepted and cultural diversity became tolerated. The fact that many of the post-World War II newcomers from Hungary were educated people also helped to improve their image.

The image of Hungarians was also linked to the image that Hungary enjoyed abroad. This image was quite favourable throughout the second half of the 19th century but began declining early during the twentieth. Rather than being seen as an upholder of freedoms the Hungary of the times began to be viewed as an "oppressor" of minorities. The transformation coincided with a revolution in European international relations manifested by the rise of an *entente* first between France and Russia and then between these powers and Britain.[29] Not surprisingly, Hungary's reputation further declined during World War I, and in the interwar years Hungary's image suffered even more. The war had been followed by revolutions in Hungary, first by moderate leftists and then by social democrats and communists. When the "old order" was restored, some two hundred thousand people who had participated in the revolutions or sympathized with their aims left Hungary. In emigration many of these people became vocal polemicists who denounced the interwar Hungarian regime in the international media, contributing to the growing negative image of Hungary.[30] Not surprisingly under these circumstances, Hungary's reputation reached its nadir during and immediately after World War II, when the country was viewed in the West, as well as the East, as "Hitler's last ally."[31]

The image of Hungary and Hungarians in the West, including Canada, underwent a most dramatic transformation in October of 1956. From former enemies, Hungarians became allies in the fight against Communism. That they had the courage to stand up against the vast "evil empire" of the Soviets made them objects of admiration. The fact that the West had not been able to help the freedom fighters in their struggle for liberty made the Western public, including Canada's, all the more eager to help the refugees. And, just about everyone was exposed to daily coverage of the situation. Television had just become the new mass media in Canada, and the images of Hungarians first fighting Soviet tanks then escaping across the Iron Curtain, were splashed in front of millions of people. Never before—or since—had the image of Hungarians been so positive. Not surprisingly the Canadian government, which was facing an election in 1957, felt that it had to appease the swelling of public sympathy and act in the most vigorous manner and allow a great number of Hungarians to come to Canada.[32]

Contributions to Hungarian-Canadian society and Canada

Under the discussion of the last dimension of the differences between the 1956 refugees and the previous Hungarian waves of immigrants to Canada we examine the contributions of each to Hungarian-Canadian society—as well as to Canada as a whole. In this connection the first observation must be that the first two waves made unique contributions in that they established a Hungarian presence in various parts of this country. The earliest newcomers created the first Hungarian colonies, whether on the prairies or in Canada's cities. Some of their institutions lasted for many decades, unlike many of the organizations of the DPs and the fifty-sixers that often began to disintegrate as soon as the first generation of immigrants began to grow old. The immigrants of the 1920s continued this process of establishing new settlements in other parts of Canada or reinforcing those that had been created by their predecessors.

The DPs who came in the wake of World War II did little to augment the immigrant organizations that had been created by the previous waves; they preferred to set up their own associations. The exception to this tendency may have been within the circles of the Hungarian ethnic churches, where Magyar immigrants of all vintages mingled. The reason for the avoidance of the old immigrants' institutions by the new arrivals was the different social backgrounds of the two groups. There were also ideological reasons for this divergence: many of the 1920s immigrants had come under the influence of Communist ideas while the newcomers were staunchly anti-Communist. The DPs were, by their very social standing, leaders, many of whom had experience in leadership positions. In this their group was different from the previous or subsequent waves of Hungarian newcomers to Canada. They, more so than the refugees of 1956, tended to provide Canada's Hungarian communities with activists, leaders, whose influence prevailed for decades.

The contributions of the 1956 refugees to Hungarian-Canadian society were also significant. Above all, they augmented the numerical strength of many Hungarian-Canadian communities, just when some of these were undergoing erosion because of the aging of their membership and the assimilation of the second and third generations. Their arrival in great numbers also resulted in the creation of Hungarian community life in parts of Canada where no such life had existed before, such as in Ottawa. All in all, the coming of some 38,000 refugees rejuvenated Hungarian-Canadian community life, created market for such products of the community as Hungarian-language newspapers and the Magyar-language theatre, and helped to fill the pews of many Hungarian ethnic churches.[33]

As far as contributions to Canada in general are concerned, there can be no doubt that the early settlers had done their share. As pioneer homesteaders, miners, and loggers, they worked hard to create farms out of prairie wilderness and to help build Canada's economy. They also assisted in populating Canada: some of these pioneer families have hundreds of descendants who can be found in all walks of Canadian life. Similar contributions were made by the members of the interwar immigration. What the DPs offered Canada was somewhat different. By bringing their skills and education, they helped to make Canada an advanced technological and cultural society. The refugees continued this tradition. Since there were many well-trained workers professionals and entrepreneurs among them, each of whom contributed to his or her specific or in some cases even unique field of expertise or enterprise. Hungarian newcomers to Canada tended to supply this country exactly with what manpower it needed at the time. As I put it some three decades ago, "In the age of frontier development, farmers, miners and navvies came [from Hungary]; in the industrial age, skilled workers and professional people...."[34]

*

In looking at the coming of the refugees in 1956–1957 in the context of the entire Hungarian-Canadian community's evolution, we can say that the 1956 refugee experience was both unique and not so unique when compared to those of the pervious waves of Hungarian immigration to Canada.

The Hungarians who arrived here in 1956–1957 certainly constituted the largest group of refugees from Hungary, but they were not the only refugees. Already after the 1848–1849 War of Independence a handful of Magyar expatriots had made their way here, although hardly any of them stayed for more than a brief period. The newcomers who followed them during the turn-of-the-century were mainly economic refugees or sojourners. Many of the latter stayed in Canada for reasons they didn't expect, especially the outbreak of World War I and the upheavals that the conflict created in their native land. Among the members of the mid- and late-1920s immigrant stream there were more people who could be deemed political refugees, especially those who came, directly or indirectly (i.e., through Hungary) from the territories that had been detached in the post-war peace settlement. The displaced persons who came after World War II were predominantly refugees, at least as much as the 1956ers.

As far as the demographics of the over one hundred years of large-scale Hungarian immigration are concerned, the fifty-sixers certainly constituted the largest group. But, in being composed mainly of young males, the group was only slightly different from the earlier waves, some of which were made up, almost exclusively, of young males. In social composition they also differed little from the first two waves of Hungarian immigration, and a lot from the post–World War II one that contained an unusual proportion of upper-middle and upper-class elements. And as far as religious composition was concerned, the refugees had a large contingent of people of Jewish background, something that hadn't been the case with the first three streams of Hungarian newcomers to Canada.

In the matter of adjustment to Canadian life, the refugees had done better in some respects and worse in others than the previous groups. Because of their technical and educational skills they often found it easier to learn the Canadian ways, but because they left Hungary in such a hurry, and often without having made a considered decision to leave, their adjustment to Canadian life was often problematic, at least for the first months or years of their stay here.

As we have seen in one respect, the refugee experience was different from that of the other immigrant streams' experiences. This was in the way the Canadian public looked upon newcomers from Hungary. The early immigrants were seen as strangers from a faraway land, with little education and few assets to recommend them for anything but menial work. The interwar immigrants were seen in similar light, in addition to being regarded as members of a nation that had been an enemy of Canada in the Great War. The post–World War II displaced persons also had to face the reality of being known as former enemies of the Western democracies. But the refugees were different. They were seen as heroes who had stood up to the mighty Soviet Union, allies in struggle against the "evil empire" of the Communists. No group of Hungarians had received as warm a welcome in Canada before or since. Such a reception, however, was a mixed blessing. It made initial settlement in Canada easier, but it created undue expectations in some, who felt abandoned once the initial welcome wore off.

As far as contributions to Canada are concerned, it is difficult to single out any of the four groups we have discussed for special mention. The members of all streams made valuable contributions, each in their own way. The fact that the last two groups had better education and training often resulted in more variegated and remarkable contributions by some of their members. However, when it comes to perseverance and hard labour, the early immigrants often also proved praiseworthy. In any case, it is somewhat difficult to differentiate the contributions, both to Canada and Hungarian-Canadian society, of the post–World War II wave and the 1956 refugees, since as time passed their collective efforts intertwined with each other—after all, less than a decade separated their arrival in Canada. In terms of their overall contribution to Canada there can be little doubt that, by bringing their customs and traditions to this country, by cherishing these after arrival, and by sharing them with Canadians at large, Hungarian immigrants helped to further Canada's cultural diversity and to enrich the quality of life in this country.[35]

As a final comment on the legacy of the refugees, it would be a mistake not to stress the great contribution they made to the development of Canada's Hungarian community. Both by their sheer numbers and by the vigour, determination, and social skills—as well as the knowledge of things Hungarian—they brought with them, they revitalized immigrant cultural life for an ethnic group that was by the middle of the century on the verge of assimilation and spiritual extinction in many parts of Canada. The decades that followed 1956–1957 were the "golden age" of Hungarian ethnic life in Canada, in which Magyar institutions flowered to the extent that they hadn't before 1956, or at the present time, when the refugees are growing old and have started to withdraw from immigrant community life. Historians looking at the evolution of Canada's Hungarian society a century from now will probably remember the refugees above all for that reason.

Notes

1. Gerald E. Dirks, "Canada and Immigration: International and Domestic Considerations in the Decade Preceding the 1956 Hungarian Exodus," in Robert H. Keyserlingk, ed., *Breaking Ground: The 1956 Hungarian Refugee Movement to Canada* (Toronto: York Lane Press, 1993), 3–11.

2. The first documented Hungarian visitor to North America was Stephen Parmenius of Buda. See David B. Quinn and N.M. Cheshire, eds. and trans., *The New Found Land of Stephen Parmenius: The Life and Writings of a Hungarian Poet Drowned on a Voyage from Newfoundland, 1583* (Toronto: University of Toronto Press, 1972); and, for a short entry on Parmenius, the *Dictionary of Canadian Biography*, Vol. 1 (Toronto: University of Toronto Press, 1966), 333–335. An important early-19th-century visitor was Alexander Bölöni Farkas. On the Canadian aspects of Farkas's tour of North America see my essay "The Critical Visitor: Alexander Bölöni Farkas' Tour of Canada in 1931," *Quarterly of Canadian Studies* 5, 3–4 (1982): 147–152. On the subject of Hungarian visitors see also J. Eugene Horvath, "Late Nineteenth Century Hungarian Tourists in America," *Hungarian Studies Review* 32, 1–2 (Spring–Fall 2005): 115–124.

3. On the earliest Hungarian settlements in the Canadian West (in the Esterhaz-Kaposvar and the Otthon-Kipling districts) see, above all, the works of Martin (Márton) L. Kovacs (1918–2000), especially his book *Peace and Strife: Some Facets of the History of an Early Prairie Community* (Kipling, Saskatchewan: Kipling District Historical Society, 1980). Kovacs also published short studies relating to the subject: "The Hungarian School Question," in M. L. Kovacs, ed., *Ethnic Canadians: Culture and Education* (Regina: Canadian Plains Research Centre, 1978), 333–358; "Searching for Land: The First Hungarian Influx into Canada," *Canadian-American Review of Hungarian Studies* 7, 1 (Spring 1980): 37–43; "From Industries to Farming," *Hungarian Studies Review* 8, 1 (Spring 1981): 45–60; as well as Chapter 3, "The Saskatchewan Era," in Dreisziger et al., *Struggle and Hope: The Hungarian-Canadian Experience* (Toronto: McClelland and Stewart, 1982). On some of the early settlements see also my article, "The Quest for Spiritual Fulfilment among Immigrants: The Rise of Organized Religious Life in Pioneer Hungarian-Canadian Communities, 1885-1939," *Magyar Egyháztörténeti Vázlatok: Essays in Church History in Hungary* 16, 3-4 (Fall–Winter 2004): 95–124.

4. For a book-length survey of the subject see my *Struggle and Hope* mentioned above. It is available also in French: *Lutte et Espoir : L'expérience des Canadiens hongrois* (Ottawa: 1983). A short survey is by Carmela Patrias, *The Hungarians*

in Canada (Ottawa: Canadian Historical Association, 1999). There is also my "Rose-gardens on Ice-floes: A Century of the Hungarian Diaspora in Canada," *Hungarian Journal of English and American Studies* 6, 2 (Fall 2000): 239–258; and "The Hungarians," in the *Encyclopedia of Canadian Ethnic Groups* (Toronto: University of Toronto Press, 1999), 660–674.

For monographs on the interwar wave of immigrants see John Kosa, *Land of Choice: Hungarians in Canada* (Toronto: University of Toronto Press, 1957) and Carmela Patrias, *Patriots and Proletarians: Politicizing Hungarian Immigrants in Interwar Canada* (Kingston and Montreal: McGill-Queen's University Press, 1994). A shorter study are by the same author is "Hungarian Immigration to Canada before the Second World War," in Susan M. Papp, ed., *Hungarians in Ontario* (Toronto: Multicultural History Society of Ontario, 1980), a special double issue of *Polyphony* 2, 2–3 (1979–80): 17–21. See also my own papers: "In Search of a Hungarian-Canadian Lobby: 1927–1951," *Canadian Ethnic Studies* 12, 3 (Fall 1980): 81–96; "Aspects of Hungarian Settlement in Central Canada, 1921–1931," in M. L. Kovacs, ed., *Hungarian-Canadian Perspectives: Selected Papers* (Ottawa: Hungarian Readers Service, 1980), 45–53; "Immigrant Lives and Lifestyles in Canada, 1924–1939," *Hungarian Studies Review* 8, 1 (Spring 1981): 61–83; "Immigration and Re-Migration: The Changing Urban-Rural Distribution of Hungarian Canadians, 1986–1986," in M. L. Kovacs and N. F. Dreisziger, eds., *The Tree of Life: Essays Honouring a Hungarian-Canadian Centenary* (Toronto: HSR, 1986); "The 'Justice for Hungary' Ocean Flight: The Trianon Syndrome in Immigrant Hungarian Society," in S. B. Várdy, ed., *Triumph in Adversity: Studies in Hungarian Civilization* (Boulder, CO: East European Monographs, 1988), 573–589; and, "Sub-ethnic Identities: Religion, Class, Ideology, etc. as Centrifugal Forces in Hungarian-Canadian Society," *Hungarian Studies* (Budapest) 7 (1992): 123–138.

On the 1956 refugees see Robert H. Keyserlingk, ed., *Breaking Ground: The 1956 Hungarian Refugee Movement to Canada* (Toronto: York Lane Press, 1993), as well as various studies by Peter I. Hidas and Greg Donaghy in this volume and elsewhere (for some of Hidas's works see also note 23 below). It should be added that the *Hungarian Studies Review* often features papers on Hungarian-Canadian subjects and has three issues devoted exclusively to them (Spring–Fall 1981, Fall 1985, and Fall 1986).

5. On Szalatnay see Stanley B. Ryerson's entry in the *Dictionary of Canadian Biography*, Vol. X (1871–1880) (Toronto: University of Toronto Press, 1972), 670–671.

6. De Dőry's ancestors were landed aristocrats in Sopron County in Western Hungary. Although a nobleman, he was not reluctant to try his hand at homesteading and settled with the group of Magyar and Slovak trans-migrants he brought from the Ohio Valley. When de Dőry died the Magyar settlers of Hun's Valley scattered to other places. By the time World War I ended, there were hardly any Hungarians among the region's settlers. Kovacs, "The Saskatchewan Era," in Dreisziger, ed., *Struggle and Hope*, 63.

7. Esterhazy claimed to be a member of one of Hungary's leading aristocratic families. His soldierly bearing and good command of English made him a successful immigration agent. In honour of his activities, the Canadian government named a community after him, Esterhazy, Saskatchewan, one that he had not helped to found. Of the many works that deal with his work and accomplishments the most important is Martin L. Kovacs, *Esterhazy and Early Hungarian Immigration to Canada* (Regina, SK: Canadian Plains Studies, 1974).

8. Jenő Ruzsa, *A kanadai magyarság története* [The History of Canada's Magyars] (Toronto: by the author, 1940), 76. Ruzsa heard about Péter Nagy during the late 1930s, when he was researching his book, from people who had known Nagy's son.

9. By the end of the war, the Kingdom of Hungary had lost 530,000 of its soldiers. In addition, 1.4 million were wounded and 833,000 were taken prisoners of war. Many of these POWs returned only years later, some of them with their health impaired, while tens of thousands never returned at all, having succumbed to malnutrition and disease in the POW camps. The severe losses of men and material on the fronts, the demands made by the war on Hungary's economy, the deteriorating relations between Hungarians and the country's Romanian and Slav minorities, and the incursions of the enemy into Hungarian territory, placed a heavy toll on Hungary's economy and society.

10. Czakó had a varied and interesting career. In order to get an education that he otherwise would not have been able to get as the child of poor parents, he joined the Cistercian Order at age fifteen. After a promising start—which saw him getting his doctorate and begin post-doctoral studies abroad—he broke with the church after his theological writings, well received by liberal clerics, were condemned by conservative church authorities. He next trained as a Calvinist minister. During the revolutionary regime of Count Mihály Károlyi, Czakó took a government position. He also translated into Hungarian theological works that were not appreciated in conservative circles. Worse still, in a journal he started Czakó criticized Hungary's establishment. Not surprisingly his periodical was suppressed and he left Hungary for Vienna with the aim of immigrating to the United States. His entry into the American Republic was denied but, in time, people who respected his work convinced the United Church of Canada to bring him to this country. He arrived in 1928, and soon he was appointed minister of the United Church's Hungarian congregation in Toronto. He saw himself not so much as a theologian but as a teacher who would educate his countrymen who had been denied a decent education in their native country. Helping in this task was the journal *Tárogató* that he launched in 1938 with the help of a subsidy from his church. In old age, Czakó returned to the Catholic Church and the teaching of art history. See my article "Social Progress and Ethnic Solidarity: Ambrosius Czakó's *Tárogató*," in *Tárogató: The Journal of the Hungarian Cultural Society of Vancouver* 27, 9 (September 2000): 55–56. (The two journals mentioned here are unrelated.)

11. The excuse for this territorial settlement was the principle of national self-determination, but in the application of this principle the rights of millions of Hungarians to self-determination were disregarded. Furthermore, Hungarian calls for plebiscites in the territories concerned were ignored, with one minor exception. The irony of the act of dismembering the multinational Kingdom of Hungary was underscored by the fact that the states that benefitted most from this process were themselves multinational, in some cases even more mixed ethnically than Hungary had been before 1918.

12. The peace settlement also disrupted Hungary's transportation and communication systems. As has been mentioned, most of Hungary's railway lines found themselves in detached territories. Even lines in the Hungarian heartland ended up with parts of them passing through foreign territory. The same happened to some roads and telegraph lines. Water transportation systems were also disrupted. Some navigable rivers that previously were entirely under Hungarian jurisdiction became either boundary waters or international waterways controlled by four different countries.

13. By far the most dangerous long-term consequence of the Trianon Treaty was the impact it had on the Hungarian national psyche. The post-1920 generations of Hungarians were preoccupied with the "tragedy of Trianon" and with schemes for reversing it. S. B. Vardy, "The Impact of Trianon upon Hungary and the Hungarian Mind: The Nature of Interwar Hungarian Irredentism," *Hungarian Studies Review* 10, 1–2 (1983): 21–42.

14. In particular by Professor Patrias in her *Patriots and Proletarians,* especially Chapter 1.

15. One immigrant who stands out among these is Baron József Csávossy. He went into ranching and his ranch was voted Canada's "best managed farm" in the late 1920s by an Alberta organization. Dreisziger, *Struggle and Hope,* 129.

16. There was some family reunification still going on in the 1930s, and during the war some refugees from Hungary made it to Canada from third countries, such as North Africa, the Caribbean, etc. Ibid., 144.

17. Dreisziger, *Struggle and Hope,* 195f.

18. Dreisziger, *Struggle and Hope,* 203–204. Only cursory studies exist about immigration from Hungary to Canada after 1956–1957. In the 1960s much of this movement was family reunification. Later migration was probably motivated as much by politics as by the much higher living standards in Canada. Still, many of the Hungarians who had come to Canada from Romania, Yugoslavia, Carpatho-Ukraine (then part of the USSR) and even Czechoslovakia came because of the unfavourable political situation of ethnic minorities in those lands, and as such can be considered political refugees.

19. Ibid., 100. The numbers are difficult to establish as Hungarians coming from the successor states were usually classified as Yugoslavs, Romanians, or

Czechoslovaks. The size of this wave is indicated not so much by immigration statistics but by the substantial increase of the people who declared themselves "Hungarian" in the 1941 census as compared to the 1921 one.

20. Ibid., 139–141. Only individuals with property or savings were allowed to bring out family members. One parish this writer knows about had a floating sum of money that was "lent" to individual parishioners for the purpose of demonstrating "savings" when they applied to bring a loved one to Canada.

21. Ibid., 207.

22. An entire school, the Sopron College of Forestry, was brought to Canada and was set up as an adjunct of the University of British Columbia's forestry program. The students were allowed to finish their studies in Hungarian, under their own professors. Laszlo Adamovich and Oscar Sziklai, *Foresters in Exile: The Sopron Forestry School in Canada* (Vancouver: University of British Columbia, 1970); and Kalman J. Roller, "Hungarian Foresters in Canada," in Sopron Alumni, ed., *Sopron Chronicle, 1919–1986*, (Toronto: Rákóczi Foundation, 1986), 1–177. Many mining engineering students from Sopron also came to Canada and some of them finished their studies at the University of Toronto, but unlike the foresters, they enrolled (after learning sufficient English) in the University of Toronto's regular program in mining engineering.

23. Dirks, *Canada's Refugee Policy*, 203. Previously only during the late 1930s and the early 1940s were Jews over-represented among Hungarians coming to Canada—but in those years Hungarian immigration to Canada was not much more than a trickle. They tended to come via third countries and they were probably among the Jews who had converted to Christianity at some point during the interwar or early war years. Statistics about them are probably impossible to find. For information on young Jewish refugees, see Peter I. Hidas, "*Menekült magyar egyetemisták Kanadában, 1956–1957*" (Hungarian refugee university students in Canada, 1956–1957) *Évkönyv* (Yearbook) III (Budapest: *Az 1956-os Magyar Forradalom Történetének Dokumentációs és Kutatóintézete*, 1994), 125–135; also published in English as "The Hungarian Refugee Student Movement of 1956–57 and Canada," *Canadian Ethnic Studies* 30, 1 (1998): 19–49.

24. The writer of these lines, with his parents and brother, had a few hours to decide whether to leave Hungary and spent only a few weeks in Austria before departing for Canada. Such rapid transfer, however, was the exception rather than the rule.

25. The major risk was imprisonment for leaving the country illegally. There was also the possibility that the new Communist regime in Hungary would make a public spectacle out of the returnees, and they would be expected to collaborate in a media campaign designed to prove that life in the West brings only disappointments to those who seek it. One person this writer knows returned, only to be profoundly disappointed about his decision to do so. He tried to escape to Austria again, was caught, and was sent to prison. In the end he did manage to come back to Canada, this time knowing that he wanted to stay for good.

26. Dreisziger, *Struggle and Hope*, 208–210 and note 56 on p. 218. For a more detailed discussion of the subject see E. K. Koranyi, A. Kerenyi and G. J. Sarwer-Foner, "On Adoptive Difficulties of Some Hungarian Immigrants: A Sociopsychiatric Study," *Medical Services Journal* 16, 6 (June 1958): 383–405.

27. Dreisziger, *Struggle and Hope*, 209f.

28. On attitudes toward the "new" Hungarian immigrants in the United States see especially Stephen Béla Várdy, "Image and Self-Image among Hungarian-Americans since the Mid-Nineteenth Century," *East European Quarterly* 35, 3 (September 2001): 309–342. For examples of the treatment of the subject in Canadian books see Ralph Connor's (Charles William Gordon) novel *The Foreigner*. In this book one Hungarian immigrant, Kalman, is portrayed favourably: he becomes a Protestant and marries a Scottish girl. But, we might ask, how many other Magyar newcomers could pay such a price for acceptance by Canadian society? Another Canadian author, Wellington Bridgman, in his book *Breaking Prairie Sod*, is even more stridently anti- "Austro-Hun." Both authors were Protestants ministers who had served as chaplains in World War I.

29. On the rise of anti-German and then anti-Austrian and, especially, anti-Hungarian sentiments in France see Dany Deschênes, "French Intellectuals and the Image of Austria-Hungary in France: Prelude to the Break-up of

Historic Hungary, 1918–20," *Hungarian Studies Review* 34, 1–2 (2006): 93–120 (in print); and on the rise of similar sentiments in Britain, see Géza Jeszenszky, *Az elvesztett presztízs: Magyarország megitélésének megváltozása Nagy-Britanniában (1894–1918)* [The lost prestige: The Transformation of Hungary's Image in Great Britain (1894–1918)] (Budapest: Magvető, 1986).

30. One study that traces the activities of some of these émigrés in North America is Thomas L. Sakmyster, "A Communist Newspaper for Hungarian-Americans: The Strange World of the *Új Eldore*," *Hungarian Studies Review* 32, 1–2 (2005): 41–70. The Canadian equivalent of the *Új Eldore*, the *Kanadai Magyar Munkás*, is examined in Patrias, *Patriots and Proletarians*. Among the non-Communist progressive émigrés in North America, the most prolific polemicist was Oscar Jaszi. On him see my own works, especially "A Hungarian Liberal in American Exile: The Life of Oscar Jaszi," *Hungarian Studies Review* 32, 1–2 (2005): 127–136; and "Oscar Jászi: Prophet and Danubian Federalist," *Hungarian Quarterly* 47, 1 (Spring 2006): 159–163 (a shorter version of the above).

31. This condemnation was not unanimous. In the United States, for example, John F. Montgomery, a former American minister to Budapest, exempted Hungary's regime of most of such charges. See his *Hungary, the Unwilling Satellite* (New York: The Devin-Adair Company, 1947; reprint edition by Morristown, NJ: Vista Books, 1993); and in the United Kingdom, C. A. Macartney, writing in the post-war period, did the same. See his *October Fifteenth: A History of Modern Hungary, 1929–1944* (Edinburgh: Edinburgh University Press, 1957; 2nd edition, 1961, 2 vols.), published in the United States as *A History of Hungary, 1929–1944* (New York: Praeger, 1957). While Montgomery can be dismissed as an inexperienced American diplomat (his background was in business administration), a similar charge can hardly be levelled against Macartney, a distinguished scholar and, at the end of his career, an Oxford academic. Hungary's association with Nazi Germany in the war can best be seen as a consequence of the harsh Treaty of Trianon of 1920. See my study "The Long Shadow of Trianon: Hungarian Alliance Policies during World War II," *Hungarian Studies* (Budapest) 17, 1 (2003): 33–55. Those who

call Hungary "Hitler's last ally" often dismiss the fact that Hungary tried to defect from the Axis alliance in October 1944 but failed. Two months earlier Romania had succeeded. The main difference between the two attempts was the fact that in August of 1944 there were only a handful of German divisions in Romania but in October there were over twenty of them in Hungary. The fact that Slovakia and Croatia were also Hitler's allies is usually ignored as these states were not recognized by the Allies.

32. Nándor Dreisziger, "The Biggest Welcome Ever: The Toronto Tories, the Ottawa Liberals, and the Admission of Hungarian Refugees to Canada in 1956," *Hungarian Studies Review* 35, 1–2 (2008): 41–83. There was some opposition to the admission of refugees. The most strident came from Hungarian-Canadian Communists. After 1957 the favourable image slowly began fading away. This story has not been told yet, but we know some of its components. One was the Peter Demeter trial and the negative publicity resulting from it. The trial revealed a Hungarian underworld in Canada. Another is probably such writing as Margaret Atwood's *Wilderness Tips,* whose Hungarian hero is depicted as a womanizer (which portrayal some Hungarians might take as a compliment). The main problem was that ninety years of anti-Hungarian propaganda could not be overcome by a few years of a favourable image generated in 1956.

33. Dreisziger, *Struggle and Hope*, 210–213; also, the same author's "The Refugee Experience in Canada and the Evolution of the Hungarian-Canadian Community," in Keyserlingk, ed., *Breaking Ground*, 76–82. On the subject of the Magyar-language theatre in Toronto from the late 1950s to the late 1970s, see Sándor Kertész, *Déryné Voltam Kanadában—Curtain at Eight* [I played Mrs. Déry in Canada...] (Toronto: by the author, 1981).

34. Dreisziger, *Struggle and Hope*, 229.

35. Ibid., 230.

10.

Arrival and Reception: Hungarian Refugees, 1956–1957

Peter Hidas

anada is a land of immigrants. Each year, decade after decade, since World
War II ended, hundreds of thousands of newcomers arrive to start a new
life, enriching themselves and their new country in the process. The government
of Canada is well organized to recruit, screen, transport, and receive large
numbers of immigrants. The situation was not different in the mid-1950s. In
1956, 165,000 immigrants landed in Canada and the following year the number
reached 282,000.[1] After some hesitation, Ottawa unconditionally threw open
the gates of Canada to the Hungarian refugees. For a good six months, between
December 1956 and June 1957, they were transported across the ocean at
government expense. But once the 1956 figure for unemployment jumped
from 3.2 percent to 6.5 percent in 1957, the Hungarian refugee movement was
restricted in order to protect wages and employment.

The refugees were airlifted or shipped to Canada from Europe. Ships and
airplanes carried British and other immigrants in addition to their Hungarian
passengers. The propeller aircrafts usually stopped on their way to Canada
in Reykjavik, Iceland, before landing in Gander, Newfoundland. Most ships
disembarked their passengers in Halifax, Nova Scotia.

In 1957 the Canadian government organized the largest airlift in Canadian
aviation history, the Air Bridge to Canada (ABC); 350 flights were allocated.
Hungarians travelled mainly by Maritime Central Airways between March 2
and May 31, 1957—45 flights in total.[2] Previously, from November to December

2, 1956, only 81 Hungarian refugees arrived to Toronto on commercial airlines. On December 3, Immigration sent Maritime Central Airways to Montreal with 68 Hungarian refugees on board. Every day from December 2 to the end of the month there were some arrivals (except on December 30). Sabena Airline made two trips to Dorval, bringing 71 refugees on December 10 and 52 on December 13. A small group of Hungarians who originally found refuge in Yugoslavia travelled to Vienna from where they were flown to Montreal on December 14 (65 persons), December 23 (68), and December 28 (147) on the non-pressurized aircrafts of Maritime Central Airways and Wheeler Airlines. Sponsored cases and a few refugees with enough money to pay for the passage form Europe came on these commercial lines. Altogether 526 Hungarian refugees arrived at either Toronto or Montreal in December. On December 4, Canadian Pacific Airlines flew 68 refugees to Vancouver from Vienna, following up with another group of 66 three days later.

The flights from Vienna were long. The mainly old warplanes used to bring the refugees to Canada were usually forced to stop in Iceland and even at the Azores Islands due to weather conditions or technical difficulties before landing in Gander, Newfoundland. The Canadian Red Cross hired Rose Vaszari, a Canadian-Hungarian welfare worker on loan form the Catholic Children's Aid in Toronto, to welcome the refugees at their first Canadian station. At a day-and-night reception centre, the Newfoundland branch of the Red Cross provided warm food, clean underclothing, mittens, sweaters, shoes, and other clothing items for the needy.[3]

Eva Balogh, one of the refugees, remembers,

> There were two stopovers. The first stop was Glasgow, Scotland, where we had a very elegant meal. The second stopover was Iceland on an American military base. Eventually we landed at the Montreal Airport, were put on a bus, without any information where we were going.[4]

The Department of Immigration secured space for the refugees on ocean liners. On December 9, 1956, the ship SS *Arosa Sun* brought the first large group of 257 Hungarians to Quebec. Four days later on the SS *Arosa Star*, 458 more arrived at Quebec City. From this time on the ships with refugees on board ported in Halifax, Nova Scotia, or St. John, New Brunswick. Halifax was the main gateway to Canada; Pier 21, Halifax, was the golden door through which half the Hungarian refugees sought a new life. On December 14 the *Empress of Britain* brought 361 Hungarians destined for Saskatchewan or Ontario. The *Invernia* (December 16) and the SS *New York* (December 19) went to Halifax with 122 and 338 refugees aboard respectively. The *Carinthia* also arrived at Halifax on December 20 with 106 refugees. On the same day the SS *Newfoundland* brought 36 Hungarians. On December 23 the *Empress of France* sailed to St. John carrying 128 refugees, while the SS *Columbia* transported 830 newcomers to Canada. In early January, the *Castel Bianco* brought 1,124 Hungarians to St. John, and the *Venezuela* disembarked 1,590 of them at Halifax.[5] The Italian line *Ascania* shipped 5,250 refugees from Southampton to Quebec and 3,450 from Le Havre also to Quebec between late April and early November 1957. Dutch vessels transported 2,100 Hungarians to Quebec and Halifax between March 11 and June 7, 1957.[6] A young refugee recalled,

> We arrived in Halifax on the afternoon of February fourth. The day was overcast and drizzly as we crowded the decks to get our first glimpse of Canada. We spent the night on the ship in harbour and in the morning we were led to a great hall for processing and from there onto our train for Winnipeg. Since most of the refugees knew little or nothing about Canada, had they been given a choice, would have wanted to go to Montreal or Toronto, the only two places they had heard about from former immigrants.[7]

From Canada's eastern harbours the railways moved the refugees inland. In early January three special trains rolled from Halifax westward carrying 1,050 refugees; 350 for Winnipeg, 200 for Edmonton, and 500 for Quebec City.[8] The Canadian National Railway carried the Hungarians along with other immigrants into the heartland of Canada. One refugee remembers,

> The train was fabulous. We had never seen anything like it. It sported luxurious plush seats, friendly black porters in crisp uniforms, shiny brass fittings, polished wood everywhere, and boxes of Kellogg's Corn Flakes in every nook and cranny. We had never seen corn flakes before and never had dry cereal for breakfast. After tasting the freebie, we decided it was the Canadian equivalent of potato chips and snacked on it dry during the whole trip.[9]

Most of the refugees were young, strong, and in good health. Only a few were ill. Nevertheless, the sick were admitted to Canada and looked after by the federal government. Of the 416 Hungarian refugees from the SS *Columbia* who were examined at Saint John, NB, on December 26, 1956, 13 were found to be suffering from tuberculosis. The *Arosa Sun* and the *Arosa Star* also shipped to Canada along with the healthy refugees 21 Hungarians who had TB.[10] Scarlet fever was detected at the West Lodge refugee centre in Toronto, but the three sick children were sent to the Riverdale Isolation Hospital. There was no epidemic, and the cases remained isolated.[11]

Hungarians not destined to be received by known sponsors, such as relatives, were accommodated on arrival at the Immigration Department reception centres at Halifax, Quebec, Montreal, Saint John, Winnipeg, Edmonton, Calgary, and Vancouver. Many were housed in the Labour Department hostel at St. Paul l'Hermite, near Montreal. In December 1956, Immigration allocated the Hungarian refugees to various provinces. Sponsored and unsponsored refugees were free to go wherever they wished to settle. The December "allocation" scheme includes that category, as well:

Ontario	2,227
Quebec	653
British Columbia	327
Manitoba	556
Alberta	34
Saskatchewan	310[12]

The Maritime provinces received their first allocation of Hungarian immigrants in January 1957. A group of 256 Hungarians were asked to stay in the Maritimes out of the 1,556 who arrived in Halifax on the SS *Venezuela* on January 4, 1957. From the *Venezuela*, Immigration assigned 75 refugees to Nova Scotia, 60 to Prince Edward Island, and 125 to New Brunswick.[13] But, from the middle of February the Department of Immigration no longer indicated on their schedules tentative allocations.

Earl E. McCarthy of the Immigration Branch told a group of scholars in 1993 at a gathering in Ottawa how he "outsmarted" the Hungarian refugees who were to travel to the Western provinces by preventing them from leaving

Windsor Station in Montreal with the aid of railway detectives and immigration guards who cordoned off the station. While flaunting his strange sense of humour, he admitted that as a rule 40 percent of the Hungarian passengers took off at Windsor Station and other transit points in order to go where they wanted and not where they were assigned.[14] One refugee remembers, "In Montreal, a few of our sponsored compatriots, as well as a few adventurous ones, decided to stay behind even though they were told that there would be no help in getting settled from the Immigration Department if they didn't continue to our assigned destination."[15]

The minister in charge of immigration, Jack Pickersgill, ordered the secret operation of dispersal himself. "We should not have any publicity we can avoid about Hungarians while en route as they are so apt to be diverted form their destination."[16] His department expected the Hungarians to go to assigned destinations and there accept whatever work was available to them, within their physical limitations, on their arrival in Canada in order to maintain themselves until they had learned one or other of the official languages and had become familiar with the methods of their own trade or profession. Pickersgill stated plainly that government assistance would be withdrawn unless the refugees cooperated with the authorities. However, he was ready to assist families with payment of rent and household services and provisions for groceries until the families began to have an income. Single men and women were to be assisted with accommodation and subsistence until their first pay cheques.[17]

Table 10.1: Hungarian Refugees Admitted to Canada[18] by Province of Intended Destination

Province	1/31/57	5/31/57	8/31/57	12/31/57	4/30/58
NL	4 (0.1%)	4 (-)	4 (-)	4 (-)	4 (-)
PE	0	11 (0.1%)	11 (0.l%)	11 (0.1%)	11 (0.1%)
NS	119 (1.2)	816 (2.8)	838 (2.4)	842 (2.4)	1,077 (3.0)
NB	167 (1.7)	589 (2.0)	646 (1.9)	652 (1.8)	835 (2.3)
QC	3,130 (32.7)	6,874 (23.9)	9,097 (26.4)	9,280 (26.3)	9,375 (26.1)
ON	3,248 (33.9)	9,325 (32.4)	11,518 (33.4)	11,860 (33.6)	11,923 (33.2)
MB	903 (9.4)	2,964 (10.3)	3,211 (9.3)	3,302 (9.4)	3,329 (9.3)
SK	121 (1.3)	832 (2.9)	944 (2.7)	972 (2.8)	980 (2.7)
AB	783 (7.8)	3,181 (11.1)	3,525 (10.2)	3,583 (10.2)	3,604 (10.1)
BC	1,137 (11.9)	4,165 (14.5)	4,705 (13.6)	4,746 (13.5)	4,774 (13.3)
YT & NT	-	-	2 (-)	2 (-)	2 (-)
Canada	9,572	28,761	34,501	35,254	35,914

The Canadian government promised the provinces to pay a sum of $3/day for each Hungarian refugee given board and lodging. It was hoped that a good number of the Hungarian refugees would be accommodated in private homes and would be supported by charitable organizations and public-spirited individuals. The federal government promised to reimburse the provinces if public response was limited. This offer also applied to the clothing needs of the newcomers. In addition, Ottawa provided the entire cost of transportation of the refugees from Europe to Canada and within Canada to their destinations and/ or places of employment. For the first year following their arrival, the refugees' hospitalization, medical treatment, and nursing assistance requirements were also to be financed by the federal government.[19]

On January 7 private subscriptions in Canada to the Red Cross Fund totaled $367,000. From the provincial governments of Alberta, Ontario, and Saskatchewan came the pitiful amounts of $7,000, $25,000 and $2,000 respectively. Popular feeling about the Hungarian tragedy ran higher in Western Europe, and relief assistance from private sources in many of the countries concerned has been on a larger scale. For example, in Sweden a voluntary subscription fund had reached $4,000,000 while a fund, established by the Lord

Mayor of London, passed £500,000 in early 1957.[20] In Canada, mainly public funds were used for the benefit of the refugees. The federal government financed the Hungarian Refugee Movement with most cooperation coming from the three largest provinces in the country and with the support of religious and other organizations, as well as individual volunteers.

The federal government was anxious to obtain the cooperation of all the provinces in the settling of the Hungarian refugees. A generous offer by Ontario was used to bring the other provinces aboard in order to spread the financial burden of the refugee movement. At the end of November 1956, a committee under chairmanship of Planning Minister W. M. Nickle was authorized by the Ontario government to do anything necessary to facilitate the arrival of Hungarians, as well as a proper reception for them.[21] In the Ontario Legislature, all parties declared their support of the provincial government's effort to give full cooperation to the federal immigration authorities in its refugee program.[22] The Ontario government quickly established reception centres and also provided medical and nursing facilities. At the end of November, Premier Leslie Frost announced that the Ontario government had taken over the Bernardo House at Jarvis and Isabella streets in Toronto. The gabled stone building was to be used as the main reception centre for Hungarian refugees.[23] Another centre was established on West Lodge Avenue. Here, a convent, the Home of the Good Shepherd, was purchased by the city of Toronto earlier in 1956 to be torn down and replaced by a new home for the aged. But when the first Hungarian refugees arrived, the city turned the home over to Hungarian relief agencies as a temporary shelter.[24]

On December 6, 1956, the first group of 67 Hungarian refugees was welcomed by officials at Jarvis Street. The Red Cross gave each immigrant a kit bag containing cigarettes, soap, a washcloth, and a razor. On the end of each bed at the centre was a towel. Officials said that it was hoped that the centre would only be a stopping-off place until the people were able to find more permanent accommodations. Offers of jobs for the men were already pouring in.[25] Soon the Red Cross took charge of the operation. At the West Lodge a religious centre was established where refugees could receive guidance from either Protestant, Roman Catholic, or Jewish counsellors. Medical teams were established at both centres while Red Cross staff members and volunteers directed recreational activities. The representative of the Toronto Welfare Council advised the refugees on loans and other financial matters. The Department of Citizenship and Immigration set up a placement office at the convent where the Hungarians were interviewed and advised about job possibilities. The Welfare Council established a committee for the housing of Hungarian refugees in Toronto.[26]

There was a general enthusiasm in the province for the anti-Communist freedom fighters and for the recent victims of Communism fleeing Hungary. The *Toronto Star* financed the trip from Australia to Canada of the Hungarian Olympic swimmer Valeria Gyenge to marry the recently arrived freedom fighter refugee Janos Garay.[27] The archdiocese of Ottawa asked Catholics from 130 parishes to offer hospitality to Hungarian refugees. The Catholic Episcopalian Committee set up a placement bureau for Hungarian Catholics to coordinate all offers of shelter for Hungarian refugees.[28] In Toronto, December 15, 1956, was declared Hungarian Day. The Salvation Army offered the entire collection, including the first day of the Christmas Cheer kettle collection for Hungarian relief.[29] Toronto high-school students collected Christmas toys for young refugees.[30] The Royal Ontario Museum hosted a special art exhibition in support of the refugees.[31] Cardinal McGuigan of Toronto invited the members of his archdiocese to open their hearts and their homes to the Hungarian refugees.[32] The Colgate-Palmolive Company sent 10,000 toothbrushes, 10,000 units of dental cream, and 10,000 bars of soap to the nine distribution points in Canada, including Toronto.[33]

Dignitaries also showed their support for the popular cause of the Hungarian refugees. Jack Pickersgill visited Jarvis Street and was photographed with the little refugee Iren Gyarfas.[34] The Right Reverand F. H. Wilkinson went to the West Lodge to welcome the newcomers.[35] By the end of January 1957, the Canadian Hungarian Relief Fund raised close to half a million dollars to be administered by the Canadian Red Cross Society.[36] The national executive committee of the Seventh Day Adventist Church in Canada established a special Hungarian Relief collection and pledged $2,500 for the relief.[37]

Most of the refugees coming to Ontario were young, well educated, and urban. According to Pickersgill, "What is striking about these people is that they are extraordinarily bright looking, and we have analyzed their occupations, skills and so on. They are way and above the average stream of immigrants that you get in ordinary times."[38] Only 6.28 percent of these Hungarians came from the countryside. Almost half of them were under the age of 25 and less than 0.01 per cent were aged 50 and over. Men outnumbered women two to one. Jewish refugees made up 11 percent of the total, about ten times the Jewish ratio in Hungary. Three hundred and seven (5 percent) university students and artists registered at the two Ontario reception centres.

Table 10.2: Hungarian Evacuees Received at Ontario Government–Red Cross Reception Centres (Part 1): West Lodge Avenue (W.L.) and 538 Jarvis Street (Jar.)[39]

Time		Total	Age							
			1–15		16–25		26–50		51+	
			male	female	male	female	male	female	male	female
Dec.'56	Jar.	383	7	3	127	39	166	29	8	5
	W.L.	1264	77	84	374	160	381	170	13	9
Jan.'57	Jar.	172	8	9	87	29	25	7	4	3
	W.L.	837	83	77	180	83	239	152	18	5
Feb.'57	Jar.	34	5	4	8	5	7	5	0	0
	W.L.	641	68	60	95	69	191	143	9	6
March '57	W.L.	586	69	60	98	69	164	109	11	6
Apr-57		1618	132	114	431	186	460	264	24	7
May-57		631	63	51	134	64	187	107	8	7
Jun-57		27	4	3	6	3	7	4	0	0
Jul-57		6	0	3	1	0	1	1	0	0

Table 10.3: *Hungarian Evacuees Received at Ontario Government–Red Cross Reception Centres (Part 2): West Lodge Avenue (W.L.) and 538 Jarvis Street (Jar.)*

Time		Total	Religion			Profession and occupation				
			Prot.	R.C.	Jewish	doctor	eng.	trades	mech.	farm lab.
Dec.'56	Jar.	383	80	259	44	28	35	96	142	72
	W.L.	1264	324	884	56	9	40	563	395	96
Jan.'57	Jar.	172	36	130	6	74	36	35	7	3
	W.L.	837	147	488	202	18	36	374	215	34
Feb.'57	Jar	34	10	24	0	5	8	10	2	0
	W.L.	641	131	312	198	6	28	354	105	20
March '57	W.L.	586	124	410	52	4	24	272	130	27
Apr-57		1618	393	1168	57	5	45	701	509	112
May-57		631	161	411	59	16	29	292	147	23
Jun-57		27	8	16	3	1	1	13	3	2
Jul-57		6	0	6	0	0	0	3	0	0
total	Jar.	589	126	413	50	107	79	141	151	75
	W.L.	5610	1288	3695	627	59	203	2572	1504	314
total	Jar.+W.L.	6199	1414	4108	677	166	282	2713	1655	389
%			22.81%	66.27%	10.92%	2.68%	4.55%	43.77%	26.70%	6.28%

Table 10.4: Hungarian Refugees: Overall Movements and Situation, October 1956–June 1960

Country	Arrivals										Departures			Situation on 30 June
	Direct from Hungary	Through Austria	Through Yugoslavia	Through France	Through Germany	Through Italy	Through Switzerland	Through United Kingdom	Through other or unspecified countries	Total	For Hungary	For other countries	Other movements[b]	
Countries of first asylum	199,540	-	410	**	-	110	70	-	530	200,660	11,180	178,780	-690	10,010
Austria	179,660[c]	-	410	**	-	110	70	-	530	180,780	8,400	162,170	-700	9,510
Yugoslavia	19,880	*	*	-	-	-	-	-	-	19,880	2,780	16,610	+10	500
Other European countries	1,060	76,800	9,220	90	170	200	110	140	1,110	88,900	6,140	20,070	+1,470	64,160
Belgium	180	3,470	2,390	80	40	20	20	10	50	6,260	470	830	+80	5,040
Denmark	-	1,180	200	-	-	-	**	**	**	1,390	70	380	+10	950
France	-	10,240	2,460	*	-	50	10	20	60	12,830	770	4,090	+140	8,110
Germany, Federal Republic of	-	14,320	1,150	**	**	70	60	60	120	15,780	310	1,310	+240	14,400
Italy	-	3,850	240	**	**	*	**	**	**	4,090	190	3,810	+30	120
Netherlands	120	3,570	90	10	20	**	10	**	20	3,860	610	550	+60	2,760
Norway	10	1,250	360	**	-	**	**	**	**	1,630	30	50	+20	1,570
Sweden	-	6,070	1,290	**	**	**	10	10	60	7,440	250	220	+110	7,080
Switzerland	***	12,140	750	**	100	30	*	30	770	13,820	1,620	2,260	+540	10,480
United Kingdom	760	20,710	290	**	**	30	10	**	20	21,820	1,820	6,570	+240	13,670
Overseas countries	-	81,670	6,930	3,960	1,150	3,000	1,670	6,420	2,700	107,470	820	550	+1,580	107,680
Argentina	-	910	100	20	10	10	10	60	220	1,320	-	-	+20	1,340
Australia	-	10,340	1,520	430	100	650	1,130	700	530	15,390	90	430	+220	15,090
Brazil	-	1,010	630	20	10	100	20	30	30	1,850	-	-	+20	1,870
Canada	-	25,620	1,770	3,070	700	1,540	120	5,250	1,120	39,190	130	**	+590	39,650
Israel	-	1,900	170	30	**	10	20	10	10	2,140	-	30	+40	2,150
New Zealand	-	1,030	80	10	10	10	**	**	30	1,210	-	-	+10	1,220
Union of South Africa	-	1,330	**	10	**	10	10	10	10	1,380	-	-	+20	1,400
U.S.A.	-	38,820	2,600	370	310	590	340	340	740	44,110	600	90	+650	44,070
Venezuela	-	710	70	**	10	40	20	20	10	880	-	-	+10	890
Other & unspec. countries[a]	-	3,690	50	30	10	500	420	30	270	5,000	80	2,070	+40	2,890
Grand total	200,600	162,160	16,610	4,090	1,310	3,810	2,260	6,570	4,620	402,030	18,220	201,470	+2,400	184,740

Notes to Table 10.4

(a) Including i.a. Iceland, Ireland, Luxembuourg, Chile, Colombia, Costa Rica, Dominican Republic, Federation of Rhodesia and Nyasaland, Turkey, and Uruguay

(b) Naturalization in Austria and natural increase in all other countries, See also footnote (c)

(c) Including natural increase in Austria

Source: Report of the Statistical Office of the United Nations High Commissioner for Refugees, National Archives, Canada, RG 25, 86-87/336, Volume 160, File 5475-EA-4-40

The Royal General Agency of Toronto appealed to the employees of the provincial capital to secure work for the newly arrived Hungarians. The Hungarians of the small Ontario community of New Lovell invited fifty Hungarian refugee families to come to their town.[40] The German Harmonie Club of the province offered to assist the refugees to find jobs.[41] Windsor, Ontario, received its share of refugees on December 6. Maritime Central Airways/TCA moved 128 Hungarians to the city.

Canadian-Hungarians were most excited about welcoming the refugees. Quickly, however, jealousies and suspicions emerged. "The newcomers were reminded how difficult it had been for their predecessors in Canada: how the pre-World War II immigrants had to work in menial jobs for years, and how the post war group had to confront strong anti-Hungarian prejudices."[42]

Meanwhile, the refugees themselves were energetically looking for jobs. Of the December group, everyone from Jarvis Street found new homes and work, as did all but 82 from the West Lodge. In January, the pattern was the same; all left Jarvis and only 53 returned to West Lodge because they were unable as yet to support themselves. By August all but 389 of the 5,610 West Lodge refugees were self-sufficient. The Hungarians moved out of the centers very quickly after their arrival. About half of the refugees remained in Toronto; 116 left for Cornwall, 132 for London, 114 for Hamilton, 134 for Sudbury, and the rest for other towns in Ontario, except for the 114 who went to other provinces.

Despite the seemingly successful transition the refugees were experiencing there was some opposition to the Hungarian refugee movement. On December 6, 1956, at a labour union meeting in Windsor, several speakers suggested the government was trying to bring cheap labour into the country.[43] The labour movement particularly worried about an oversupply of labour, while some simply opposed the "dilution" of British stock.

The Town Council of Little Current decided to ignore a request from the Northern Ontario Hungarian Relief Organization to help the Hungarian refugees. One of the town's councilors said, "They [the Hungarians] can't get along in their own country. They will just make trouble here." An editorial of the *Globe and Mail* branded the behaviour as "priggish xenophobia."[44] Later, the town's mayor reversed his original position in the hope of gaining federal aid. The Brampton town council also voted down a request to house Hungarian refugees. A United Steelworker spokesman gave expression to organized labour's fears of "indiscriminate dumping of immigrants unto the labor market."[45] In Ottawa, the president of the 100,000-member Canadian and Catholic Confederation of Labor declared that "some employers are dismissing Canadian workers and hiring Hungarian refugees at lower salaries." "However," Mr. Picard said, "the CCCL approves of government action to help refugees of the Hungarian revolution get to Canada."[46] A *Globe and Mail* editorial in February 1957 accused labour of speaking with two voices—the leaders supporting the Hungarian immigration movement while the membership remaining generally hostile.[47]

Early in December, the Ontario government consulted municipal officials throughout the province, asking for their cooperation in caring for the new arrivals. Their response was less than had been hoped. Recalling the seasonal unemployment of the past winters, the municipalities were fearful that the influx of refugees would place an unbearable strain upon their resources.[48] There was a whispering campaign aimed at the Hungarian refugees claiming that they would ruin the British stock of the province, as well as upset the balance of Protestants and Catholics.[49] To an accusation of Communist infiltration, Pickersgill responded by saying that a few bad eggs will not spoil the overall high quality of Hungarian refugees.[50] When W. Bev Lewis, a member of the Ontario Legislature, complained that more attention was being paid to Hungarian refugees than British immigrants, the *Globe and Mail* accused the legislator of being maudlin, a person who failed to grasp the fundamental difference between refugees and immigrants.[51] The *Globe* also attacked the Ontario Welfare Council for its criticism of the Federal Immigration Department's open-door policy to Hungarian refugees.[52]

By June of 1957, approximately 7,000 Hungarian refugees were received at Toronto reception centres and another 1,500 sponsored refugees passed through the city. About 5,000 settled in jobs in Toronto. An estimated 80 to 85 percent of these were employed at permanent work; the remaining 15 to 20 percent were in temporary jobs. In the summer of 1957, only 600 men, women, and children were still in the centres.[53]

With 140,000 other immigrants arriving to Canada in 1956 and an additional 100,000 expected in 1957, Canada reached its absorptive capacity. By July 1957 Ottawa imposed radical restrictions on Hungarian immigration, and, as a result, the operations of the Ontario Red Cross reception centres closed their doors after eight months of existence.

In the province of Quebec, just as in Ontario, the reception of the Hungarian refugees was a mixed one. When Prime Minister Louis St. Laurent invited Maurice L. Duplessis, the premier of Quebec, to provide assistance to the Hungarian refugees,[54] the premier of Quebec responded in the affirmative: "The Province of Quebec will be happy to do everything reasonably possible under the circumstances to relieve the sufferings and misery of the victims of the inhuman Russian persecution in Hungary."[55] Acting Minister of Citizenship and Immigration Walter E. Harris asked Duplessis for details. Harris wrote the premier that upon their arrival, the 6,000 Hungarians assigned to Quebec would be sheltered in the immigration reception centres. Two of those were in the province of Quebec—one in Quebec City and the other in Montreal—where they were to undergo medical examination and be interviewed concerning their occupations. They were also to be asked whether they had close relatives or friends in Canada where they could be accommodated. The federal government offered to search for jobs for all those who could work. Then Harris asked the premier, "Can you take care of the sick and provide all that you provide your citizens? Can you handle the overflow?"[56] In the provincial capital the Quebec

Assembly responded by passing Bill No. 38, an act to constitute the Provincial Relief Committee for Hungarian Refugees in Montreal in charge of the coordination and the carrying out of social, educational, and medical services intended for the relief of Hungarian refugees in the province. The assembly authorized cabinet to contribute up to $100,000 for the cause.[57]

Cardinal P. E. Léger of Montreal appealed to the Canadian public to welcome the Hungarian refugees. He then set up the Hungarian Refugees' Service in Montreal. The president of the group was General George Vanier, who set up two shelters in Montreal to look after the refugees.[58] Pickersgill was delighted at the prompt and timely action. He offered Quebec $3/day in support of the refugees in any provincial centre. He also offered to reimburse the province for medical and social assistance expenses for one year. Pickersgill hoped that volunteers would provide the clothing needed by the refugees, but if that was not sufficient he was willing to make up the deficit. He also offered to pay 50 percent of language course costs plus reimbursement for books.[59]

Looking for concrete provincial government measures Harris now asked Duplessis whether Quebec could take care of both the healthy and the sick and provide all benefits that the province provided its own citizens. Harris stated that 6,000 Hungarian refugees were expected in the near future.[60] Harris's telegram was not answered for a long time.[61] By the end of 1957 there was still no agreement between Quebec and Ottawa on financial co-responsibility for Hungarian refugees. However, major support did come from Catholic, Protestant, and Jewish organizations, as well as churches, private firms, and individuals, located mainly in greater Montreal.

There were three federal reception centres in Quebec. There were immigration halls in Quebec City and Montreal and a labour hostel in St. Paul L'Ermite outside of Montreal. There were also two shelters on St. Antoine Street; one for individuals and families and a second, a former convent run by Leger's organization for women and families. Eva Balogh remembers,

> We were taken to Montreal and placed in a former nunnery on St.
> Antoine Street. A Hungarian priest appeared on the scene and called on
> people to attend morning mass. Every morning three hours of French, in

the afternoon, taught by the same French-speaking man, three hours of English. Soon I was transferred to the Montreal YWCA.[62]

The Protestant churches in Montreal were anxious to aid the refugees and were not pleased that the Roman Catholic Church had taken the lead in the matter. The Reverand Mihály Fehér of the United Church of Canada complained, "If the refugees are handled by this organization, called Hungarian Refugee Service, we lose track of our Protestant Hungarians."[63] He suggested the setting up of a Protestant reception centre, but this idea was not supported by the leadership of the United Church of Canada. Instead, the Montreal Council of Churches, a Protestant organization, set up the Protestant Hungarian Refugee Service Association, which, with the help of [Protestant] Traveller's Aid, provided professional advice, guidance, and material aid to the refugees. The Home Mission of the United Church of Canada extended its charitable services to Hungarian refugees by appointing Edmund Seres as lay helper to the Hungarian United Church in Montreal.[64] They also hired a full-time social worker to assist the refugees. The minister and the social worker met the new arrivals at the Montreal airport and at the railway station, visited them at the various hostels, invited them to church services, and provided transportation to the church and back to the shelter. Within the church a clothing depot was set up, and articles were given free to the needy. Donated furniture was forwarded to some refugee families, who were also helped with their first few rent payments. English classes were organized and conducted throughout 1957. Of the refugees arriving in Montreal, every third was Protestant. But only 150 of these joined the Hungarian United Church of Montreal.[65]

During the winter of 1956–1957 there were jobs available in the Montreal region and therefore finding work for refugees was not a major problem. Neither was it difficult to place refugees with Montreal families.[66]

While most of the refugees arriving at the province of Quebec settled in the Montreal region and integrated into the English community, there were a number of refugees who moved to the Eastern Townships of the province and attempted to fit into the French milieu. The Roman Catholic Church was most active in the towns of Drummondville and Victoriaville. French courses were given, the refugees were encouraged to attend religious services, and an attempt was made to revive the refugees' knowledge of their faith. In the meantime, within three weeks of their arrival most of these refugees found work.[67]

A quarter of the Hungarian refugees, 9,375 to be exact, settled in the province of Quebec, mainly in the Montreal region. The newcomers were more attracted to the English community because it was urban, concentrated in the Montreal region, and had experience in absorbing immigrants. The Hungarian community there was English speaking. The negative experiences of those refugees who spent time in French camps on their way to Canada resulted in them not wishing to align themselves with the Quebec French community. It did not help that the Quebec government showed little interest in welcoming the Hungarians, mirroring the sentiment of the general population. The charitable work of the Catholic Church and the positive attitude of the University of Montreal could not significantly impact the English orientation of the Hungarian refugees who landed in Quebec.

In the westernmost province of Canada the reception of the Hungarians was equally complex. British Columbia, in need of workers, welcomed the Hungarian refugees. This province was most anxious to receive new Canadians. The Mining Association of BC (MABC) requested the federal agent district superintendent of immigration to provide a list of all Hungarian refugees who were in need of accommodations and employment. The MABC's representative, Professor Howard, "inferred that it would be almost a tragedy were British Columbia to be faced with a similar labour shortage in 1957 as existed in 1956—when such a worthwhile pool of labour existed in Vienna from which to draw." He concluded, "There appears to be a growing conviction in all management circles that British Columbia for some reason or another is being by-passed in the matter of immigrants by Dominion authority."[68]

On December 5, 1956, British Columbia established a special cabinet committee on the Hungarian refugee situation headed by Attorney General Robert W. Bonner. Bonner initially showed little enthusiasm for the cause. Dr. Bonner considered the reception and placement of Hungarian refugees in British Columbia a federal responsibility.[69] Pickersgill tried to convince Bonner of the benefits of accepting the Hungarians. He wrote to him, "From my observations I am convinced that the majority of the refugees are an excellent type of immigrants who should not have great difficulty in becoming established in this country and who, I am sure, will in future be an asset to the province in which they settle."[70] In contrast to Bonner, Dr. G. F. Amyot, provincial deputy minister of health, declared that should any of the refugees require hospital accommodation, either for tuberculosis or any others disease, the full facilities of his department would be available. Responsibility for medical examinations, X-rays, and vaccinations had already been undertaken. He told his federal colleagues that they would talk about cost later.[71] The provincial Department of Education was also more than eager to cooperate by providing adequate English classes.[72] The Immigration Branch soon began to operate reception centres in Abbotsford, Victoria, and Vancouver. Up to February 5, 1957, 1,639 out of 11,558 Hungarian refugees were destined for BC, and 1,000 more had been allocated to the province before the end of February.[73] In that month the government of British Columbia agreed to the proposal of the federal government, according to which Ottawa was to become responsible for expenses incurred on behalf of all Hungarian refugees for social assistance, hospitalization, medical treatment, and nursing assistance during the first year of their residence in Canada. This was identical to the agreement agreed to with Saskatchewan.[74] The two governments—provincial and federal—as well as business, academia, and the population at large were now in support of the refugee movement. Some misgivings, however, came from labour.

The Hungarians arrived during the peak season of unemployment in the Vancouver area. Most of the 25,000 unemployed, however, were wood workers and construction workers who were accustomed to seasonal layoffs. Some Vancouverites resented the newcomers. People commented as follows: "I think they're Communists"; "We're only adding to the leftist vote"; "We're doing too much for them, we should look after our own first"; and "I guess I won't be getting as many jobs now that these Hungarians are here." The Mine and Mill Workers' Union insisted that the Hungarians must have an adequate working knowledge of English before they could be allowed to work safely below ground. On the other hand, in Abbotsford 70 people volunteered to teach English. One woman was quite prepared to spend $4 of the $6/day she received to pay her taxi fares to and from the camp. The Hungarian community of about 5,000 in BC was doing its best to aid their arriving compatriots.[75]

On March 1, 1957, the *Globe and Mail* reported that the "Hungarians [were] Winning a New Life in B.C." Government officials and volunteer agencies estimated that one-third of the Hungarian refugees were already employed and entirely self-supported. The number would have been higher but for an abnormally severe winter and the unusually high level of unemployment in the forest industry. Enthusiasm for the freedom fighters turned to indifference and there were cases of exploitation; long hours and underpaying. Some unsuccessful attempts were made to work refugees at slave labour conditions—work for room and board and no pay— but immigration officials nipped these attempts in the bud. Most families, however, who took in Hungarian refugees, usually for three months, advised the new Canadians about labour and rental conditions in their area. English classes were well attended by the Hungarians.[76]

Despite strikes, lockouts, and generally unfavourable conditions in the economy of British Columbia, by May of 1958 only about 400 Hungarian single men and heads of families required welfare. Officials expected to have all employable single Hungarian refugees off the welfare roll within two weeks.[77] By then, the Canadian total for Hungarian refugees on welfare was 791 out of more than 36,000 arrivals.[78]

Over 13 percent of the Hungarian refugees, or 4,774 people, settled in British Columbia. The (Hungarian) Forestry School of the University of British Columbia was operating in Hungarian and in English. The rest of the refugees went to work and smoothly fitted into Canadian life.

The people of Canada's easternmost prairie province, Manitoba, looked sympathetically on the plight of the Hungarians fleeing their country, as many Manitobans themselves had before settling in Canada. On November 27, 1956, provincial officials contacted the Department of Immigration regarding inquiries they had received from persons in Manitoba about the possibility of adopting Hungarian refugee children or offering foster care for them. Since there were very few unaccompanied children among the refugees, help was offered to assist in the settlement and employment of the newly arrived.[79] There was a large immigration hall in Winnipeg for the reception of the Hungarians. Eva Kende remembers:

> On February 8th, we arrived in Winnipeg. On the platform, a contingent of middle-aged ladies, wearing silk dresses, straw hats, and fur jackets, waited to welcome us, to minister to us and help ease our way into becoming Canadian. Our ragtag group, emerging from the train, suppressed a collective giggle at their elegance that clashed with our own dilapidated clothes. Nevertheless, the intentions of the ladies soon proved to be very genuine, even if their understanding of our plight was somewhat deficient. The ladies spoke no Hungarian and we spoke no English. We communicated with hands and smiles.
>
> With their kind help and that of countless others, we started our long and often arduous trek into becoming Canadians.[80]

Another prairie province, Alberta, also provided a welcome for the Hungarian refugees. At the November 30 invitation of the prime minister of Canada, the premier of Alberta, in a telegram dated December 3, 1956, offered to accept the Hungarian refugees and to provide the same services as were provided to all immigrants through the various provincial departments, including Social Welfare and Public Health. Alberta offered to cooperate in every way possible with the federal officials to facilitate and to assist in the necessary care and rehabilitation of the Hungarian refugees. The federal Department of Veterans Affairs immediately turned over the convalescence wing of Colonel Belcher Hospital in Calgary to the Province of Alberta and invited the province to operate it as a reception centre.[81] Two reception centres, as well as an immigration hall in Edmonton and another one in Calgary, were already prepared to accept the Hungarians to Alberta.

Calgary, already the home of many European immigrants, welcomed the Hungarian revolution of 1956 and was ready to receive refugees once Canada began dispersing the new arrivals throughout the country. The Roman Catholic bishop of Calgary spearheaded the drive to settle the Hungarians. He asked his parishioners to open their homes to refugees and make material contributions for their welfare. A clothing depot was soon opened at the Hungarian Catholic Church. Five local Hungarian groups; the Hungarian Relief Fund, the

Hungarian-Canadian Club, the Hungarian Kossuth Club, and the Hungarian Presbyterian and Catholic churches joined together to amass clothing, money, and accommodation for the expected influx.[82] Approximately one out of every hundred Calgarians was Hungarian or of Hungarian origin before the refugees arrived.[83] Calgarians even enlisted, albeit with little success, the support of Mike Kadar of Elnora, Alberta, the brother of János Kádár, the new leader of Hungary.[84] The Dutch Reformed Church offered to house 100 persons, while the members of the Knights of Columbus prepared rooms in their club to accommodate some of the refugees. The local branch of the Canadian Citizenship Council attempted to secure wings in two hospitals as a stopover for refugees until they could be placed.[85] The mayor of Calgary set up a central steering committee and 30 representatives from 116 Calgary agencies and organizations pledged their support to coordinate efforts to receive and to absorb the refugees. This was done despite the fact that in Calgary and its vicinity, 4,500 persons were unemployed and the figure was expected to remain high throughout the cold weather and possibly the winter.[86]

The first few arrivals were sponsored relatives, but before mid-December most Hungarians bypassed Calgary. There were already charges of exploitation. Some Calgarians were offering domestic work to refugees at wages of $25 a month and accommodation.[87] A provincial civil servant was convinced that the Hungarians were potentially good maids and farm workers.[88] In fact, as reported in the *Calgary Herald*, a large proportion of the refugees were professional, skilled, or semi-skilled people.[89] Of the first 3,000 male refugees 44.5 percent were skilled workers compared with an average of 29 percent in the ordinary immigration movement between 1953 and 1955.[90]

Although there was no word on any group arrival after Christmas, Calgary managed to prepare a "package" accommodation (jobs [domestics, farm workers], housing, food, clothing) for a mere 45 Hungarian refugees,[91] who duly arrived two days before the end of the year. But S. R. Purdy of the National Employment Service sadly admitted that he had only "50 jobs right now for domestic employees."[92] Soon work was found for about half the job-seekers. They were employed as woodcutters, car washers, domestics, and farm workers. The employment situation was better in the provincial capital, Edmonton, and as a result many Hungarians stayed in the north. In Calgary many of those who were offered accommodation received vacant rooms but no beds or bedding.[93] Nevertheless, by February 1957, 385 refugees had arrived in Calgary, and all but 20 were placed in homes or at a local reception centre. An estimated 140 of the 260 job applicants had been placed, albeit many of them in casual or temporary positions.[94]

Lack of proper placement, problems with housing, and shifting from place to place embittered many of the newcomers in Calgary. When the authorities transferred a group of the newcomers from their dormitory at the Knights of Columbus to the hostel of the Salvation Army, the Hungarian refugees staged a small protest march in early March 1957.[95] The hostel, which the Hungarians described as a place "not fit for pigs," was partially filled with transients.[96] The refugees refused to stay and proceeded to the Canadian Pacific Railway station, where they endeavoured to bed down for the night but were ejected by the railway and the city police. From here they went to the Empire Café, where they remained until three in the morning, later going to the Palliser Hotel lobby. They were persuaded to leave there and all went to the Hungarian Club, where they remained until about five in the morning, when they were convinced to return to the Salvation Army quarters. The following afternoon they were dispatched to an immigration hall in Edmonton, hundreds of miles away.[97]

In the spring of 1957, Hungarian refugees were still coming coming. About 1,700 arrived at Calgary, of which 1,000 were working and living in their own homes by mid-June.[98] The majority of these refugees quickly and successfully integrated into the community. In July the reception centre was closed, and the few (46) remaining refugees were moved to a hotel at government expense.[99]

In another Alberta town, Lethbridge, the refugees had an easier time. The local Red Cross opened a small hostel housing about two dozen refugees. By mid-January, 16 Hungarians found employment, an additional 16 had been provided with housing, 9 had been transferred to Medicine Hat, 2 girls were in hospital, and only 4 persons remained in the hostel. Local officials soon asked for 25 more refugees, to fill the capacity of their hostel.[100] The town of Grande Prairie found refuge for a group of 25 Hungarians, who were transferred from Edmonton, but finding jobs for them was not easy.[101]

The third prairie province, Saskatchewan, accepted about one thousand Hungarian refugees. On December 20, 1956, Canada's minister of citizenship and immigration and the premier of the province of Saskatchewan announced an agreement to cooperate concerning the reception and care for Hungarian refugees. Saskatchewan promised to establish reception centres, to provide food and shelter for the refugees, and to pay for X-rays and vaccinations. Saskatchewan also promised to employ the necessary staff to operate these centres. The two levels of government agreed to share the expenses for citizenship and language classes. Ottawa planned to use this agreement as a model to reach agreements with other provinces. The governments of Manitoba, Alberta, and Newfoundland eventually signed identical cost-sharing formulas. The Northwest Territories and Yukon Territory were not invited to participate.[102]

Soon the premier of Saskatchewan, T.C. Douglas, offered to

1. receive, register, billet, clothe and feed Hungarian refugees sent by joint agreement, until suitable employment is arranged or until they have completed one year of residence in the Province;

2. arrange for medical, hospital and nursing services if required;

3. provide orientation and basic English instruction in reception centres;

4. check employment conditions offered to see that they meet provincial employment standards and also that suitable accommodation is available;

5. arrange the movement of the immigrants to employment locations, including issue of travel warrants.

The Saskatchewan government proceeded with this plan and did an exceptionally fine job of preparation, according to a local federal agent.[103]

However, the province did demand advance notice of the delivery of the refugees. At first Ottawa was not able or willing to do that and therefore halted the transport of the Hungarians to Saskatchewan until late in January 1957, when the province waived its request for an advance nominal roll.[104] In fact, Ottawa suspected that Saskatchewan was attempting to gain greater control of the Hungarian refugee movement as a first step toward controlling all immigration to Saskatchewan.[105] As a result of this argument between the province and the federal government, Saskatchewan received the lowest number of refugees of the prairie provinces.

The refugees were processed quickly once the notification dispute was settled. Premier T. C. Douglas personally welcomed the first group on the evening of their arrival after they had had a chance to clean up and rest in the comfortable hotel, which was turned into a reception centre. The premier told the refugees that they would find no gold on the streets, but if they were willing to work and be honest, they would find a better way of life in a province where everyone was equal, where people attended the church of their choice, and where they were members of any organization they wished. T. C. Douglas rejected organized labour's objections to the welcome of Hungarian refugees to Saskatchewan with this sarcastic statement: "If organized labor's attitude toward immigration is right, then we should have left the Prairies to the Indians."[106]

As the refugees arrived, the authorities immediately began to disperse them throughout the province. The first group of 70 Hungarians was sent from the Edmonton Hall refugee centre to Saskatoon, Prince Albert, Battleford, or Weyburn, and 50 more from Winnipeg to Regina.[107] At the Regina centre, the refugees were asked to elect spokesmen from their group and to form a refugee committee. Orientation courses were given for each group. They lasted about a week. Shortage of winter employment and some misguided efforts on behalf of the authorities delayed satisfactory placements. Refugees themselves resisted postings to alternative available work, such as employment on farms. In fact, there were very few among the Hungarians who possessed agricultural skills. When they were sent to farms, after a few days many of them "escaped" and returned to urban centres.[108] Toward the end of January, four groups of Hungarian refugees, numbering about six hundred, arrived in Saskatchewan. All but a few found jobs, even though this was the annual period of winter unemployment. About half of them were processed through Regina. By the end of January, 280 of them were already employed. Many with highly developed specialized skills quickly found lucrative jobs.

On May 7, in Winnipeg, the Regina hostel was closed and local welfare agencies and the local immigration officer became responsible for the remaining Hungarians. Some of the refugees stayed for a while in the Fort Qu'Appelle

Valley Centre, from where they could be dispatched to farms or to the Metropole Hotel in Regina.[109]

According to the federal government, 980 refugees arrived to Saskatchewan. Since the provincial Department of Social Welfare issued 1,154 health service cards to Hungarian refugees, this latter figure seems to be more reliable.[110]

Since the Maritime provinces contained none of the major urban centres of Canada, the Hungarian refugees showed little interest in settling in the sparsely populated easternmost parts of the country. But since many refugees landed first in these provinces and Immigration wanted to disperse the Hungarians throughout the country, the federal government asked for the cooperation of New Brunswick, Nova Scotia, Prince Edward Island, and Newfoundland in settling the new Canadians.

Ottawa invited New Brunswick to organize a reception centre for about one hundred persons. There were two federal reception centres in the province: one in St. John and another at the RCAF base in Moncton. The premier of the province showed little enthusiasm for any action. "I feel that we cannot make additional concessions to Hungarian refugees which are not already enjoyed by our own residents," wrote H. J. Fleming to J. Pickersgill.[111] At the time, New Brunswick had no hospitalization scheme. Municipalities provided care and hospitalization for people who resided within their jurisdiction for at least five years. Hungarian refugees in the province were left without medical coverage. Taking all of the above into consideration, Ottawa decided to reduce the flow of refugees to the province. On January 7, 1957, Laval Fortier, deputy minister of immigration, telephoned Fleming informing him that a provincial reception centre would not be needed at that time.[112] Most of the refugees moved on to the major urban centres of Canada.

Very few refugees settled in the Maritime provinces of Canada. One of the refugees on board an Eastern Maritime Airline plane was Jeno Galfi, with his family. The plane developed engine trouble en route to Canada and was forced to land in Keflavik, Iceland. There, at a US army base, the family experienced true American hospitality. After a brief stay, they arrived at a Moncton, NB, army base, where the mayor of Moncton welcomed them. "They looked after us very well for a couple of days while they processed our landing papers," reads the testimony of Mr. Galfi.[113] A total of 835 Hungarians, 2.3 percent of all the refugees, arrived to New Brunswick. Prince Edward Island took in a mere 11.

The government of Prince Edward Island agreed on December 6, 1956, to set up a refugee centre that was to provide medical and nursing facilities for Hungarian refugees. But by mid-February 1957, there was only one Hungarian refugee in Prince Edward Island, and by the end of the year eleven. Newfoundland was also shunned by the Hungarians. The premier of Newfoundland, on December 5, 1956, offered all medical and nursing facilities of Newfoundland to any Hungarian refugees who settled in the province. One did. Nova Scotia received about one thousand Hungarians. The Nova Scotia Technical College invited the Hungarian Forestry School to join it, but these refugees opted to settle in British Columbia. However, the main landing area, Halifax, proved most attractive to many Hungarians. The last Hungarians allowed to enter Canada as refugees were the ones that originally had escaped to Yugoslavia from Hungary. On January 20, 1958, the SS *Vulcania* arrived at Halifax with 499 Hungarians on board; they moved to other parts of Canada very quickly.[114]

There were a small number of Hungarian refugees who caused difficulties to Canadian government officials. Some refused to leave hostels or centres, others refused to accept employment, while a few refused to remain in hospital and accept treatment. Pickersgill's deputy Laval Fortier suggested, rather harshly, that such people should be invited to apply for repatriation or be deported at government expense. A change of government during the summer of 1957 prevented Fortier's proposals from being implemented.[115] By November 8, 1957, only 629 Hungarian refugees were in reception centres and 4,891 of them living outside these halls still received some federal support.[116] Not quite a year later, in June of 1958, 791 refugees received federal assistance out of the 36,541 arrivals.

As of July 1, 1958, 435 Hungarian refugees had been repatriated at the expense of Canada.[117] According to a Hungarian source, 30 refugees returned from Canada to Hungary in 1956, and between July 1 to December 31, 1957, 280 returned.[118] But, as the new (acting) minister of Immigration stated at the end of the Hungarian immigration movement, "many thousands of Hungarians are quietly settling into our Canadian way of life and already are making their contribution to our economy and culture."[119]

Notes

1. John W. P. Veugelers and Thomas R. Klassen, "Continuity and Change in Canada's Unemployment-Immigration Linkage (1946-1993)," *The Canadian Journal of Sociology* 19, 3 (Summer 1994): 367.
2. Acting Deputy Minister's Memorandum to The Minister re: Airlift for Immigrants–Statement, February 27, 1957, National Archives of Canada (NAC), RG 26, Volume 94, File 3-7-2 (ABC) part 1.
3. "Touch Frozen Soil in Gratitude, Gander Heaven to Refugees," *Globe and Mail,* December 6, 1956.
4. E-mail from Eva Balogh to Peter I. Hidas, July 17, 2005.
5. National Archives of Canada, Mg 32, Int. 2, B 34, File I-2-5545, pt.1.
6. NAC, RG 26, Volume 95, File 3-7-12.
7. Eva Kende, *The Tale of One Refugee,* manuscript. http://www.arjay.bc.ca/www0/canthology/eAnthology.htm#Refugee.
8. "Hungarian Arrival Tell of Fight, Flight," *Globe and Mail*, January 7, 1957.
9. Kende, *Tale of One Refugee.*
10. NAC, MG 32, Volume 56, File I-2-5545-C.
11. *Globe and Mail,* January 5, 1957.
12. Arrivals and allocation of Hungarian refugees as of January 7, 1957, NAC, MG 32, Int.2, B 34, I-2-5545, pt.1; Movement Order, December 6, 1956, NAC, RG 26, Box 36, File 3-37-4; Maritime Central Airways Trans-Atlantic Schedule, January 1957.
13. Arrivals and Allocation of Hungarian refugees as of January 7th 1957, NAC, MG 32, Int.2, B 34, I-2-5545, pt.1; Movement Order, December 6, 1956, NAC, RG 26, Box 36, File 3-37-4; Maritime Central Airways Trans-Atlantic Schedule, January, 1957.

14. Earl E. McCarthy, "Hungarian Refugee Movement: Transportation and Settlement in Canada," in Robert H. Keyserlingk, ed., *Breaking Ground: The 1956 Hungarian Refugee Movement to Canada* (Toronto: York Lanes Press, 1993), 61.

15. Kende, *Tale of One Refugee.*

16. December 21, 1956, NAC, RG 26, Volume 93, File 3-5-12.

17. March 6, 1957, J. W. Pickersgill to George Mayer, Chairman of the Citizen's Committee for Hungarian Refugees, Kingston, Ontario, NAC, RG 32, B 34, Volume 56, File I-2-5545 C.

18. The distribution in this figure is approximate. In several instances, the destination could not be established with accuracy (Statistics Section, Department of Citizenship and Immigration). Source: National Archives of Canada, Records of the Privy Council Office (RG 2), Box 862, file 555-54-565, parts 2-5.

19. RG 76, Interim 151, Box 910, File 580-10-654.

20. L. B. Pearson to Secretary of State for External Affairs to Minister of Finance [Ottawa], January 11, 1957, NAC, DEA/12476-40, Department of Foreign Affairs and International Trade, Canada and the World, Departmental History, Documents, Documents on Canadian External Relations, Volume #23 – 492, Chapter 3, Eastern Europe and the Soviet Union, part 1, Hungarian revolution, 492.

21. "Pickersgill Going to Vienna Soon," *Globe and Mail*, November 29, 1956.

22. "Ontario Plans to Pay Full Cost of Refugees until Cost of Refugees Settled," *Globe and Mail*, February 5, 1957.

23. "Use Barnardo House to Receive Refugees," *Globe and Mail*, November 30, 1956.

24. "Mob with Rope Attacks Refugee," *Globe and Mail*, December 20, 1956.

25. "Final Gap to Freedom Bridged for Refugees," *Globe and Mail*, December 7, 1956.

26. Kay Kritzwiser, "Hungarians in Canada: Sudden Freedom Mental Hazard," *Globe and Mail*, March 6, 1957.

27. *The Toronto Star*, December 4, 1956; *Globe and Mail*, December 21, 1956.

28. "Lack of Shipping Space May Retard Refugee Movement," *Globe and Mail*, December 5, 1956.

29. "Sally Ann Aiding Hungarians," *Globe and Mail*, December 10, 1956.

30. "Gift Awaits 67 Hungarians," *Toronto Star*, December 25, 1956.

31. "Museum Like Three-Ring Circus for Festival to Aid Students," *Globe and Mail*, January 9, 1957.

32. "Opening Homes to Refugees Urged," *Toronto Star*, December 23, 1956.

33. "Toothbrushes for Hungarians," *Globe and Mail*, December 11, 1956.

34. *Toronto Star*, December 24, 1956.

35. "Bishop Visits Newcomers," *Globe and Mail*, January 18, 1957.

36. "Raise $422,601 for Hungarians," *Globe and Mail*, January 24, 1957.

37. "Adventist Church to Aid Refugees," *Globe and Mail*, January 26, 1957.

38. CBC Television, *Citizen's Forum*, January 13, 1957, p. 14, NAC, MG 32, B34, Box 80, File I-2-9390.

39. RG 76, Box 910, File 580-10-651.

40. *Kanadai Magyarság*, November 24, 1956.

41. Ibid., December 1, 1956.

42. Nandor F. Dreisziger, "Sub-Ethnic Identities: Religion, Class, Ideology, Etc. As Centrifugal Forces in Hungarian-Canadian-Society," *Hungarian Studies*, 7/1–2 (1991–1992): 135.

43. "Labor Council View on Hungry Refugees Far from Unanimous," *Globe and Mail*, December 7, 1956.

44. "For Shame," *Globe and Mail*, December 18, 1956.

45. "Jobless Workers Concerned Lest Refugees Take Their Jobs," *Canadian Tribune*, December 24, 1956.

46. "Being Replaced by Refugees," *Globe and Mail*, January 25, 1957.

47. "Labor's Two Voices," *Globe and Mail*, February 1, 1957.

48. James Eayrs, *Canada in World Affairs, October 1955 to June 1957* (Toronto: Oxford University Press, 1959), 48.

49. "Bad Handling of Refugees Is Charged," *Globe and Mail*, January 23, 1957.

50. "Takes 3,382 Refugees, Ontario Top Provinces; Expect Some 'Bad Eggs,'" *Globe and Mail*, January 26, 1957.

51. "The Welcome Wagon; An Editorial in the Peterborough Examiner," *Globe and Mail*, April 1, 1957.

52. "Caught Short," *Globe and Mail*, June 7, 1957.

53. "Most Have Jobs, Few Hungarians Would Go Back," *Globe and Mail*, June 10, 1957.

54. Louis St. Laurent to Maurice L. Duplessis, Premier of Québec, November 30, 1957, telegram, NAC RG 76, Box 911, File 580-10-660; Provincial Co-Operation in the Reception & Welfare of Refugees; Quebec.

55. Maurice L. Duplessis to St. Laurent, December 5, 1956, NAC RG 76, Box 911, File 580-10-660; Provincial Co-Operation in the Reception & Welfare of Refugees; Quebec.

56. December 7, 1956, NAC RG 76, Box 911, File 580-10-660; Provincial Co-Operation in the Reception & Welfare of Refugees; Quebec.

57. Legislative Assembly of Quebec, First Session, Twenty-Fifth Legislature, 5 Elizabeth II, 1956-57. Québec: Rédempti Paradis, 1957.

58. MG 32, B 34, BOX 56, File I-2-5545C, Quebec, 3 January 1957, Hungarian Refugees' Service to Laval Fortier, Deputy Minister.

59. NAC RG 76, Box 911, File 580-10-660; Provincial Co-Operation in the Reception & Welfare of Refugees; Quebec, J.W. Pickersgill to Maurice Forget, January 11, 1957, Hungarian Refugees' Service, 117 St. Catherine St. West, Montreal.

60. Acting Minister of Citizenship and Immigration Walter E. Harris to M. L. Duplessis, December 7, 1956, NAC RG 76, Box 911, File 580-10-660; Provincial Co-Operation in the Reception & Welfare of Refugees; Quebec.

61. Bill No. 38, Legislative Assembly of Quebec, First Session, Twenty-Fifth Legislature, 5 Elizabeth II, 1956-57. Québec: Rédempti Paradis, 1957.

62. E-mail from Eva Balogh to Peter I. Hidas, July 17, 2005.

63. Mihaly Feher to Rev. M.C.Macdonald, December 11, 1956, MG 8, G 76, Volume 2.

64. *Globe and Mail*, March 9, 1957.

65. M. Feher [?], Hungarian Refugees in Canada and in Montreal, NAC, MG 8, G 70, Volume 2.

66. *La Patrie*, January 20, 1957.

67. NAC, MG 32, B34, Volume 56, File I-25S45C, Quebec.

68. P. W. Bird, District Superintendent, Vancouver, to Director of Immigration, December 20, 1956, NAC, RG 7, Vol.862, File 555-54-565 pt.1.

69. British Columbia Archives (BCA), GR 1724, reel B-7518, file 172-3, Immigration ct, General.

70. December 24, 1956, NAC, RG 76, Volume 910, file 580-10-653.

71 NAC, RG 76, wt 151m Box 910, File 580-10.

72. P.W. Bird, District Superintendent of Immigration to Director of Immigration, Ottawa, December 10, 1956, NAC, RG 76, Box 910, Int. 51, File 580-10-653.

73. Summary of Correspondence Exchanged between the Federal Government and the Province of British Columbia Regarding Care of Hungarian Refugees, NAC, RG 76, Volume 910, File 580-10-654.

74. Ibid.

75. Grant Deschman, Executive Secretary (of the B.C. Liberal Association) to H. E. Kidd, General Secretary, National Liberal Federation of Canada, January 21, 1957, NAC, MG 32, B34, Box 80, File I-2-9469.

76. Nigel Dunn, "Hungarians Winning a New Life in B.C.," *Globe and Mail*, March 1, 1957, page 6.

77. P.W. Bird, district Superintendent of Immigration to Director of Immigration, Ottawa, May 28, 1958, NAC, RG 76, Box 910, Int. 151, File 580-10-653.

78. Laval Fortier to the Minister, July 4, 1958, NAC, RG 76, Int. 151, Box 910, 580-10.

79. Summary of Correspondence Exchanged between the Federal Government and the Province of Manitoba Regarding Care of Hungarian Refugees, NAC, RG 76, Volume 910, File 580-10-654.

80. Kende, *Tale of One Refugee.*

81. NAC, RG 76, wt 151, Box 76, File 580-10.

82. "Many Groups Planning Hungarian Assistance," *Calgary Herald*, November 30 [?], 1956.

83. "Two Main Groups in Calgary," *Calgary Herald*, May 2, 1953.

84. "Mike to Try Again to Contact Premier," *Calgary Herald*, December 5, 1956. Another Kadar brother, George, at that time lived in Niagara Falls, Ontario.

85. "Calgary Plans For Refugees," *Calgary Herald*, December 6, 1956.

86. "Plans Agreed for Refugees," *Calgary Herald*, December 12, 1956; "Immigration Dep't to Take Hungarian Responsibility," *Calgary Herald*, December 11, 1956.

87. "Exploitation Charges Criticized," *Calgary Herald*, December 20, 1956.

88. "Will Endeavor to Place Hungarian Farm Refugees," *Calgary Herald*, December 22, 1956.

89. "Helping Hand Extended to Refugees in Canada," *Calgary Herald*, December 24, 1956.

90. "Enlightened Humanitarianism," *Calgary Herald*, December 29, 1956.

91. "'Package' Plan Ready For 45 Hungarians," *Calgary Herald*, December 27, 1956.

92. "Job Need Great for Hungarians," *Calgary Herald*, January 2, 1957.

93. "Equipment Needed for Refugees," *Calgary Herald*, January 24, 1957.

94. "Hungarians Require Comforts," *Calgary Herald*, February 5, 1957.

95. *Globe and Mail*, March 7, 1957.

96. "Hungarians Stage Protest," *Calgary Herald*, March 6, 1957.

97. March 11, 1957, NAC, RG 26, Volume 93, File 3-5-12.

98. "Hungarians Being Assimilated," *Calgary Herald*, June 15, 1957.

99. "1,900 Hungarian Refugees in City," *Calgary Herald*, July 17, 1957.

100. C. E. Smith to the Deputy Director, January 16, 1957, NAC, MG 32, B34, Box 56, File 1-2-5545C, 1956-1957, Hungarian Refugees, Alberta.

101. May 17, 1957, NAC, MG 32, B34, Volume 56, File I-2-5545C, Alberta.

102. Department of Citizenship and Immigration; Immigration Branch; Press Release, December 20, 1956, NAC, RG 76, Box 862, File 555-54-565. Pt.1.

103. Western District Superintendent, Winnipeg, Man., to Chief of Operations, Ottawa, January 3, 1957, NAC, RG 76, Vol.911, File 580-10-661: Provincial Co-Operation in the Reception & Welfare of Refugees. Saskatchewan.

104. Summary of Correspondence Exchanged between the Federal Government and the Province of Saskatchewan Regarding Care of Hungarian Refugees. NAC, RG 76, Volume 911, File 580-10-661. Movements to Saskatchewan of 300 refugees who landed on January 7, 1957, and 100 who landed on

February 11, 1957, were cancelled without notification to the Province of Saskatchewan.

105. Western District Superintendent, Winnipeg, to A/Chief of Operations, Ottawa, February 1, 1957, Ibid.

106. "Hungarians Finding a Place in the West," *Globe and Mail*, February 7, 1957.

107. Western District Superintendent, Winnipeg, to A/Chief of Operations, Ottawa, May 7, 1957, Ibid.

108. T. G. Bentley to J. W. Pickersgill, February 6, 1957, NAC, RG 32, B34, Volume 56, file I-2-5545, Saskatchewan.

109. Western District Superintendent, Winnipeg, to Director, Ottawa, May 9, 1957, Ibid.

110. H.L. Voisey, District Superintendent to Chief of Administration Division, Ottawa, October 24, 1958, NAC, RG 76, Volume 910, File 580-10-661.

111. February 14, 1957, NAC, RG 76, Volume 910, File 580-10-655.

112. NAC, RG 76, Volume 910, File 580-10-655.

113. Note to the author, July 20, 1991.

114. Acting Chief, Operations Division for Distribution to Ottawa, December 6, 1957, RG 26, Box 95, File 3-7-12, Air and Shipping arrangements for Hungarian refugees, 1956-1957, part 1.; Inter-District Placement Co-ordinator, J. B. Bissett to Acting Chief, Operations Division, Immigration Branch, January 27, 1958, NAC, RG 76, Volume 864, File 555-54-565-9, pt.2.

115. Fortier's Memorandum for the Minister, June 10, 1957, NAC, RG 26, Volume 95, File 3-7-13.

116. NAC, RG 76, Int 151, Box 910, File 580-10.

117. Ibid.

118. Seasick Ferenc, "*Adatok a magyar kivándorlás történetéhez, 1945–1989.*" [Addendum to the History of Emigration, 1945–1989] *Történelmi Szemle* 35, No. 3–4 (1993): 334.

119. E. D. Fulton, Ottawa, to Hebert W. Herridge, M.P., December 20, 1957, NAC, RG 26, Volume 120, File 3-25-19.

11.

"An Unselfish Interest?": Canada and the Hungarian Revolution, 1954–1957

Greg Donaghy

A s he left his office in the Woods Building on a grey November afternoon, soon after Soviet troops had re-entered the Hungarian capital of Budapest, Earl McCarthy, the new chief of movement and control for Canada's Department of Immigration, was hailed by his deputy minister, Colonel Laval Fortier. "How," the stately colonel demanded, "can we get these poor Hungarians, who are streaming out of their country under Russian oppression, to Canada as quickly as possible?" Though shaken by this sudden encounter with his distant chief, McCarthy, with a can-do attitude that promised to slash through red tape, burst out in reply, "Fly them over!"[1] These bold words amply illustrate the main motifs of the celebrated national myth that has grown up around Canada's response to the Hungarian crisis: it was swift, unorthodox, and generous. Freda Hawkins, one of the leading authorities on Canadian immigration, elegantly describes it as "a brief moment of splendour."[2]

There are grounds for a strong sense of self-satisfaction in the Canadian reaction to the Central European crisis of November 1956. Of the 200,000 or so refugees that spilled out of Hungary into Austria, Yugoslavia, and Italy in the wake of Moscow's decision to crush the Hungarian revolt, Canada welcomed almost 40,000—the largest contingent received by any country and a number disproportionate to Canada's size. The arrival of these migrants, as well as their lasting significance for Canada's immigration and refugee policy, has naturally dominated the discussion of the Canadian role during the revolution. The inaccessibility of government records for the period and the overriding importance to Canada of the Suez Crisis, which erupted simultaneously, has reinforced this tendency to focus on Canada as a haven for refugees.

Canada's response to the Hungarian crisis was more complex and its implications further reaching than this narrow perspective suggests. Though the refugees and their significance for Canadian immigration policy remain central in any retelling of this story, the documentary record suggests a less triumphant view of Ottawa's handling of the Hungarian exodus, with policy in the hands of an uncertain and hesitant government. Moreover, the Hungarian revolution had important implications for Canadian foreign policy. This paper explores Canada's nuanced diplomatic reaction to the crisis against the backdrop of Ottawa's evolving attitudes toward the Soviet Union after the death of its dictator, Joseph Stalin. The moderation in Canada's Soviet policy beginning in 1954 conditioned the country's response to the Soviet challenge in Hungary and defined Ottawa's long-term relations with the USSR and Eastern Europe, despite the dramatic events of November 1956.

The prospects for peace and security in Europe appeared better in January 1956 than they had since the end of World War II. For almost a decade, relations between the totalitarian Soviet Union and the American-led Western democracies, including Canada, had been gripped in the rigid and dangerous Cold War. Bilateral contact had virtually ceased by 1947, while multilateral exchanges at the new United Nations (UN) were largely reduced to bitter volleys of ill-tempered recriminations in an endless search for propaganda advantage. It was worse in Asia. There the two sides and their proxies traded bombs and bullets in a series of vicious post-colonial struggles that often flirted with atomic annihilation. Stalin's death in 1953, the Geneva Conference on the Korean War and Southeast Asia in the spring of 1954, and the July 1955 summit in Geneva, where Western leaders met with their Soviet counterparts for the first time since 1945, seemed to herald a period of reduced global tensions.

In Ottawa, Robert Ford, who had become head of the European division of the Department of External Affairs in April 1954, was responsible for making sense of these developments and charting Canadian policy toward Moscow and the Communist bloc. Ford was admirably equipped for the job. Educated at the universities of Western Ontario and Cornell, where he studied Russian history and language, he joined Canada's small foreign ministry in 1940. After serving in the Soviet Union in 1946–1947, he returned to Moscow in March 1951 as chargé d'affaires and head of the Canadian embassy. A reserved intellectual with a burgeoning national reputation as a poet, Ford was an ambitious and self-assured political analyst whose pronouncements on Soviet domestic and foreign policy trends were influential among Canadian policymakers by the mid-1950s.[3]

Ford sensed the currents of change early. "[W]e felt that a thaw was on the way," he wrote of the period after Stalin's death. "There were little signs: an advertisement at Lomonsov University for a lecture on the popular poet of the twenties, Evgenny Esenin...The Russian wives of some foreign correspondents... were suddenly given exit visas. The travel regulations for foreigners were slightly liberalized."[4]

During the summer of 1954, in a widely circulated memorandum that was eventually adopted as the departmental view, Ford set out to define Canada's policy toward the Soviet Union.[5] Like most of his colleagues in external affairs, he was a consummate realist whose understanding of Soviet diplomacy was rooted in his reading of Russian history. Warning against expecting dramatic change in Eastern Europe, the diplomat argued that Soviet policies of outward pressure on its western borders and large standing military forces reflected traditional Russian preoccupations and enjoyed widespread support among Stalin's successors. These new leaders, whom Ford characterized as "practical men," were less certain of Stalin's tactics and questioned his handling of Tito's independent-minded Yugoslavia, his misreading of American strength, and his disastrous decision to support the Communist assault on South Korea in June 1950. They were, the analyst concluded, anxious to abandon Stalin's aggressive posturing, which they feared had weakened the Soviet Union and reduced its chances for further expansion in Europe.

Moscow's new caution and determination to avoid war was reinforced by the development of the hydrogen bomb in 1953. Other factors were also at work. The lopsided expansion of the Soviet Union's post-war economy, where massive capital expenditures left unhappy consumers grasping for basic supplies, and the growing political and ethnic divisions within the union, underscored the country's basic weakness and made it unlikely that Moscow would resort to war. The post-war emergence of an established party "bourgeoisie," with a stake in the existing Soviet system, strengthened the country's basic conservative outlook. What Moscow wanted, Ford suggested, was a "workable division of the world more or less along the present lines."[6]

It was a wrenching departure for Canadian policy to accept the status quo in Central Europe as permanent. Ford described his conclusion as "a pessimistic counsel...[which] requires abandoning the peoples of Eastern Europe to their fate." He continued, "It is the only realistic policy unless we are prepared to fight to liberate the satellites or to destroy communism. If we are not going to do the latter we must accept the alternative, which is to try and live in a divided world." This policy promised important dividends. Canada and its Western allies might eventually reduce their heavy defence burdens while still deterring a more complacent Soviet Union from expanding. Meanwhile, Ford proposed that Canada increase its trade, scientific, and cultural links with the Soviet Union, insisting that even such small steps "may in time have some mellowing effect on the Soviet concept of living with their neighbours."[7]

Canadian engagement with the USSR increased sharply the following spring, when Soviet Foreign Minister V. M. Molotov surprised Canada's secretary of state for External Affairs, Lester Pearson, with an invitation to visit the USSR. As historian John English recounts, Pearson's encounter with the landscape and its people rekindled in him the admiration he had earlier felt for the Soviet effort in the battle against Hitler.[8] He delighted, too, in his encounter with the Soviet leader, Nikita Khrushchev, whom he found "as blunt and volatile as only a Ukrainian peasant, turned one of the most powerful political figures in the world, can be."[9] Despite a clash over the role of the North Atlantic Treaty Organization (NATO), Pearson assured his cabinet colleagues that the party secretary "seemed incapable of not saying what he actually believed and that he seemed perfectly frank in his statements that the Russians did not want war."[10] Indeed, the foreign minister was more worried by the Soviet leadership's self-imposed isolation and its dangerous ignorance of the outside world.

"Canada should meet Soviet overtures halfway," he told cabinet, "and indicate a willingness to settle problems as they arose." Consequently, in late 1955, Ottawa proceeded with plans for a stepped-up program of official exchanges and agreed to continue talks with Moscow on a bilateral trade agreement.

Ottawa's confidence in Moscow's intentions was reinforced when Khrushchev denounced Stalin during the 20th Communist Party Congress in February 1956. "There can be little doubt that the myth of Stalin is being completely demolished," exulted Pearson. "[N]ow the body of Stalin like that of Oliver Cromwell, is, post-mortem, likely to be hanged, drawn and quartered."[11] Improved relations with Moscow brought a quickening in Canada's contacts with the East European satellites, including Hungary. Ottawa's links with the government in Budapest, which had deeply angered Canadian Catholics by imprisoning Cardinal Josef Mindszenty in 1948, had been especially distant during the darkest days of the Cold War from 1947 to 1953. Repeated efforts by Hungary to revive the relationship following Stalin's death were resisted in the Department of External Affairs for a variety of reasons. In part, policymakers worried that a Hungarian mission might be used to spy on or intimidate the Hungarian-Canadian community. Moreover, officials were concerned about Budapest's human rights violations and the absence of any direct Canadian interest in Hungary.[12] This detached view began to change during the spring of 1956.

Pressure for a shift in Canadian policy came primarily from Ford, who had been tracking political and social unrest in Eastern Europe since the 20th Party Congress. Ford's hopes for the region were restrained, and he warned that Moscow would insist on maintaining some form of control over the satellites for the foreseeable future. Even so, he argued that Khrushchev's rapprochement with Tito, the denigration of Stalin, and the rehabilitation of nationalist leaders in Hungary, Poland, and Czechoslovakia were evidence of a movement toward "some liberalization" that "may offer some degree of Titoism."[13]

To exploit these developments, Ford urged the West to abandon its rhetorical commitment to the liberation of the satellites, which only alarmed Moscow and raised impossible expectations among the people of Eastern Europe. Instead, he believed that Canada and its allies should increase their contacts with the satellites, encouraging closer commercial, cultural, and scientific ties. "Our object," Ford told Pearson, "is to wean them away to some degree from extreme dependence on the Soviet Union and to encourage any developments which will ameliorate the lot of the satellite peoples."[14]

The new approach had an immediate impact on Canada's relations with Hungary, which was then seeking a trade agreement with Ottawa in exchange for a promise to purchase Canadian wheat. Cautiously welcoming this initiative, the under-secretary of state for external affairs, Jules Léger, warned Pearson that the deal would almost inevitably mean an exchange of diplomatic representatives and the opening of a Hungarian mission in Canada.[15] Despite the risk of domestic opposition, cabinet welcomed the proposal, and in mid-October 1956, a Hungarian trade delegation arrived in Ottawa. Within a matter of weeks, officials concluded a trade deal, arranged to sell Canadian wheat to Hungary on credit, and agreed that Budapest might open a trade office in Ottawa as a prelude to the establishment of full diplomatic relations.[16] Even as ministers considered the new trade deal, its future was cast in doubt by reports of growing unrest in Hungary.

Policymakers in Ottawa (and other Western capitals) were surprised when protesting students and workers in Budapest clashed with Soviet troops on the night of October 23, igniting a full-scale popular assault on the Communist regime. Dependent on newspapers and second-hand reports from Washington and London for its information, Prime Minister Louis St. Laurent's Liberal government was happy to leave Western policy-making to its great power allies, the United States, France, and Britain. On October 26, Pearson associated Canada with an Anglo-American request to have the Security Council discuss the Hungarian crisis and the question of foreign military intervention, a position he made public the following day.[17] Like its NATO allies, which had agreed in Paris to follow a similar policy, Canada hoped the restrained Security Council resolution, properly framed to attract the support of non-aligned India and Yugoslavia, would isolate, but not aggravate, the Soviet Union or provide pro-Soviet forces in Hungary with a rallying point. More important, Ottawa hoped the UN proceedings might halt the bloodshed in Hungary and allow

Hungarian Premier Imre Nagy room to negotiate an end to the crisis "on terms which would be better than mere repression of anti-Soviet rioters."[18]

Initially, at least, there appeared to be some evidence that this cautious strategy would meet both the government's domestic and foreign policy requirements. While Eastern European émigrés from across Ontario and Quebec, packed into four hundred "banner-decked" cars, petitioned the government to do more, most Canadian opinion-makers showed little real interest during the first days of the crisis. Léger assured Pearson that editorial comment on events in Hungary and Poland, which was also convulsed by anti-government riots, was largely factual and non-committal, with several papers echoing the *Ottawa Citizen's* view that the West could "best serve its ends" by letting the Poles and Hungarians "settle their own affairs without interference from outside."[19]

From the foreign policy perspective, the cautious Western strategy also seemed to be working. Pearson was "encouraged" by the pause in fighting that followed the withdrawal of Soviet troops from Budapest on October 29 and Moscow's declaration on October 30 that it was ready to re-examine its relations with Eastern Europe. Even as late as October 31, worried about forcing the Soviet Union onto the defensive and reducing Moscow's options unnecessarily, the minister argued that it might be wise to postpone any UN discussion of the crisis until the situation was clarified.[20] Indeed, a distraught Ford would later argue that the West might have used this pause to launch "a diplomatic initiative to guarantee Soviet security interests in Eastern Europe...[taking] advantage of the declared Soviet willingness to discuss the withdrawal of troops from Hungary."[21]

But with Hungary still in the balance, the UN was suddenly gripped by a second crisis. On October 29, Israel attacked Egypt, providing Anglo-French forces with a trumped-up excuse to seize the Suez Canal two days later. A Western initiative on Hungary was clearly impossible. The Suez Crisis, which outraged Washington and threatened the unity of the North Atlantic Alliance, absorbed Western attention. Pearson emerged as the vital intermediary in the effort to rescue France and Britain from their folly and restore harmonious relations between London and Washington, Canada's two closest allies.[22] As the world's focus on Hungary wavered in the first days of November, Soviet forces tightened their noose around Budapest, launching a bloody attack on the city on November 4. "The international situation is taking on an nightmare aspect," scribbled the diarist Charles Ritchie, Canada's ambassador to West Germany.[23]

The Soviet attack stunned Pearson, already exhausted by his efforts to broker a cease fire in Egypt. "So far as the brutal and bloody suppression of freedom in Hungary...is concerned," he wrote a friend, "there are no words of mine to express the horror and distress that we feel."[24] In his memoirs, the minister recalled being "tempted.... to have a UN Assembly Committee fly straight to Budapest with the UN flag and some men in UN uniforms."[25] Ever the realist, the foreign minister dismissed the idea as "an emotional reaction," aware that there was little Canada or the UN could do short of war to reverse the Soviet intervention. All Canada and the West could do, Léger told the prime minister, was to "bring it in upon the Russians that... they stand alone and isolated before world opinion."[26]

Like other Western leaders, Pearson and St. Laurent savaged the Soviet Union in public statements and rallied behind a series of UN resolutions condemning the Communist state. The government suspended upcoming cultural and scientific contacts with the USSR and declined to sign the recent trade deal with the Soviet-installed regime of János Kádár in Hungary. Canadian efforts to punish Moscow were influenced, however, by several considerations. Canadian diplomats continued to hope throughout the crisis that Moscow could be persuaded to treat the defeated Hungarians generously: they advised the prime minister that "we must not go so far that we nullify whatever chances may remain of moderating to some extent the severity of Soviet repression by a genuine humanitarian appeal."[27] Canadians were worried too about the danger of driving the Soviet Union back into "Stalinist isolation" and the possibility that the UN general assembly might pursue such "extreme" action as the expulsion of Hungary. As early as mid-December, Canada sought a reduced role in the UN debates on Hungary and began to cast around for a mechanism to move the discussion beyond futile condemnatory resolutions.[28]

The Suez Crisis introduced other factors that constrained Canadian diplomacy. This was especially true of Canada's approach to the non-aligned movement and its leader, India. Since the late 1940s, Canada had made a sustained effort to court India and its prime minister, Jawaharlal Nehru.[29] Escott Reid, Canada's high commissioner in New Delhi, long championed this policy and as the crises erupted in Egypt and Hungary, he was swept by a tide of emotions. "I was shaken by feelings of terror, pity and anger," he wrote, "pity for the people of Hungary, anger at the actions of the Soviet Union."[30] Nehru's haste to condemn the Anglo-French assault on Egypt and his reluctance to denounce the USSR distressed Reid. He urged Ottawa to mount a major initiative to win Nehru's support and truly isolate Moscow.

Reid's crusade was hampered by Pearson's struggle in New York to create a UN peacekeeping force for the Middle East, an initiative that depended on Indian and non-aligned goodwill. When he asked St. Laurent (whose relations with Nehru were warm) to urge the Indian prime minister to be more forthcoming, Reid received a "banal" reply that ignored the crisis in Hungary and stressed Indo-Canadian cooperation over Suez.[31] Pearson was equally unhelpful, warning the high commissioner that "we should not...press further at the risk of turning the Indians sour."[32] Though Pearson, and his main advisors in New York, John Holmes and R. A. MacKay, accepted the diplomatic trade-off philosophically, India's refusal to rally to the Hungarian cause left many Canadian officials feeling bitter and betrayed. "I think we must agree," concluded Ford, "that the action of the UN on Hungary was largely a failure.... The one lesson that might profitably have been learned by the Arab-Asian group concerning the nature of the Soviet system has been obstinately refused."[33]

Although Canadian diplomats subtly pulled their punches in the global effort to isolate Moscow, they were among the first in Ottawa to recognize the fleeing Hungarian refugees as a problem that Canada, with its empty spaces and booming post-war resource economy, could address effectively. Even before the final Soviet assault on Budapest, the Austrian government, still burdened by almost 190,000 displaced persons from World War II, had issued an urgent appeal for help, prompting Marcel Cadieux, head of the department's consular division, to observe that "if we were to move fast we might relieve a serious situation and admit useful people."[34]

This was not yet the view held by the Department of Citizenship and Immigration (DC&I) or its affable minister, Jack Pickersgill. A long-time and powerful aide to prime ministers W. L. Mackenzie King and St. Laurent, Pickersgill joined the cabinet as immigration minister in 1953. Though smart and armed with strong progressive credentials, his influence in Ottawa had waned with his promotion and he sometimes found it tough to bring his department into line.[35] Thus, despite the steady flow of immigrants into Canada since 1945, DC&I retained the restrictive ethos of an earlier generation that included the notorious F. C. Blair and A. L. Jolliffre. Tough officials saw themselves as Canada's "gate-keepers" rather than immigration facilitators,[36] a role encouraged by the provisions of the 1952 immigration act, "a poor and illiberal piece of legislation."[37] Moreover, the department viewed East European émigrés through a lens of cold war suspicion and thought they provided ideal cover for a legion of Soviet spies and agitators, who wished to slip into Canada; at best, immigrants from the satellites remained subject to coercive pressure from their home governments.[38]

Thus, after consulting only the prime minister, Pickersgill declined to move very dramatically to address the emerging refugee crisis in central Europe. As a gesture to the events unfolding in Budapest, the minister announced on November 6 that he had instructed the immigration office in Vienna to give priority to Hungarian applicants. They would also become eligible under the government's assisted passage scheme to borrow federal funds to pay for their transportation to Canada. However, he added, the normal immigration criteria remained in place and applicants were required to have a Canadian sponsor, as well as a suitable occupation. They also had to demonstrate that they were "not likely to become a public charge" and to prove that they did not pose a security threat.[39]

Few refugees met the standard. Over the next two weeks, while thousands of Hungarians poured into Austrian camps, only thirty applicants were approved for entry into Canada.[40] "All through November, when the rush of refugees went as high as eight thousand in a single day, Stage B [the security clearance process] remained in full operation in Vienna," recalled the veteran journalist, Blair Fraser. "Three harried policemen interviewed twenty-eight hundred people during the month....Needless to say, they didn't learn much about the political background of the people they were interviewing, many of whom had no papers of any sort. But they had no orders to stop, so they had to keep plodding on."[41]

It was clear that the government's initial response, which included a small grant of $200,000 to be divided between the Red Cross and the UN high commissioner for refugees, fell far short of expectations. The liberal *Winnipeg Free Press* endorsed the Conservative Party's demand for "unrestricted asylum," adding that "this is no time for petty, niggling thinking."[42] The *Globe and Mail* condemned the government's "cold, calculating attitude," while its crosstown rival, the *Toronto Telegram*, urged Ottawa to "quit the double talk and let the Hungarian refugees know that this country is prepared to do more than offer words of sympathy."[43] Pearson, too, was upset with Pickersgill's offer, which he warned would appear a "meagre one compared with...[the] unconditional quota offered by a number of other countries."[44] He urged the minister to waive the normal immigration regulations.

Pickersgill was unmoved. After a trip to Toronto to consult with East European immigrant groups, he reassured his cabinet colleagues in mid-November that the government was on the right track. He insisted that Canadians appreciated how far Ottawa had gone in giving Hungarian applicants priority and realized that the government was "interested and sympathetic." Defending his policy, he explained that there were "very few" applicants in Vienna who wanted to come to Canada, and he derided comparisons with American proposals to accept five thousand refugees, which "meant nothing" until passed into law. Finally, he reminded the frugal ministers, it was much cheaper to house unemployed refugees in low-cost Austria than scattered in expensive camps across Canada.[45]

Not everyone was convinced. Ford, handling the crisis in external affairs, was especially sceptical. He had his own source on Pickersgill's meetings in Toronto, Dr. Bill Stanbury, the respected head of the Canadian Red Cross. Stanbury, who worked closely with the department on a range of issues, warned Ford that the Hungarian-Canadian community remained "extremely dissatisfied" with government policy.[46] There were other signs of trouble, as well. Regular reports from New York on the assistance provided by Western countries underscored Canada's poor performance, and at least one Canadian diplomat complained of embarrassment when confronted by the probing questions of his NATO colleagues.[47] An aide-memoire from the Austrian government, increasingly besieged by refugees, begged for more help, noting that the acceptance of refugees on the basis of their "human and economic qualifications...would not constitute effective assistance."[48] The pointed diplomatic barbs were echoed, less politely, in the domestic press. "In its response to the Hungarian tragedy," the *Globe and Mail* sneered, "the Canadian government has deployed the warmth and sensitivity of a codfish."[49] Late that week, Pearson again pressed Pickersgill to amend his policy.

External affairs used the growing pressure for a more generous policy to secure cabinet's support for an additional relief contribution of $800,000.[50] Pickersgill, too, cast about for a new approach. He did so slowly and by stages. On November 23, the embattled minister admitted to his ministerial colleagues that DC&I's facilities could no longer handle the flood of applicants in Austria and that "red tape was nullifying the plans announced to help these refugees."[51] To ease the backlog, Pickersgill proposed to waive medical examinations for most refugees until they arrived in Canada. He also sought cabinet permission to charter commercial aircraft to fly the refugees to Canada, an expense the government hoped to recoup from the fleeing Hungarians.

Though cabinet approved these measures, Pickersgill refrained from immediately unveiling the amended policy. Instead, he summoned church and ethnic groups, as well as provincial and municipal representatives, to a one-day conference in Ottawa on November 27 to gauge domestic support for a large-scale refugee movement.[52] Reassured by the reaction and spooked by news that the Conservative government in Ontario was itself ready to bring over Hungarian refugees, the minister returned to cabinet for a more generous offer. As Canada was the only country making the refugees pay for their transportation, he proposed to take the unprecedented step of having DC&I pay for these costs. Cabinet agreed, sending Pickersgill himself to Europe to signal the government's new resolve.[53]

The more forthright policy, announced on November 28, and Pickersgill's high-profile trip to the refugee camps in Austria, sharply increased Canada's intake of refugees. By mid-December, according to one contemporary account, refugees were arriving in Toronto at a rate of 100 a day; by month's end, more than 4,000 Hungarians were scattered in homes and reception centres across Canada.[54] Despite the regular drop-off in arrivals over the winter, refugees travelled to Canada at comparable rates during the first six months of 1957. More than 31,000 Hungarians had arrived by the end of June 1957, while another 4,000 waited for transportation. By the time the program formally ended in September 1958, the total had climbed to 36,718 refugees.[55]

Even before the refugee flow had ceased, the implications of the Hungarian crisis for Canadian diplomacy and immigration policy were evident. This profound crisis reinforced the trend toward moderation in the approach of the Department of External Affairs to Khrushchev's Soviet Union and its East European allies. While some, like the ardent anti-Communist Cadieux, favoured a hard-line policy, most, despite Hungary, continued to support Ford's policy of constructive engagement. In this interpretation, the "[r]evolution in Eastern Europe and Soviet military intervention demonstrate[d] the failure of Russian policy"[58] and were "proof that [Canada's] policy of encouraging the trend towards liberalism...was the correct one."[59] The USSR's ongoing inability to find an appropriate balance between its investment and consumer needs remained the defining weakness of the Soviet regime, a failing made acute by the effort to maintain its control over Eastern Europe.[60] "Taking a broad view, then," wrote the under-secretary in the spring of 1957, "we doubt whether the thaw is really over....In spite of Hungary... internal pressures within the Soviet Bloc and within the USSR...will probably be sufficient to keep Moscow moving – slowly, carefully and pragmatically – but in the direction of more liberal attitudes."[61] The department's cautious moderation offset the more strident anti-Soviet inclinations of the Conservative prime minister, John G. Diefenbaker, who took office in June 1957 and ensured that Canadian policy—despite the occasional detour—remained temperate on most East–West questions during the next decade. Significantly, the Diefenbaker government renewed scientific and cultural contacts with the Soviet Union in the summer of 1957 and renegotiated the Canada–USSR trade agreement in 1959.

The tragic events of November 1956 had a more ambiguous impact on Canada's relations with Hungary. There was much more substance to the bilateral relationship after November 1956 since the revolution had rendered Hungary politically relevant and the refugee exodus had produced a dramatic increase in bilateral consular disputes as families divided by the crisis later tried to reunite. Consequently, in October 1957, Léger arranged for Canadian representatives in Vienna and Belgrade to pay regular unofficial visits to Hungary, quietly gathering intelligence on the Communist state and helping the British, who handled Ottawa's affairs in Budapest, deal with the more difficult consular cases.[62] Nevertheless Hungary, alone of all the East European states, remained excluded from the benefits of Canada's liberal policy of constructive engagement. This was virtually guaranteed by the large number of vocal Hungarian refugees in Canada and the many new grievances that followed futile attempts at family reunification. Indeed, Budapest's efforts to pursue normal relations were so firmly rebuffed by Canada throughout the late 1950s that one Hungarian interlocutor wondered why Ottawa "thought it necessary to be more purist than [the] major Western allies in [its] relations with Hungary."[63]

The crisis also had a lasting impact on Canadian immigration and refugee policy, notwithstanding Pickersgill's initial hesitant efforts at policy-making. Though his caution reflected the government's modest view of Canada's place in the world, it undermines any Canadian claim to a particularly heroic role during the crisis. But the decision to admit almost 40,000 Hungarian refugees—however reluctantly it was reached—was not inconsequential, and Canadian immigration historians largely agree on its significance. Reg Whitaker's history of immigration policy argues persuasively that the Hungarian exodus made it clear that East European migrants were unlikely to be Soviet agents, finally ending the post-war ban on immigration from Communist countries.[56] Equally important, the vital role of domestic pressure in convincing Ottawa to open its borders established a precedent for those Canadians who wanted to persuade the government to adopt a more generous attitude toward other migrants. Drawing on the Hungarian model, Canadian refugee advocates joined with community groups in responding to refugee crises in Uganda in 1970, Chile in 1973–1974, and Southeast Asia in 1979–1980, forcing Ottawa to liberalize its refugee policy and changing the very face of contemporary Canada.[57]

Notes

1. Earl E. McCarthy, "The Hungarian Refugee Movement: Transportation and Settlement in Canada," in Robert H. Keyserlingk, ed., *Breaking Ground: the 1956 Hungarian Refugee Movement to Canada* (Toronto: York Lanes Press, 1993), 58.

2. Freda Hawkins, *Canada and Immigration: Public Policy and Public Concern* (Kingston & Montreal: McGill-Queen's University Press, 1972), 114.

3. Alan Barnes, "Robert Ford Was Our Man in Moscow," *Toronto Star*, April 17, 1998, B5; James Macgowen, "Robert Arthur Douglas Ford," *Globe and Mail*, May 4, 1998, A14; confidential interviews.

4. R. A. D. Ford, *Our Man in Moscow: A Diplomat's Reflections on the Soviet Union* (Toronto: University of Toronto Press, 1989), 27–28.

5. R. A. D. Ford, "Memorandum by European Division: Relations with the USSR—A Re-Assessment," November 1954, reprinted in Greg Donaghy, ed., *Documents on Canadian External Relations [DCER], Volume 20: 1954* (Ottawa: Minister of Public Works and Government Services, 1997), 1569–1591. See also John Holmes, *The Shaping of Peace: Canada and the Search for World Order*, Volume 2 (Toronto: University of Toronto Press, 1982), 382–383.

6. Ibid., Ford.

7. Ibid.

8. John English, *The Worldly Years: The Life of Lester Pearson, Volume 2: 1949-1972* (Toronto: Alfred A. Knopf, 1992), 99.

9. Bonn (from Pearson) to Ottawa, Telegram 237, October 15, 1955, reprinted in Greg Donaghy, *DCER, Volume 21: 1955* (Ottawa: Canadian Government Publishing, 1999), 1167.

10. Cabinet Conclusions, November 16, 1955, re-printed in Donaghy, *DCER, Volume 21: 1955*, 1173–1174.

11. L. B. Pearson, "Memorandum for the Prime Minister," March 27, 1956, reprinted in Greg Donaghy, ed., *DCER: Volume 23: 1956-57 Part II* (Ottawa: Canadian Government Publishing, 2002), 911.

12. Secretary of State for External Affairs [SSEA] to High Commissioner in the United Kingdom, Telegrams 1896 and 2016, October 27 and November 15, 1949; Charles Ritchie, Memorandum for SSEA, October 22, 1953; Ford,

Memorandum for Under-Secretary of State for External Affairs [USSEA], April 7, 1955, and Blair Seaborn, draft Memorandum for the SSEA, May 3, 1956, Department of External Affairs [DEA] File 9959-40, Volume 6258, Library and Archives Canada [LAC].

13. Jules Léger, "Memorandum to the SSEA, 12 June 1956 and attached Memorandum from Head of the European Division (Ford), 12 June 1956," reprinted in Donaghy, ed., *DCER, Volume 23: 1956-57, Part 11*, 867–877.

14. Ibid.

15. Jules Léger, Memorandum for the SSEA, July 30, 1956, DEA File 9959-40, Volume 6258, LAC.

16. Cabinet Conclusions, October 3 and October 25, 1956, reprinted in Donaghy, ed., *DCER, Volume 23: 1956-57, Part 11*, 1069–1070; 1075–1077.

17. SSEA to the High Commissioner in the United Kingdom, Telegram SS-220, October 26, 1956, reprinted in Ibid., 749–760.

18. Ibid. See also SSEA to High Commissioner in the United Kingdom, Telegram SS-227, October 31, 1956, reprinted in Ibid., 754.

19. Jules Léger, Memoranda for the Minister, October 29, 1956, DEA File 8619-40, Vol 8216, LAC.

20. High Commissioner in the United Kingdom to SSEA, Telegram 1484, October 30, 1956, and SSEA to High Commissioner in the United Kingdom, Telegram SS-227, October 31, 1956, reprinted in Donaghy, ed., *DCER, Volume 23, 1956-57 Part 11*, 751–752; 754.

21. Jules Léger (drafted by Ford), Memorandum for the Acting SSEA, November 7, 1956, reprinted in Ibid., 762–766.

22. See John Hilliker and Greg Donaghy, "Canadian Relations with the United Kingdom at the End of Empire, 1956-73," in Philip Buckner, ed., *Canada and the End of Empire* (Vancouver: University of British Columbia Press, 2005), 26–30.

23. Charles Ritchie, *Diplomatic Passport: More Undiplomatic Diaries, 1946-62* (Toronto: Macmillan, 1981), p. 120.

24. Draft of a letter written by Mr. Pearson for a friend, November 8, 1956, DEA File 8619, Vol 8216, LAC.

25. L. B. Pearson, *Mike: The Memoirs of the Rt. Hon. Lester B. Pearson,* John Munro and Alex Inglis, eds. (Toronto: University of Toronto Press, 1973), 254–255.

26. Léger, Memorandum for the Prime Minster, November 12, 1956, reprinted in Donaghy, ed., *DCER, Volume 23: 1956-57,* 771–772.

27. Ibid.

28. John Watkins to Trevor Pyman, Acting High Commissioner for Australia, December 3, 1956; SSEA to the Canadian Delegation in New York, Telegram SS-302, December 10, 1956; Jim George, Memorandum for the USSEA, December 10, 1956; and Washington to SSEA, Telegram 2296, December 13, 1956, DEA File 8619-40, Vol 7104, LAC.

29. Greg Donaghy, "'The Most Important Country in the World:' Escott in India, 1952-57," in Greg Donaghy and Stéphane Roussel, eds., *Escott Reid: Diplomat and Scholar* (Montreal & Kingston: McGill-Queen's University Press, 2004), 67–84.

30. Escott Reid, *Radical Mandarin: The Memoirs of Escott Reid* (Toronto: University of Toronto Press, 1989), 282.

31. Donaghy, "'The Most Important Country in the World,'" 79.

32. Ottawa to High Commissioner in New Delhi, Telegram SS-251, November 9, reprinted in Donaghy, ed., *DCER, Volume 23: 1956-57,* 770.

33. R. A. D. Ford, Memorandum, [April 1957] reprinted in Donaghy, ed., *DCER, Volume 23: 1956-57,* 826–828.

34. Marcel Cadieux marginal note on James Reed, Deputy UN High Commissioner for Refugees to SSEA, 3 November 1956, DEA File 5475-EA-4-40, Vol 6967, LAC.

35. Hutchinson and English, *The Worldly Years,* 76–77.

36. Gerald Dirks, "Canada and Immigration: International and Domestic Considerations in the Decade Preceding the 1956 Hungarian Exodus," in Robert Keyserlingk, ed., *The 1956 Hungarian Refugee Movement,* 7.

37. Freda Hawkins, *Canada and Immigration,* 118.

38. Reg Whitaker, *Double Standard: The Secret History of Canadian Immigration* (Toronto: Lester & Orpen Dennys, 1987), 74–75.

39. Canada, Department of External Affairs, *External Affairs*, Volume 8, No. 11, p. 325; see also James Eayrs, *Canada and World Affairs, 1955-57* (Toronto: Oxford University Press, 1969), 44–47.

40. Figure supplied in Jules Léger, Memorandum for the SSEA, November 24, 1956, DEA File 5475-EA-4-40, Vol 6967, LAC.

41. Blair Fraser, "How Red Tape Is Stalling Our Refugee Program," *Maclean's Magazine*, March 1957.

42. "Be Bigger Yet," *Winnipeg Free Press*, November 7, 1956.

43. "Cold Charity," *Globe and Mail*, November 12, 1956, and "Let Refugees In," *Toronto Telegram*, November 12, 1956.

44. L. B. Pearson to J. W. Pickersgill, November 9, 1956, reprinted in Donaghy, ed., *DCER, Volume 23: 1956-57*, 769–770.

45. Cabinet Conclusions, November 14, 1956, reprinted in Ibid., 775–776. See also, "Report of the Meeting convened with the Hon. J.W. Pickersgill and Ethnic Representatives from behind the Iron Curtain," November 12, 1956, Pickersgill Papers, Vol 57, File 1-2-5545J, LAC. To be fair to Pickersgill, the minister may have found it hard to pick up the depth of concern over Hungary as each of the several groups used this rare opportunity to lobby him regarding their own concerns.

46. R. A. D. Ford, Memorandum for the USSEA, November 14, 1956, reprinted in Donaghy, ed., *DCER, Volume 23: 1956-57*, 776–778.

47. Canadian Delegation in New York to Ottawa, Telegram 1225, November 13, 1956; Geneva to Ottawa, Telegram 276, November 23, 1956, DEA File 5475-EA-4-40, Vol 6967, LAC.

48. R. A. D. Ford, Memorandum for the USSEA, November 19, 1956, DEA File 5475-EA-4-40, Vol 6967, LAC.

49. Cited in Dirks, *Canada's Refugee Policy*, 193.

50. Cabinet Conclusions, November 22, 1956, reprinted in Donaghy, ed., *DCER, Volume 23*, 783–784.

51. Cabinet Conclusions, November 23, 1956, reprinted in Donaghy, ed., *DCER, Volume 23: 1956-57*, 785–786.

52. Dirks, *Canada's Refugee Policy*, 197.

53. Cabinet Conclusions, November 27, 1956, reprinted in Ibid.

54. Figures are drawn from James Eayrs, *Canada in World Affairs, 1955-57*, 47; and E. D. Fulton, Memorandum to Cabinet, July 19, 1957, reprinted in Michael Stevenson, ed., *DCER, Volume 25: 1957-58 Part 11* (Ottawa: Canadian Government Publishing, 2004), 956–960.

55. Figures are reproduced in Dirks, *Canada's Refugee Policy*, 202. The final figure for the movement of refugees was 37,565 in December 1959.

58. R. A. D. Ford, Memorandum by European Division, November 27, 1956, reprinted in Donaghy, ed., *DCER, Volume 23*, 968–973.

59. Léger (drafted by Ford), Memorandum for the SSEA, December 5, 1956, reprinted in Ibid., 973–976.

60. Léger, Memorandum for the SSEA and attached Memorandum by Ford, March 11, 1957, reprinted in Ibid., 980–986.

61. SSEA to the Ambassador in France, Telegram S-46, January 30, 1957, reprinted in Ibid., 977–978.

62. Jules Léger to Sir Leslie Fry, British Ambassador to Hungary, October 16, 1957, DEA File 9959-40, Vol 6258, LAC.

63. Henry Davis, Head of European Division, to USSEA, March 16, 1959, DEA File 9959-40, Vol 6258, LAC.

56. Whitaker, *Double Standard*, 86.

57. Dirk, *Canada's Refugee Policy*, 211.

12.

Changing Times: *Kanadai Magyar Munkás* (The Canadian-Hungarian Worker) and the 1956 Hungarian Revolution

Christopher Adam

The refugee crisis following the 1956 Hungarian Revolution initiated a time of change, growth, and transformation for Canada's Hungarian communities. The arrival of almost 38,000 refugees in 1956–1957 had a significant impact on the Hungarian-Canadian press, and newspapers found themselves with the possibility of attracting thousands of new readers from a group that reflected great cultural, class, educational, and political diversity. The *Kanadai Magyar Munkás* (Canadian-Hungarian Worker), the second-largest Hungarian weekly printed in Canada, one that was openly affiliated with the country's Communist Party and was a supporter of Hungary's post-war regime, found itself in a very delicate situation following the 1956 revolution.

Canada's two major anti-Communist, conservative weeklies were, at first, in a celebratory mood at the apparent fall of Hungary's Communist regime, but this was followed by ferocious indignation after the Soviet repression of the revolt, on November 4, 1956. The *Munkás*, however, was unsure how to handle the situation and how, in retrospect, it would explain its jingoistic support for Hungary's discredited Stalinist regime, as well as what approach it would take when faced with the wave of refugees arriving in Canada. At first, the *Munkás* found itself having to explain to its readers why the paper had been so supportive of a Stalinist regime, which by then had been discredited by Nikita

Khrushchev in his speech at the 20th Party Congress in February 1956. This, however, was followed by a campaign aimed at encouraging the 1956 refugees to return home. The *Munkás* asserted that the refugees had been victimized by Canadian authorities and their Hungarian-Canadian collaborators, while trying to convince them that they were unwanted by the country's working class and offering the asylum-seekers assurances that repatriation to Hungary was their best option.

The primary goal of the Hungarian-Canadian press focused less on language maintenance and the preservation of the group's cultural heritage and much more on infusing the community with specific political messages, relating to Hungarian politics. Hungarians were not the only ethnic groups in Canada to use their press as a tool to maintain a sense of patriotism among immigrants and to participate in political battles taking place in their home county. Joseph M. Kirschbaum, for example, argued that Slavic groups in Canada used their newspapers as a forum to vent grievances and present opinions about the political and social situation back home.[1] A close examination of these newspapers revealed that Slavs in Canada were often divided along the same political and ideological lines as their compatriots living in the home country. Although most Hungarian-Canadian newspapers were nationalistic, just like Slavic papers, tension and conflicts between various Hungarian papers of different political stripes characterized the Hungarian-Canadian press. Conservative, liberal, and far-right publications competed with each other for the prized "ownership" of the 1956 revolution and its memory. Unlike most other ethnic papers, almost all Hungarian publications rallied around a single event, and each camp tried to interpret the legacy of the revolution in light of its respective ideology.

The impetus behind the formation of Hungarian ethnic newspapers after 1956 and their raison d'etre also appears to be different from that of most other immigrant communities in Canada and the United States. Sociologist Susan Olzak argues that most white ethnic newspapers in the United States were established out of group solidarity, during a period of hostility toward the immigrant community on the part of both the majority population and other minorities.[2] In the case of Hungarian-Canadian newspapers published after 1956, competing periodicals often arose and flourished not because of external attacks directed toward the community but due to pervasive ideological differences within the community itself and the complicated memory of a recently suppressed revolution, as well as the refugee crisis.[3]

As with most East European ethnic groups in Canada during the interwar period, Hungarian communities across the country—especially those in industrial areas of southern Ontario and a few districts in Winnipeg—were also home to declared Communists and Communist organizations. In the case of the Hungarians, however, the 1956 revolution and the arrival to Canada of tens of thousands of refugees from Hungary reshaped previously existing Hungarian communities and caused significant consternation for Canada's staunch Hungarian Communists. The *Munkás* had published editorials similar to the rhetoric and agitprop produced by the central organ of Hungary's Communist Party, even during the harsher Stalinist dictatorship of Mátyás Rákosi. The paper's initial approach to the 1956 revolution reflected this attitude as it attempted to explain away the "tragic October events" as a brief episode of fascist reactionary behaviour.[4] Nevertheless, the paper's largely uncritical support of political developments in Hungary from 1947 to 1956 served as a source of great embarrassment after the revolution.[5]

The *Kanadai Magyar Munkás* originated in 1929 in Hamilton and served as one of two major Hungarian weekly newspapers in Canada, the other being the *Kanadai Magyar Ujság* (Canadian Hungarian News), during the interwar period and the years before the 1956 revolution.[6] During the interwar period, these two papers served to divide the Hungarian communities of Canada, based on political and ideological lines, with the *Ujság* representing a nationalist-conservative ideology, generally loyal to Hungary's authoritarian interwar regime, and the *Munkás* representing left-leaning secular forces with close ties to Communists in Hungary, trade unions, and the Communist Party of Canada.[7]

The *Munkás* was an out-and-out Communist paper published during this period by István Szőke, who also wrote a book on Hungarian Canadians, ran literary organizations in Toronto, and stood at the head of Canada's "progressive" Hungarian émigré communities. The paper's key goal was to encourage Hungarian immigrants to rally under the banner of the Communist Party of Canada and affiliated trade unions, ostensibly in an effort to improve working conditions.[8] The founders, first editors, and journalists of the *Munkás* were Hungarian Communists who had been involved in the short-lived Hungarian Soviet Republic of 1919 and had fled to the United States following the regime's collapse and the subsequent establishment of a conservative anti-Communist regime in Hungary in 1920. With the founding of the *Munkás* in 1929, several of these left-leaning émigrés moved to Canada, hoping to win over members of the fast-growing Hungarian-Canadian communities to the Communist cause and draw them into the wings of the Communist Party of Canada.[9]

Under Szőke's leadership, the *Munkás* also made a point of fighting political battles being waged in Hungary during the country's interwar regime. For example, in 1936, the *Munkás* organized a Hungarian-Canadian campaign to free a Hungarian Communist leader, Mátyás Rákosi, who would later become Hungary's Stalinist dictator. Rákosi was then languishing in prison in Hungary for his political views. The campaign included a petition containing 11,000 signatures and a political demonstration of some four hundred Communist supporters in Winnipeg, who picketed the editorial offices of the *Újság*.[10]

After the 1956 revolution broke out, the *Munkás* subtly aligned itself with the peaceful student demonstrations of October 23, 1956, all the while arguing that these had been hijacked by "reactionary" forces. Szőke noted that he and his paper "observed with great sorrow and anxiety, how certain groups and elements have turned the demonstrations, aimed at hastening the just demands of the people, into a bloody war."[11] The paper appeared to also offer lukewarm support for Prime Minister Imre Nagy's new government, mainly for its calls to halt the violence on the streets, but was not impressed by the prime minister's decision to create a coalition with non-Communist parties and politicians. As such, the Soviet suppression of the revolt, the fall of the Nagy government, and the establishment of János Kádár's regime served as a welcome relief for the editors of the *Munkás*. "With Soviet help, the attempt to turn the Hungarian uprising into a counter-revolution was brought to an end. Moreover, the Nagy government, which tolerated an orgy of white terror, has been removed from power by Kádár's government of socialist independence."[12] This was the only time that the paper referred to the demonstrations of October 23 as an "uprising," terminology which would not be used again.

The paper's standard interpretation of the events in Hungary was published on November 15, 1956, and this was the version that appeared again, in different words, on a number of occasions.

> The just and peaceful movement of the people was utilized by reaction for counter-revolutionary purposes....Imre Nagy could not and did not want to wage a struggle against the dark forces of reaction....But the working people of Hungary did not permit the internal and external counter-revolution to trample upon their great socialist gains. They resolutely said "no!" to all those who wanted to utilize the legitimate and just demands of the working people and the serious errors of the past leadership in order to swerve the country from the path of socialism.[13]

The *Munkás*'s most important activities during the revolution and immediately, however, focused on relief efforts organized by the Red Cross. Through various community fundraisers, usually spearheaded by the Kossuth Fraternal Benefit Society, a federation of local chapters closely associated with the *Munkás*, Canada's Hungarian Communist organizations raised over $7,000 within a matter of six weeks.[14]

Following the 1956 revolution the *Munkás* was, quite literally, at a loss for words. Due to its earlier support of Stalinism, the paper found itself in a rather prickly situation. It took several weeks for the paper to formulate a coherent detailed response, as well as an *apologia* to claims that it had misled its readers regarding the situation in Hungary. The paper launched a series entitled *The Hungarian Question* starting on January 3, 1957, in which the paper provided its viewpoint on the "October events" and tried to explain the paper's support for the old Rákosi regime. There was a sense of betrayal among some readers of the *Munkás*—and the paper's editors admitted as much—but from simply reading the journal, it is difficult to determine how significant this was, as the weekly did not publish any critical letters from its readers. It did, however, concede that some subscribers believed that "everything that we wrote about Hungary was false and that we attempted to conceal reality."[15]

> One of our errors, which we cannot deny, was that while we praised the grand results, we did not mention clearly enough that the road to socialism in these (Eastern European) countries is a long and painful process and it is nowhere near complete. Reactionary forces must be defeated one

step at a time. In our efforts aimed at dispelling the accusations found in reactionary propaganda and appropriately assessing the successes of socialism, we presented this development in a one-sided, uncritical way.[16]

The editors of the *Munkás* were walking on precarious ground as they had to demonstrate a certain amount of humility and regret for not having presented the "full picture" vis-à-vis Hungary, yet it was also important that they convinced their readers that this was, at most, an innocent error of omission and nothing more sinister.

Despite this apparent apology and the fact that the editors agreed that the demonstrations on October 23, 1956, had started off as a legitimate protest before being hijacked by reactionary rightist elements, the paper was fully supportive of the Soviet intervention of November 4, 1956, and had harsh words for Hungarian-Canadians who supported the revolt, especially those who vowed to return to Hungary to fight with the revolutionaries. In fact, Szőke was convinced that the Soviet re-invasion could not have come too soon, and he expressed these views in his correspondence with officials from Budapest. Szőke observed that the so-called Soviet intervention was "rather late and delayed."[17] At the same time, Szőke also recognized that these views and those expressed in the *Munkás* have turned supporters away from the movement. "The majority of our supporters behave coldly towards us and some even reject us. It is very difficult for us to change this situation."[18]

The *Munkás* was by no means the only paper to publish polemical editorials on the 1956 revolution, the subsequent refugee crisis, and the way in which Hungarian-Canadians of differing political persuasions reacted to the crisis. *Kanadai Magyarság*, a Toronto-based weekly founded in 1951 by László F. Kenesei—who arrived in Canada in 1949—was perhaps the most vehemently anti-Communist in its critique of left-leaning Hungarian-Canadians and their primary press organ.[19] On November 17, 1956, less than two weeks after the Soviet suppression of the uprising, Kenesei launched one of several diatribes against Canada's Hungarian Communists.

> Here in Canada there are a couple of evil-doers, who edit a Hungarian-language newspaper, which portrays these heroes (of 1956) as "reactionary and racist elements."…Anyone who gives money to a Communist

newspaper also supports the murderers of the Hungarian people....God will punish you, you ignominious quislings. Yes, *He* will punish you, because we won't so much as dirty our hands with you. At most, we will spit in your face, if we see you on the street. We must not spend another day negotiating with the red butchers, but rather send them straight to the gallows, or line them up before the barrels of guns. The weapons are already loaded and tomorrow comes the day of reckoning. But until then, we demand that the Canadian government lock up these dirty, red creeps, or send them off to Russia.[20]

Kenesei boasted that the *Magyarság* was the most consistently anti-Communist Hungarian paper in the entire world, and in an editorial he claimed that his publication was successfully dividing the Hungarian-Canadian Communist community. Szőke responded in short order to Kenesei's call to deport and execute Communists by calling him a "scoundrel" who "clings on desperately" to a crushed uprising and all the vain hopes associated with it.[21] Despite all this, Kenesei was convinced that "a significant proportion of former Hungarian Canadian Communists have been cured of the red curse, they have joined other readers of our paper and are fighting together with us until the final victory."[22] Kenesei continued to publish *Magyarság* until 1963, when the paper was bought by István Vörösváry, who maintained the paper's right-wing staunchly anti-Communist profile.[23]

Canada's third major Hungarian weekly, *Magyar Élet* (Hungarian Life) was also an essentially conservative journal, but it started off on a much less combative footing. The paper had been printed in Buenos Aires since 1948 but was transferred to Canada in early 1957. In its first editorial, published on March 9, 1957, *Magyar Élet*'s editors called on the entire Hungarian immigration to unite and rally around 1956, claiming that the revolution served as a common cause that could effectively break down all ideological, political, and class divisions among immigrants.[24] During the first several months of publication, the paper's editors, themselves recent immigrants to Canada, were seemingly oblivious to the long history of conflict between Canadian Hungarian Communists and the more conservative immigrants.

In December 1956, once tens of thousands of refugees had already poured into Austria and were awaiting asylum in Western Europe and North America, the *Munkás* was becoming increasingly alarmed at the prospect of a large wave being accepted into to Canada. The paper's campaign began to shift from collecting donations for the Hungarian Red Cross and serving as an apologist for Hungary's new post-revolution Kádár regime, to sounding the alarm bells in terms of what the refugee crisis would mean for Canada. "It is clear from the Canadian government's propaganda and actions that it is not only helping the fleeing fascists and the remains of the generally well-dressed and portly capitalists, but that it is also trying to tempt young men and women, workers, peasants and athletes filled with doubt about fleeing by providing them with aid."[25] Szőke and most Communist leaders were concerned not only about the arrival of anti-Communist crowds to Canada but also (at least ostensibly) about an impending brain drain caused by the exit of thousands of skilled labourers, intellectuals, and others from Hungary. "Experienced fascists and Horthyites— who dared not remain for fear of the consequences of their counter-revolutionary actions—are not the only ones who fled to Austria, but also hundreds, possibly thousands, who left amidst great doubts."[26]

Beginning in February 1957, the *Munkás* made the case on numerous occasions that a significant number of 1956 refugees wanted to go home, en masse, due to their ill treatment in Canada, a lack of employment, and crushed hopes. Quoting an unnamed "well-informed Hungarian newcomer," the *Munkás* claimed that more than half of all refugees in Montreal and Toronto yearned to go home and that they would proceed to make their travel plans once they were "permitted contact with the Hungarian government."[27]

The paper's coverage of the wave of refugees willing to return to Hungary included headline articles alleging that several thousand Hungarians who had fled to Western Europe, the United States, Canada, and Australia were considering repatriation. For example, the *Munkás* knew of some thirty refugees living in Windsor who planned to return home, after a disappointing stay in Canada.[28]

Occasionally, the paper also published letters to the editor from refugees who desired to return to Hungary but who had inadequate funds for the trip. The *Munkás* published the letter of one such anonymous refugee, staying in

Calgary, who begged the paper's editors to help him return and offered a humble *mea culpa* for having left Hungary in the first place.

> I have only been here a few weeks, but I have made a very, very grave mistake, like so many of my compatriots...I have had enough of life here and wish for nothing more than to find myself in my home country again. I will never leave Hungary again, nor will I listen to others. I know that your paper represents the working class, of which I am a part. I made a mistake, but I dare not turn to anyone else. Please do everything in your power to help me return home. I want to live in my home country, even if they will lock me up for having left. But I know that they will understand and that they will forgive me for my mistake.[29]

In the June 27, 1957, issue of the *Munkás*, the paper noted the number of letters they received from refugees who had been "led astray," but who later realized that it had been a mistake to leave Hungary. As usual, the *Munkás* continued to publish anonymous letters, ostensibly because the paper did not want them to "suffer further disadvantage and discrimination at the hands of Hungarian counter-revolutionary terrorists."[30] One of the letter writers, from "a large city in Western Canada," expressed the familiar themes of regret, sorrow, shame, and forgiveness. "Today I see, as do so many other honest, misled people, that we have been shamefully tricked. Many of our Hungarian brothers are languishing in camps throughout Canada, instead of experiencing all the shiny, hopeful promises....I see nothing else in Canada, other than the scramble and mad rush for the dollar....My only comfort is that here, as well, progressive forces are fighting for a better existence."[31]

The theme of Hungarians who had made mistakes out of poor judgement, or because they were "led astray" by seditious forces, but were just as willing to admit their errors and mend their ways, was present not only in the Communist press but also among anti-Communist conservative Hungarians. Kenesei and his weekly *Kanadai Magyarság* asserted that the paper helped Hungarian Communists see the light. "We know of several Hungarian Canadian Communists who, after they realized their mistake, have waged the most dedicated battle against those who led them astray. These people are now church-going, good Hungarians, who respect our paper as they do the Bible...we are pleased that we are able to bring so many Hungarians into respectable society."[32] *Magyarság* and the *Munkás* both framed the revolution, the refugee crisis, and the ideological divide in the most dramatic and apocalyptic terms. The frequent polemics of both newspaper editors suggests that there was a battle if not purely on ideological grounds but also to attract new readers and subscribers during a time of great change within Canada's Hungarian communities.

The editors of the *Munkás* were, indeed, quite willing to help refugees return home, and they offered to forward repatriation requests on behalf of their readers to the Hungarian Division of the Polish Legation in Ottawa.[33] By May 1957, the *Munkás* asserted that "several hundred" were interested in returning to Hungary and cited the same three reasons given by the anonymous letter writer from Calgary. "An ever increasing number of people are demanding forcefully that they be transported back home, partly because they had regretted their poorly thought-out decision to leave and also because despite all the rosy promises, they have found only unemployment, dupery and misery."[34]

The experience of great disappointment allegedly felt among refugees upon their arrival in Canada was presented as the standard refugee story on the pages of the *Munkás*. A series of anonymous statements, letters, and recollections from refugees were meant to demonstrate how so many refugees were duped into coming to Canada and how disenchanting it was when the promises of material wealth and well-being did not immediately materialize. One such refugee writing from British Columbia, who signed his article as "S.G." wrote about how he and his dreams were shattered almost immediately after landing on the shores of Canada.

> It is only now that we truly understand what our homeland meant. It is only now that we found out what it meant to work for each other, for our homeland, our well-being, peace and for our freedom. Now we have to work, so that the capitalists can make more money. It was obvious that the Canadian workers did not like us very much, because they knew that with us the number of unemployed will increase and that wages will go down. Many of us, at first, lost track of what was important, as we saw that Canadian workers own cars and televisions....But where are their social and recreational institutions? Where are their factory libraries and their cultural institutions? Our life was not based on a car and a castle built of

cards. Our work was a strong bastion and it offered a secure existence. This
is what we threw away.[35]

The *Munkás* used the testimonies of unnamed refugees to create the impression
that a very significant number of Hungarian refugees were so deeply disappointed
with Canada that they seriously contemplated returning to Hungary. One
such anonymous refugee observed, "We, who were not counter-revolutionaries
can see with our own eyes, what is behind the bewildering propaganda....We
can see that everything here is business, including human rights, health care,
employment and the only reason we were accepted by Canada is to provide
cheap labour for employers."[36]

Yet if Hungarian refugees felt unwanted and sometimes abused in Canada,
the *Munkás* tended to reinforce this perception by publishing articles that implied
that Canadian workers and labour unions did not appreciate the presence of so
many refugees. The paper pitted the Liberal government of Louis St. Laurent,
which they believed aligned itself with the refugees, against labour unions,
Canadian workers, and the Labour Progressive Party. For example, the paper
quoted a group of Hungarian refugees in Vancouver who allegedly proclaimed
that there is "no need to worry about trade unions, because we are under the
protection of the Canadian government."[37] The implication was that both the
Hungarian refugees and the St. Laurent government were in a strategic alliance
to marginalize the unions. The *Munkás* also quoted an article from *Ship and
Shop*, a Vancouver-based paper published by dockyard workers, which asserted
that Hungarian refugees were "used as tools in European conflicts and when that
thing called the 'freedom fight' ended, they dumped them here among us. Now
[the government] is trying to use them as tools against Canadian workers."[38]

By June 6, 1957, a front-page headline in the *Munkás* declared that the
"outcry is growing" regarding the continued arrival of refugees, as well as their
alleged poor treatment in Canada. According to the Communist weekly, just
about everyone, on all sides of the crisis, was unhappy with the situation.
The paper insinuated that scores of refugees desired to return to Hungary
but were unable to do so, due to a lack of funds, the obstructionist tactics of
Hungarian Canadians involved in the relief effort, and the alleged unwillingness
of Canadian authorities to transport them back to their home country. The

Munkás illustrated this point by referring to the case of Lajos Rajki, a young Hungarian actor who left his twenty-three-year-old wife, his family, and his career in Budapest, and ended up committing suicide in Montreal "due to the hopelessness of his situation."[39] The *Munkás* claimed that a member of the local Hungarian community who—according to the paper—was once a "fascist captain" of the Hungarian military and now served as a translator at a refugee camp in Montreal, where he "maintained a state of terror against those refugees that wish to return to Hungary."[40]

According to the *Munkás*, the refugees, therefore, were victims of three forces. First, they had fallen prey to people who encouraged them to flee to the West in the hope of a better life. Second, their return to Hungary was obstructed due to pressure from anti-Communist Hungarian-Canadians and the unwillingness of Canadian authorities to help them in returning home. Third, the St. Laurent government used the refugees as pawns in a Cold War struggle against Communists abroad, and left-leaning pro-Communist unions in Canada, by "flooding" the country with workers who would be loyal to the government, rather than to the trade unions. The fourth victim of these alleged political machinations was the Canadian workforce, as well as unions in general.

As the federal election of 1957 approached, the paper's critique of the St. Laurent government also increased, for undermining Canada's unions and for augmenting Cold War rivalries. The *Munkás*, however, reserved even stronger criticism for the Conservative party and John Diefenbaker, who, according to Szőke, maintained contacts with the most extremist anti-Communist Hungarians.[41] At the same time, the paper campaigned openly for the Labour Progressive party, which ended up garnering 7,760 votes, as well as for the Co-Operative Commonwealth Federation.[42]

The defeat of St. Laurent's government was the paper's most evident goal, in terms of Canadian politics, mainly because the editors felt that it would serve to repudiate the government's approach to Hungarian refugees. At the same time, the paper was no more pleased with John Diefenbaker, who, Szőke charged, had broken bread with reactionaries and former fascists at Hungarian community events.[43] Once the Tories had ended twenty-two years of Liberal government, the *Munkás* credited this to the party's demagogical approach during the campaign.

The 1956 refugees and what Canada's Hungarian Communists could do with them, however, remained the paper's long-term problem and contributed to the publication's eventual downfall. It is interesting to note that almost no efforts were made to try to convince some of them—who may well have been left-leaning—to join their ranks and take part in an array of affiliated social clubs and organizations. The World Federation of Hungarians (MVSZ), a government organization based in Budapest closely affiliated with the Hungarian Socialist Workers' Party (MSZMP), tried on numerous occasions to encourage Canada's Hungarian Communists to reach out to left-leaning fifty-sixers, but their efforts, as well as those of the Hungarian embassy in Ottawa after 1964, were in vain. MVSZ officials concluded that the Communist movement held "sectarian views" and had a propensity to turn inward.[44] Hungary's Ministry of Foreign Affairs also found it problematic that the *Munkás* was so closely affiliated with the Communist Party of Canada, as this "did not make it possible for the paper to become influential among (politically) indifferent crowds, or have any influence over them."[45] Hungary wanted to use the *Munkás*—which in 1964 had a weekly circulation of 1,800 copies—as a forum to challenge the politics of the Hungarian-Canadian right and to publish propaganda pieces on contemporary post-1956 Hungary. Yet even if the paper's editors might have been more willing to open up to new content, in-fighting within the Communist movement made this even more difficult. Foreign Ministry and MVSZ officials were also genuinely stunned by Szőke's main solution for all the ills of the Hungarian Communist movement. Szőke hoped for the economic situation to become worse in Canada, which would lead to higher unemployment and lower wages, all of which would strengthen the movement's raison d'etre.[46]

Unable and unwilling to open up to left-leaning refugees, the *Munkás* simply wanted them to return home. The Hungarian government also tried to support the case of some refugees during the years following the revolution. The paper used a dual approach in achieving its goals. First, it tried to convince the refugees that many of their compatriots were deeply unsatisfied with their situation in Canada and wanted nothing more than to return to Hungary.

Second, the *Munkás* attempted to demonstrate that the refugees were unwanted and disliked by ordinary Canadian workers, who saw them as part of the government's Cold War plot to weaken unions at home and strike a blow at the Soviet Union abroad. Despite all efforts, the vast majority of Hungarian refugees remained in Canada, and the *Munkás* struggled with what to do with them and how to overcome its unpopular portrayal of the revolution in 1956 and the Soviet intervention.

Notes

1. J. M. Kirschbaum, "The Ideological Orientation of the Canadian Slavic Press," *Slavs in Canada* Vol. 3 (Toronto: Inter-University Committee on Canadian Slavs, 1971), 297.
2. Susan Olzak, "Ethnic Conflict and the Rise and Fall of Ethnic Newspapers," *American Sociological Review*, 56:4 (August 1991): 459.
3. A large number of Hungarian periodicals, newsletters, and other publications were established shortly after 1956, and in each case, their key goal was to examine politics in Hungary. These publications represented the full political spectrum, from far-right press organs to more liberal publications. These included *Honfitárs* (1956), *Hungarista Tájékoztató* (1957), *Magyar Élet* (which moved from Buenos Aires to Toronto in 1957), *Magyar Hírlap* (1958), *Montreáli Figyelő* (1958), and *Szittyakürt* (1962). There was also a handful of post-1956 publications that were not overtly political but focused more on local community news. These included *Hagyomány* (1962), *Menora Egyenlőség* (1966), and an array of community newsletters.
4. "*Ellenforradalom*" (Counter-Revolution), *Kanadai Magyar Munkás* (Canadian Hungarian Worker), November 8, 1956, p. 1.
5. "Canada and the Hungarian Revolution of 1956: A Canadian Chronicle," *Hungarian Studies* 12: 1-2 (1997): http://www3.sympatico.ca/thidas/ Hungarian-history/chronicle.html (accessed April 12, 2007).
6. The *Kanadai Magyar Újság* [Canadian Hungarian News] was, in fact, the product of the merger of two smaller newspapers, namely the *Canadai Magyar*

Farmer [Canadian Hungarian Farmer] (1918) and the *Kanadai Magyar Hírlap* [Canadian Hungarian Journal]. The paper received subsidies from Hungary's interwar regime, led by Regent Miklós Horthy, which explains the editorial board's overall support for Hungarian politics until 1944.

Carmela Patrias, *The Kanadai Magyar Újság and the Politics of the Hungarian Canadian Elite* (Toronto: Multicultural History Society of Ontario, November 1978), 6.

7. For an in-depth analysis of the ideological divide between Hungarian-Canadian conservatives and Communists, see Carmela Patrias's book, *Patriots and Proletariats: Politicizing Hungarian Immigrants in Interwar Canada* (Montreal: McGill-Queen's University Press, 1994).

8. Carmela Patrias, "*The Hungarians in Canada,*" Booklet No. 27 of *Canada's Ethnic Group Series* (Ottawa: The Canadian Historical Association, 1999), 16.

9. Ibid., 18.

10. István Szőke, *We Are Canadians—The National Group of the Hungarian-Canadians* (Toronto: Hungarian Literature Association, 1954), 84.

11. "*Segélyt a magyar népnek a Vöröskereszten át*" [Aid to the Hungarian People through the Red Cross] *Kanadai Magyar Munkás*, November 1, 1956, p. 1.

12. *Kanadai Magyar Munkás,* November 8, 1956, p. 1.

13. *Kanadai Magyar Munkás*, November 15, 1956, p. 12.

14. *Kanadai Magyar Munkás*, December 6, 1956, p. 12.

15. "*A Magyar kérdés!*" [The Hungarian Question], *Kanadai Magyar Munkás*, January 3, 1957, p. 3.

16. Ibid., 3.

17. István Szőke's letter to Lajos Biró (MVSZ), March 28, 1957, P975 – *Magyarok Világszövetsége – Kanada – Egyesületek A-V, Magyar Országos Levéltár* – National Archives of Hungary (MOL), Budapest.

18. Ibid., Szőke's letter to Biró.

19. At first, the *Magyarság* was quite popular among the recently arrived DPs, who tended to embrace more radical right-wing views, and for a short time the paper even catered to those who supported the by then defunct Arrow

Cross Party and Hungary's former Nazi leader, Ferenc Szálasi. Patrias, "The Hungarians in Canada," 25.

20. László F. Kenesei, "*Népünk gyilkosait dicséri a Kanadai 'Magyar' Munkás,*" [The Canadian "Hungarian" Worker applauds the Murderers of our People], *Kanadai Magyarság*, November 17, 1956, p. 3.

21. *Kanadai Magyar Munkás*, November 22, 1956, p. 3.

22. Editorial, *Kanadai Magyarság*, December 22, 1956, p. 4.

23. István Vörösváry (b. 1913) once published a radical right-wing paper in Hungary, with ties to the Arrow Cross Party. He left Hungary in 1948, first settling in Argentina and eventually establishing a Hungarian paper in Buenos Aires entitled *Magyarok Útja* [The Hungarian Way]. Vörösváry moved to Toronto in 1955. For biographical information, see Gyula Borbándi, *Nyugati Magyar Irodalmi Lexicon és Bibliográfia* [The Encyclopedia and Bibliography of Western Hungarian Literature] (Budapest: Hitel, 1992).

24. *Magyar Élet*, March 9, 1957, p. 2.

25. Editorial, *Kanadai Magyar Munkás*, December 13, 1956, p. 12.

26. Ibid., 12.

27. "Refugees: We Want to Go Home," *Kanadai Magyar Munkás*, February 7, 1957, p. 8.

28. "*Hazatérnek Magyarországba*" [They are Returning to Hungary], *Kanadai Magyar Munkás*, February 21, 1957, p. 1.

29. "*Az itteni életet[megelégelte*" (He has had Enough of Life Here], *Kanadai Magyar Munkás*, May 18, 1957, p. 12.

30. "*Hibák voltak…tévedtünk…becsaptak…szégyeljük magunkat és félünk is*" [We Made Mistakes...We Were Cheated...We are Ashamed of Ourselves and We are Scared], *Kanadai Magyar Munkás*, June 27, 1957, p. 10.

31. Ibid., 12.

32. Editorial, *Kanadai Magyarság*, December 22, 1956, p. 4.

33. Ibid., 12.

34. Ibid., 12.

35. "*Az álom és a valóság*" [The Dream and the Reality], *Kanadai Magyar Munkás*, May 30, 1957, p. 10.

36. "*Miért akarunk hazamenni?*" [Why do We Want to go Home?], *Kanadai Magyar Munkás*, May 30, 1957, p. 10.

37. "*Szakszervezeti vélemény magyar emigránsokkal kapcsolatban*" [The Opinion of Trade Unions with Regards to the Hungarian Immigrants], *Kanadai Magyar Munkás*, May 30, 1957, p. 11.

38. Ibid., 11.

39. "*Nő a felháborodás és tiltakozás a menekültek ügyében*" [Growing Outcry over the Situation of the Refugees], *Kanadai Magyar Munkás*, June 6, 1957, p. 1.

40. Ibid., 1.

41. *Kanadai Magyar Munkás*, June 2, 1957, p. 1.

42. "The History of Federal Ridings since 1867," Parliament of Canada website
http://www2.parl.gc.ca/Sites/LOP/HFER/hfer.asp?Language=E.

43. *Kanadai Magyar Munkás*, May 28, 1957, pp. 1–2.

44. "*Feljegyzés—Az MVSZ-nek a kanadai magyar emigrációban lévő kapcsolatairól, ismereteiről*" [Observations on the MVSZ's contacts and information on the Hungarian Canadian immigrant communities], 66.053/1964, XIX-J-1-j-Can, 1952-1964, *Magyar Országos Levéltár* - National Archives of Hungary, (MOL) Budapest, 3.

45. Ibid., 4.

46. "*Feljegyzés a kanadai Magyar haladó mozgalom vezetőivel folytatott beszélgetésről*" [Observations on Talks with the Hungarian Canadian progressive movement's leaders], 265/1957, XIX-J-1-j, TÜK Iratok, 1952–1964, MOL. Budapest.

Appendix: Conference Notes

There were a number of presentations at the conference that are not included in this volume either because they were to be published elsewhere or were not intended for publication at this time by their authors. A few words should be said about these here.

*

The conference was opened by Dr. Mark Pittaway, Senior Lecturer in European Studies at Great Britain's Open University. Pittaway, a specialist in twentieth-century Hungarian history, gave a keynote address, in which he examined the 1956 revolution from the perspective of social history, focusing on how these events unfolded in a specific county in Hungary.

*

Complementing this social history approach, Dr. Peter Pastor, a professor of History at Montclair University in New Jersey, employed the methods of political history in comparing the 1956 uprising to the Hungarian revolutions of 1848–1849, 1918, and 1919. Professor Tadeusz Kopys of Poland's Jagellonian University took a historiographical approach and examined how Hungarians in Canada and Western Europe commemorated the revolution on the occasion of its tenth anniversary.

*

Susan Papp-Aykler of Toronto's Rákoczi Foundation presented an oral history project she had conducted in collaboration with the Multicultural History Society of Ontario, involving the taping of interviews with hundreds of Hungarians who arrived to Canada as refugees in 1956–1957. Papp-Aykler's presentation was supplemented by an exhibit, entitled Hungarian Exodus, on the arrival and integration of about 38,000 Hungarian refugees to Canada.

Eniko Pitter, a Ph.D. candidate in Theory and Policy Studies at the University of Toronto, brought a multimedia component to the conference, with a video presentation of the interviews she had conducted as part of a documentary film on Hungarian-Canadian philanthropist and prominent civil engineer George Vari.

*

The last session of the conference was devoted to an exploration of the contributions made by Hungarian refugees to Canadian cultural expression. Four panelists, representing four artistic disciplines, had been asked to review some of the creative works produced by 1956 refugees in Canada. They were also asked to discuss some of the issues that arise when we consider the participation of immigrant writers, visual artists, filmmakers, and musicians in the diverse cultural life of Canada. Since this session was more of a round-table discussion than the formal presentation of papers, a summary is provided in the following paragraphs.

Perhaps because the 1956 Hungarian refugees integrated so well into Canadian life, not much research has been undertaken on their integration and contributions to Canada in comparison to those of earlier waves of immigration. This is even truer for the arts, despite the fact that significant contributions have been made by Hungarians in many artistic domains. The panel attempted to make a stab at filling this void.

Oliver Botar, a professor of Art History at the University of Manitoba, gave an illustrated presentation about two Modernist Hungarian-Canadian artists and their differing styles in the memorialization of the Hungarian Revolution. Gyula (Julius) Marosan's *Revolutionary Series* of paintings were placed in their context—modelled on Picasso in some measure—and contrasted with sculptor Victor Tolgyessy, whose work drew on American abstract sculptural models. In analyzing works relating to the revolution, Botar raised the question of what the stylistic choices of the individual artists tell us about their intentions, ambitions, and alliances in their creative lives.

Professor George Bisztray, until recently Chair of Hungarian Studies at the University of Toronto, spoke about the contributions of a number of Hungarian refugee writers to Canada. He specifically dealt with writers who continued to use their mother tongue for their work, noting that there was a "flourishing" of Hungarian Canadian literature for two or three decades after 1956. Bio-bibliographic works on this aspect of Canadian writing include Bisztray (1987) and Miska (1990). Professor Bisztray raised the question of the integration of such writers into Canadian literature—as compared to those usually second- or third-generation writers who use English or French and whose work clearly belongs to Canadian literature, both in content and in form. William New's *Encyclopedia of Literature in Canada* (2002) includes Canadian writers of Hungarian origin as part of Canadian literature in several sections of the volume, such as "Exile," "Cultural Plurality," and "European Influences," and it has a separate entry on "Hungarian," which mentions the following: Tamas Dobozy, George Faludy, John Hirsch, John Marlyn, Eva Tihanyi, Stephen Vizinczey, Robert Zend, and the publisher/writer Anna Porter.

Janos Csaba, recently retired viola player of the National Arts Centre Orchestra, spoke about the very rich tradition of Hungarian musicians and composers in Canadian music from the early days of the Hart House Quartet founded by Geza de Kresz, to contemporary musicians engaged actively in the Canadian music world and who arrived after 1956. Among these were the ones who joined the National Arts Centre Orchestra when it was founded in the late 1960s, as well as a number of internationally recognized music teachers at The Banff Centre for the Arts. Others, like conductor and teacher Miklos Takacs of Montreal, came later but integrated into Canadian musical life nevertheless. Musicologists and folk music practitioners of Hungarian origin have also contributed significantly to Canadian musical life since 1956. The *Encyclopedia of Music in Canada* (digital version available at www.thecanadianencyclopedia. com) contains a long article written by George Zaduban about Hungarian influences on Canadian music.

Unfortunately, one of the panelists, Steven Totossy de Zepetnek of Boston and Halle, was unable to participate at the last minute, so film and video representations about the 1956 Hungarian Revolution were barely discussed. It is a fact that the Canadian film industry has benefitted from the arrival of Hungarians after 1956. Included in Canada's filmmaking ranks are such luminaries as producer Robert Lantos, whose film adaptation of Stephen Vizinczey's *In Praise of Older Women*, has become an international success story. The National Film Board of Canada, as well as Canadian TV, has been greatly enriched by individuals such as László Barna, George Kaczender, John Kemeny, and Albert Kish, among many others.

Following their presentations, panellists discussed with the audience various questions raised about the nature of these contributions and forms of artistic expression, such as: Are these artists and works to be considered part of Canadian or Hungarian culture and what special perspectives do they add to our knowledge and understanding of the two main conference themes: the 1956 revolution and the refugee experience? This panel thus complemented the scholarly examination of the themes presented in the earlier parts of the conference.

Further Reading

Bisztray, George. *Hungarian Canadian Literature*. Toronto: University of Toronto Press, 1987.

Miska, John. *Ethnic and Native Canadian Literature*. A Bibliography. Toronto: University of Toronto Press, 1990.

New, William H., ed. *An Encyclopedia of Literature in Canada*. Toronto: University of Toronto Press, 2002.

Contributors

Christopher Adam is a sessional lecturer at Carleton University and a PhD candidate in history at the University of Ottawa.

Csaba Békés is the founding director of the Cold War History Research Centre in Budapest and Senior Research Fellow at the Institute for the History of the 1956 Hungarian Revolution.

Greg Donaghy is the director of the Historical Section of the Canadian Department of External Affairs and International Trade.

Nandor Dreisziger is professor emeritus at the Royal Military College and editor of the *Hungarian Studies Review.*

Tibor Egervari is former acting dean of the Faculty of Arts at the University of Ottawa and professor emeritus, Department of Theatre.

Susan Glanz is professor of administration and economics at St. John's University.

Peter Hidas is emeritus professor of history, Dawson College.

Judith Kesserü Némethy is professor of language and literature at New York University.

Leslie Laczko is professor in the Department of Sociology and Anthropology at the University of Ottawa.

Heino Nyyssönen is professor in the University of Jyväskylä's Department of Social Sciences and Philosophy.

Mária Palasik is Senior Researcher, Historical Archives of the Hungarian State Security.

János Rainer is director of the Institute for the History of the 1956 Hungarian Revolution.

Harold Troper is professor in the University of Toronto's Department of Theory and Policy Studies in Education.

Júlia Vajda is research fellow of the Hungarian Academy of Sciences' Institute of Sociology and of ELTE University, Budapest.

Judy Young is president of the Canada-Hungary Educational Foundation and editor of a website on the Hungarian presence in Canada (www.hungarianpresence.ca).